The Anti-Nuclear Game

Gordon Sims

University of Ottawa Press

Ottawa • London • Paris

© University of Ottawa Press, 1990
ISBN 0-7766-0285-3
Printed and bound in Canada

Canadian Cataloguing in Publication Data

Sims, Gordon H. E.
The anti-nuclear game

ISBN 0-7766-0285-3

1. Nuclear energy.   2. Antinuclear movement.
I. Title.

QC792.S45 1990   333.792′4   C90-090081-4

UNIVERSITÉ UNIVERSITY
D'OTTAWA OF OTTAWA

Design: Judith Gregory
Cover illustration: Canvas Digital Art Productions Inc.

*To my friends and colleagues
in the nuclear industry who have endured misrepresentation
from some members of the anti-nuclear establishment
without recourse*

Contents

The Anti-Nuclear Game

Acknowledgements

THE NUMBER OF PEOPLE WHO HAVE CONTRIBUTED DIRECTLY AND indirectly to this book is very large and it would not be possible to thank them all individually.

One person cannot be expected to have expert knowledge of all the different areas of nuclear energy dealt with in this book. In order to ensure technical accuracy, each chapter has been read by an expert in the field. The contributions of these experts have been invaluable.

I would particularly like to acknowledge the editorial skills of Elizabeth Bowen and Peter Martin who both read the entire manuscript and made many suggestions.

Despite the considerable help I have received from friends and colleagues in the nuclear industry in preparing this book, any errors or omissions are solely my responsibility.

CHAPTER 1

Introduction

CANADA IS ONE OF A SMALL NUMBER OF COUNTRIES IN THE world blessed with large quantities of all conventional forms of energy. It has oil (including enormous tar-sands reserves), gas, coal, uranium, and hydro energy. However, in common with other energy resource–rich countries, Canada finds some disadvantages to exploiting its resources. For example, burning oil, gas, and coal pollutes the environment, and there are increasingly strong suggestions that these resources should be conserved for future use as chemical feed-stocks rather than consumed to produce energy. Hydro sources devastate large areas of the landscape, and in some parts of Canada economic hydro sites are already fully utilised.

The one energy source which Canada possesses in abundance, which is economic to use, and which has a minimal effect on the environment is uranium. Canada has also devised a unique and highly efficient nuclear power reactor, the CANDU, which uses uranium to generate electricity.[1] It would appear that nuclear energy should have a secure future in Canada. Unfortunately it does not.

Over the last fifteen years a segment of the public has expressed doubts about the use of nuclear energy. According to public opinion polls these doubts vary from mild distrust to genuine fear. This book will examine how and why these doubts and fears have been formed. In doing so, it will pose and answer such questions as the following:

> How can people be convinced that nuclear energy, one of the safest forms of large-scale energy production, is by far the most dangerous?

> How can people be persuaded that nuclear energy is completely uneconomic when, in fact, it is one of the cheapest forms of electricity production?

> How can people be made to believe that the safe disposal of nuclear waste, which simply involves digging a hole in the ground and burying it, is completely beyond the capability of today's technology?

Persuading people to believe something when the opposite is true is not easy. However, this has been accomplished by a type of game which is being played in Canada and other countries throughout the world. This "game" has persuaded some people to accept unsupported statements over demonstrated facts, to believe distortions rather than veracities, and to prefer specious reasoning over common sense. Many people have been so convinced by it that they not only accept it, they defend it with a passionate intensity.

It is a game which, if successful, will cost many lives while claiming to be in the interests of safety, will cost many billions of dollars while claiming to be in the interests of economy, and will inexorably dictate our choice of lifestyles while claiming to be in the interest of personal freedom. It is a deadly serious game related to the use of nuclear energy. It is the **anti-nuclear game**.

The anti-nuclear game is being practised in many industrialised countries to the exasperation of their governments and to the dismay of most scientists. It has many players and diverse dimensions, but with always the same aim: **to abolish the use of nuclear energy**. Its character is evident to many people in responsible scientific and government positions. One of the reasons for its success is that those who realise its character are inhibited by the nature of their occupations from speaking out frankly about the game or its players. Even less are they allowed to openly deride anti-nuclear opinions.

This book assesses the nature of the game largely from a Canadian perspective. However, it is a global phenomenon, spread among many of the industrialised countries of the world. Many examples of the game exhibited in Canada have their counterparts elsewhere. Indeed, much of the misinformation on which it depends has been generated outside Canada, so that exposing the Canadian anti-nuclear game also exposes this wider collaboration.

Leadership in the game is held by a relatively small number of people who have evolved an international network of support. Public inquiries into nuclear power have been held all over the world, and an examination of the witnesses giving evidence against nuclear power often turns up the same names. There is a network of peripatetic anti-nuclear activists prepared to drop into any inquiry in any country to give their opinions. They enjoy a prestige among their peers which must give them considerable personal satisfaction.

The local supporters of the game receive support, encouragement, and the latest twist from the national and international coteries. The resulting cohesiveness of the anti-nuclear game contrasts sharply with the fragmented defences put up by the pro-nuclear supporters in their individual countries. When the inhibitions of the pro-nuclear supporters due to their establishment positions in government bureaucracies, industry, and crown corporations are combined with their fragmented voices, they give the pro-nuclear arguments a muted air. When this is compared with the strident voices of some anti-nuclear activists, it is not surprising that the average person may be left wondering hesitantly who is right, and whether the benefits of nuclear power are indeed worth its loudly proclaimed dangers.[2]

Since the Second World War the public's view of nuclear energy has fluctuated. At first, the post-war enthusiasm for all things scientific embraced nuclear science and led to optimistic, if inaccurate, media stories about atomic-powered cars and electricity "too cheap to meter." Thirty years later, in the mid-1970s, a reaction had set in because the promises of a nuclear-powered utopia were obviously unrealistic. In this climate, the increasingly critical voices of the anti-nuclear establishment began to receive wider media coverage.[3]

A major turn-around in public opinion occurred after the accident at Three Mile Island (TMI) in 1979. The accident, caused by a combination of equipment failure and operator error, led to a partial melt-down of the reactor core. The reactor containment structure behaved as designed, and very little radioactive material escaped outside the reactor building.[4] No one was killed or injured, and the long-term health effects were expected to be less than one statistical death in a surrounding population of about five million.

The media treated TMI as a major disaster rather than as an expensive industrial accident. In this they were assisted by an inept display of public relations by the nuclear industry and exaggerated claims by the anti-nuclear establishment. The accident was a lead story in the media for about two weeks. Even after the accident was well over and the clean-up had begun, stories generated by the anti-nuclear establishment about giant dandelion leaves, two-headed calves, and prematurely greying hair continued to be published in the media. The TMI accident decreased considerably the level of confidence in nuclear power as a safe source of electricity generation. However, as time passed without another accident, confidence improved.

Then in April 1986 there was a second reactor accident, this time at Chernobyl in the U.S.S.R. This was a much more serious event than TMI, with 31 reactor workers and fire-fighters killed and 200 injured. About 135,000 people in a 30 kilometre zone around the reactor were evacuated, and most of them have not been allowed to return. Low-level radioactive contamination was carried by the wind over large areas of the U.S.S.R. and Europe.

About four months after the accident, a meeting of the world's top nuclear scientists and engineers was held in Vienna, at which the Soviet scientists explained how and why the accident had happened. The accident will be described more fully in chapter 3; it will only be noted here that the differences in regulatory structure, as well as reactor design and operation, between Canada and the U.S.S.R. made it almost impossible to draw any useful lessons from Chernobyl which were relevant to Canadian experience.[5]

There was an immediate drop in confidence in nuclear power after the Chernobyl accident, but public opinion polls have shown a quicker and stronger rebound than there was after TMI. Chernobyl was about the worst possible nuclear accident which could occur, and the public appears to have realised that even a worst-case nuclear accident does not produce the horrendous results they have been led to believe in. Assisting the improved climate for nuclear power has been the rise in public importance of environmental issues such as acid rain and the greenhouse effect. Both of these environmental issues could be alleviated significantly by using nuclear generated electricity instead of coal.

Currently there seems to be a continuing small increase in the public acceptance of nuclear power. It is hoped this book will nudge this increase even higher by providing some of the facts about nuclear energy and exposing some of the myths used in the anti-nuclear game. Each chapter considers one nuclear-related issue which has been the subject of inaccurate or misleading information. The first part of each chapter gives the facts relating to the issue. The second part describes the game. Individual statements on which the game is based are quoted, and comments are made on each. The final chapter in the book suggests a reliable method by which an ordinary member of the public, with no special knowledge of any of the issues, can decide who is more likely correct, the pro- or the anti-nuclear establishment.

An attempt has been made to keep technicalities to a minimum in describing what are basically technical subject matters. An attempt has also been made to make the book a "good read" as distinct from a technical tome. Inevitably, some strict scientific purists will object to the way in which some facts are presented or in which some arguments are used. They may be right, but it was necessary to write in a way which would reach the widest possible audience.

ORIGINS OF THE ANTI-NUCLEAR ESTABLISHMENT

The anti-nuclear movement is remarkable in that it stands at the confluence of several other movements that have developed in the second half of the twentieth century. It has satisfied parts of their mandates or aspirations and has, in turn, provided them with a sharp focus for one or more aspects of their activities.

It is possible to dissect some of the original motivations which may have led members to the anti-nuclear movement, or at least made them participants in the anti-nuclear game. It is their firm belief in the principles from which their original concerns arose that makes them susceptible. It is the same beliefs that, once they have been converted, make them disciples.

The first, and probably the most predictable, group to join the anti–nuclear-power movement were the left-overs from the ban-the-bomb protests of the 1950s. When the U.S.S.R. exploded its first nuclear weapon in 1949, followed by the U.K. in 1952, nuclear weapons proliferation was underway on a world scale. In most industrialised countries ban-the-bomb groups sprang up to protest what was perceived to be an immediate threat to civilisation. Demands were made for national governments to ban the manufacture and forbid the use of nuclear weapons.

The passions aroused by this crusade were genuine and very strongly felt. Marches of people, thousands strong, were made regularly to military nuclear establishments. Sit-down protests, non-violent (though not always) resistance to the police, slogans, and speeches, all the methods later adopted by other demonstrators for other causes which followed in the 1960s and 1970s were first introduced by the ban-the-bomb marchers. But by the mid-1970s, after thirty years without the promised holocaust, the movement had begun to run out of steam. The ban-the-bomb protestors had not had a good rally in years, so that when the anti–nuclear-power movement began to take hold, many of them migrated to it as a natural haven.

In the late 1970s and early 1980s, the nuclear disarmament movement came to life again. This time, the introduction of cruise missiles and, later, the strategic defence initiative provided rallying points. Today it can be expected that many of the revived nuclear disarmers will also be anti–nuclear-power protestors. The reason often given is that the possession of nuclear power reactors must lead to the development of nuclear weapons.[6] This notion will be discussed in chapter 6.

A second movement which fed into the anti-nuclear crusade is more difficult to define, but for the want of a better word it can be called the "environmentalist" movement. No injustice is meant to the word *environmentalist* by using it to describe a particular group, because these days everyone is an environmentalist. There is no reasonable person who does not prefer to swim in clean water rather than in dirty, or to breathe clean air rather than foul.

In the mid- to late 1970s, a number of environmental groups rose to prominence in the industrial world, all of them concerned with the increasing rate of pollution in our environment. Much of what they had to say made sound common sense, and their activities have made us all aware that continued contamination at present rates will have increasingly serious effects on our quality of life. Unfortunately, many of these environmental groups have been susceptible to the claim by the anti-nuclear establishment that the ultimate pollutant in our society is radiation. This has led them to take up positions against the use of nuclear power. The fact that nuclear power generation is less polluting than almost any other form of electricity generation is ignored. As a result, it sometimes appears that environmental groups consider very low-level radiation pollution from nuclear power plants to be more hazardous than acid rain or carbon dioxide in the atmosphere.

REDUCING ACID RAIN

Some of our acid rain comes from coal-fired electrical generating stations. One way to remove this acid rain would be to replace coal-fired plants with nuclear plants.

During a 1985 seminar at the Niagara Institute, the leader of the Canadian Acid Rain Coalition, Michael Perley, was questioned on this matter. Like many "environmentalists," he could not bring himself to accept nuclear power even as a method for removing part of his major concern. His stated view at that time was that the Acid Rain Coalition had no opinion on replacing coal with nuclear.

A third source of supporters are those people, and there seems to be an increasing number of them, who are just plain anti-technology. Usually they do not have a scientific or technical background and, as a result, find themselves increasingly at sea in the modern technological world. An instinctive reaction of self-preservation leads some of them to oppose any further extension of technology in today's society.

The rejection of technology has a long history which includes the reaction to the discoveries of Galileo and the activities of the Luddites. In the seventeenth century there was opposition to the replacement of wood as a fuel by coal. In the early nineteenth century the introduction of railways was seen as a despoiler of the countryside. In the early twentieth century motor cars in England were considered so dangerous that they had to be preceded by a man with a red flag.[7] These instances now seem quaintly amusing, but as the twentieth century technological revolution gathered pace the number of objectors to further changes increased.

Nuclear science has produced a complicated technological achievement in the nuclear power reactor. Some people have taken nuclear power as a symbol of all that is wrong with this technically directed world and have joined the anti-nuclear movement hoping to stop this one achievement of our technical culture. As will be seen later, one of the anti-nuclear arguments has been particularly useful in playing upon the fears of these potential members, promising a return to simpler and more understandable alternative energy sources once nuclear power has been defeated. This must sound like a siren song to the anti-technologists although, in reality, the aerodynamics and mechanics of a windmill are as difficult for the layman to understand as the theory of nuclear fission.

The last group which will be mentioned as feeding into the anti-nuclear confluence is also difficult to define because its own philosophy is rather woolly. Again, for the want of a better word, this group will be called the "communalists" (not to be confused with communists). These are the people who look at the large structural systems necessary to support modern civilisation and yearn to return to a simpler form of lifestyle. In their belief that "small is beautiful," they view the present system as creating remote government which in turn tends to promote its own needs rather than the needs of the people it is meant to serve. They want to return to a smaller scale of government in which the voice of the people could be heard in day-to-day decision making.[8]

For these people the large-scale generation of energy is a paradigm for all that is wrong with modern society. They claim it is remote, unresponsive to human needs, and out of the control of the people. How much better it would be in their view if energy generation were small-scale, carried out at the local level, and thus put back under the control of the people it was meant to serve. When discussing alternatives to nuclear power, the anti-nuclear game offers these people a different lifestyle, but it is already too late to turn back the clock. Most people, having experienced the convenience, the efficiency and the favourable economics of large-scale energy production are unlikely to welcome a return to small-scale, do-it-yourself operations.

This suggested list of the origins of the anti-nuclear establishment is not complete. Many other personal and emotional factors cause individuals to become involved. Perhaps the most common characteristic of the average anti-nuclear activist is an absence of general scientific knowledge. This factor makes it very difficult for these individuals to distinguish fact from fiction in the anti-nuclear game.

CANADA'S ANTI-NUCLEAR ESTABLISHMENT

Like most industrialised countries, Canada has its own recognisable anti-nuclear establishment. However, trying to pin it down is a bit like trying to put a thumb on a blob of mercury. It splits apart into globules which then coalesce in different sizes in different places. There are only a limited number of anti-nuclear activists in Canada, and they tend to form, disperse, and re-group according to which specific aspect of the nuclear industry they are interested in attacking at any particular time. Sometimes they form groups with cute names like PANDA (People Against Nuclear Development Anywhere); at other times the names are more uncompromising, such as Direct Action Network Against Military Racism—a group objecting to uranium mining.

There are a few anti-nuclear groups which have lasted for many years and three of these in particular can claim to speak for the movement as a whole in Canada. It is from these organisations that most of the smaller groups get the latest word on the anti-nuclear game. They are Energy Probe (formed in 1974), the Canadian Coalition for Nuclear Responsibility (formed in 1975), and the International Institute of Concern for Public Health (formed in 1984). There are other groups that receive and transmit information without the knowledge to make a significant contribution to the debate themselves, but first the three major actors will be described.

ENERGY PROBE

The forerunner of Energy Probe was the Energy and Resources Group formed by Pollution Probe, Toronto, in 1970. The group changed its name to Energy Probe in 1974, and in 1980 it separated from Pollution Probe and received separate charitable tax status and a new name, the Energy Probe Research Foundation.[9]

According to its Registered Charities Public Information Return, the primary purpose of Energy Probe is:

> to promote policies for Canada, based on conservation and renewable energy, that will secure long-term energy self-sufficiency in the shortest possible time, with the fewest disruptive effects, and with the greatest societal, economic and environmental benefits; to promote the democratic process by encouraging individual responsibility and accountability; to provide business, government and the public with information on energy and energy-related issues; to help Canada contribute to global harmony and prosperity.

The word *nuclear* does not appear in the description of purpose even though much of the organisation's efforts and resources are devoted to anti-nuclear activities.

ACTIVISTS

Those who are opposed to nuclear energy often find themselves associated with other activists who may be less committed to the anti-nuclear cause but who can always be relied upon to take part in a protest—any protest.

Some years ago, the offices of the Atomic Energy Control Board in Ottawa were picketed by an anti-nuclear group who were protesting the "secrecy" of the Board. In activist language this means that the Board would not allow them to rummage around in its files.

I watched the group with its placards for a few days and then started a conversation with one of them. I asked if he had been on protests like this one before. It seems he was an old hand at it, and he was particularly proud of having taken part in the Chicago riots.

I asked him if he didn't get bored out of his skull just standing around doing nothing all day. He looked at the inactivity of his fellow activists a bit sourly and said, "Heck, it sure ain't like Chicago."

Energy Probe is responsible and accountable for its actions and opinions only to its members. It is a secretive organisation; neither its board meetings nor its minutes are usually open to the public. Those who wish to attend the meetings must so request the chairman, stating the reason for the request.[10] However, Energy Probe is the most assiduous Canadian organisation in its chosen field. It carefully cultivates the media, and its literature claims it is in the news on average twice a day.

The major reason for this success is that Energy Probe can afford to employ full-time paid staff to develop its literature and cultivate the media. The staff are provided with various titles, such as Director of Nuclear

CRITICISM

Ever since it started criticising the nuclear industry, the anti-nuclear establishment has considered itself to be above criticism. It has had good reason for this attitude. The organisations it has attacked have been respected public bodies such as Atomic Energy of Canada Limited, the Atomic Energy Control Board, and Ontario Hydro. These organisations do not usually engage in public controversy, so that most of the shots against the pro-nuclear establishment remain unanswered.

On the rare occasions when a reply has been given, the anti-nuclear establishment has been outraged. For example, in one of its attacks on Ontario Hydro, Energy Probe accused the utility of extravagance including, "chauffeured limousines for the top brass, the most expensive office space in the country."

Concerned about the effects of these allegations on its staff, Hydro sent an internal one-page information leaflet to its employees, replying to these and other statements by Energy Probe. According to the leaflet, "Hydro's Chairman has a 1981 Pontiac Parisienne (more than 121,000 km on the odometer) and the President's car is a 1979 Parisienne with 107,000 km logged so far . . . . Hydro's head office space costs $17 per square foot. The average in the same downtown Toronto area ranges from $25–45 per square foot."

Energy Probe did not admit it had misled the public. Instead, its response was to hold a press conference to denounce the fact that Hydro had defended itself to its employees and to demand equal access to Hydro's employees.

Research, Energy Advocate, or Lawyer, and in addition there are clerical staff. Staff members vary from time to time, but the total salaries for personnel seem to run about $200,000–$300,000 annually.

To raise money for staff salaries as well as for its activities, Energy Probe needs a large core of supporters and a large mailing list. It also needs to be able to obtain contributions from both. One method of raising funds is to send out a newsletter describing the latest infamy of the nuclear establishment and pleading for money to combat it. These letters must be sufficiently dramatic to shock their readers and sufficiently persuasive to loosen their purse strings. The appeals appear to be designed to be emotive rather than reasoned, stimulating anger rather than discussion. On average, about two "infamies" a year are used as a basis for this type of letter pleading for funds.

As fund-raising ventures, these letters seem to be successful because Energy Probe keeps its financial head above water. However, as will be shown later, they usually contain inaccurate or misleading statements, so that they cannot be taken seriously by anyone with a knowledge of the industry. After reading these newsletters, it may be difficult for some people to take seriously Energy Probe's claim to be an "independent think-tank."

CANADIAN COALITION FOR NUCLEAR RESPONSIBILITY (CCNR)

The CCNR was formed in 1975 as an "umbrella" group to co-ordinate the activities of the many individual anti-nuclear organisations spread across Canada at that time. It was the centre from which the anti-nuclear arguments could be passed on to the individual organisations and their members.

The chairman of the Coalition from its creation has been Dr. Gordon Edwards, a mathematician at Vanier College in Montreal. He has been assisted by a board of directors. Since its formation, the CCNR has gone from an umbrella organisation actively spreading the anti-nuclear gospel among its two to three hundred member groups to a resource group operating an information centre.

One possible reason for the change in the CCNR's activities is lack of money. For many years it promoted the idea of a moratorium on nuclear reactor construction and a national inquiry into nuclear energy. These ideas excited the membership in the 1970s, but today they seem to have become stale. Energy Probe, with its much more active process of continual confrontation, seems to have gathered contributions much more effectively than the CCNR. Its budget, which used to run at about $50,000 annually, is now down to about $15,000–$20,000 per year.[11]

The CCNR resource centre provides much of the information needed to attack the nuclear establishment, some of it derived from U.S. antinuclear sources. The U.S. nuclear program has had its successes, but it has also had some monumental failures. These latter are cited as warnings of what could happen in Canada. Literature from other countries with successful nuclear programs, such as from France and Japan, is cited hardly at all.

THE PUBLIC SPEAKS

A normal tactic of the anti-nuclear establishment is to claim to speak on behalf of the public. However, claiming public support and actually obtaining public support are two different matters. Some anti-nuclear activists on one occasion did expose themselves and their opinions to the public. The occasion was the Canadian general election of February 1980.

A number of them decided to run for Parliament on anti-nuclear platforms. They campaigned hard and spoke their anti-nuclear pieces at every available opportunity.

Typical of their fortunes was that of Gordon Edwards. Perhaps to maximise the effect of his message, he ran in the Mount Royal riding of Montreal against Prime Minister Pierre Trudeau and others. Even if he did not win, a good showing in the poll would strengthen the political credibility of the anti-nuclear cause.

Edwards gathered only 149 votes, which was about 0.36 per cent of the total votes cast. It was also about one-fifth the number of votes received by the Rhinoceros Party candidate, representing Canada's perennial joke party which tries to enliven our national elections.

INTERNATIONAL INSTITUTE OF CONCERN FOR PUBLIC HEALTH

Despite its name, the Institute is essentially the creation of one person, Dr. Rosalie Bertell, Ph.D. It was incorporated in Toronto in 1984. The two other founding members were Dr. Ursula Franklin, Ph.D., and Dr. Dermot McLoughlin, Ph.D. The Institute is "primarily concerned with public health problems related to military, industrial and technological pollution of the living space and environment." The goal of the Institute is "holistic health on a global scale through empowering people to understand, define and address [these] major health problems. Together we must all press for accurate information and become actively involved and responsible in decisions affecting the use of nuclear power and our health and survival."[12]

Although its goal is "holistic health," the Institute is an active antinuclear organisation. Dr. Bertell believes that many different health ailments from asthma to low birth weight infants are caused by low levels of radiation and that the road to health must involve shutting down all nuclear establishments, whether civilian or military. In that way, radiation levels will be reduced and the health of the global population will be improved.

Dr. Bertell is an American citizen who was first a Carmelite nun and then entered the Grey Nuns community. She obtained a Ph.D. in mathematics in 1966 and went to work at the cancer research centre at the Rosswell Park Memorial Institute in the U.S.A. While there, she began working on data obtained from the Tri-State Leukemia Survey. This was a survey of children under fifteen years in New York, Maryland, and Minnesota who had received X-ray treatment. A follow-up of these patients was carried out to see whether they had suffered an increase in the incidence of leukemia due to the X-rays, and whether this could be correlated with the X-ray doses the patients had received. Leukemia is a useful index of the effects of radiation in producing cancer, since it is the cancer which is produced in the shortest period after irradiation.

The survey produced an enormous amount of data which could have been a mathematician's delight. Unfortunately, the survey was flawed. For one thing, it showed a correlation between irradiation dose and leukemia in males but not in females. The conclusion of Dr. John Gofman, M.D., a well-known anti-nuclear critic in the U.S.A., is that "the findings from the Tri-State data appear internally inconsistent. This may be the consequence of some undetected and undetectable bias introduced long ago, when the data were collected and assembled."[13] Other experts agree with this view and have not used the data as a reliable source of information on the relationship between radiation and cancer.

However, Dr. Bertell has conducted analyses of the data. Using an original statistical method, and using only the data for males, she produced a paper purporting to show that radiation had the effect of increasing the apparent age of a population. She came up with the slogan that "1 rem equals 1 year" (a rem is a unit of radiation).[14] The unusual methodology used by Dr. Bertell, and the fact that she was using what most experts considered a flawed data base, have led to this paper being widely ignored by the scientific community. Since its publication (in 1977) Dr. Bertell appears to have published little in the peer-reviewed scientific literature. As she has said herself, "I've always considered my primary responsibility to report back to the people who have paid for it [the research] not just to publish in some obscure journal and go on to something else."[15] Dr. Bertell's Institute now publishes its own journal, *International Perspectives in Public Health*, in which her papers can appear.

Meanwhile, Dr. Bertell has been very active on the lecture circuit preaching her gospel that radiation protection regulations are "ridiculous" and that ". . . thanks to nuclear pollution, radioactivity can be found in all humans." More will be said about Dr. Bertell's views on the effects of radiation on people in chapter 2.

OTHER ORGANISATIONS

Apart from the "Big Three," there are a number of other organisations in Canada which hold anti-nuclear views, and their activities sometimes receive media attention. However, they add little that is original to the anti-nuclear game. They usually repeat statements originating from the "Big Three."

GREENPEACE

This is one of Canada's largest and best-known "environmental" organisations. It was established in Vancouver in 1970 and then spread world-wide.

URANIUM

At the end of 1987 Greenpeace undertook a campaign to prevent Canada from mining or exporting uranium (annual value at that time about $1 billion—85 per cent of it from exports). The campaign was launched with a press conference and was duly reported in the media.

One of the first major media events staged by Greenpeace in its campaign was a demonstration outside the Ottawa headquarters of the Department of Energy, Mines and Resources. The demonstration was timed for a Monday morning so as to get maximum coverage on evening television.

Unfortunately, it got no coverage at all. Greenpeace had chosen Black Monday, October 19, 1987, for its demonstration—the day the bottom fell out of the stock market.

Greenpeace started as an organisation devoted to preserving marine mammals, and it later developed land-based environmental concerns. One of its environmental concerns has been opposition to the use of nuclear power. Greenpeace members appear unable to accept that, compared with available alternatives, nuclear power is one of our most environmentally benign sources of energy.

Greenpeace has organised demonstrations against nuclear power at Ontario Hydro's Bruce nuclear station and at the Darlington nuclear station. It has also organised media events involving the waste disposal site in southern Ontario used by Eldorado Mining and Refining Company and uranium mining in Saskatchewan.

FRIENDS OF THE EARTH

This U.S.-based ecological organisation now has branches in other countries. A Canadian branch was formed in Ottawa in 1978. Its views on energy policy have been largely formed by the writings of Amory Lovins, who advocates an exclusively "soft path" approach to future energy supplies. The soft path would consist of a mixture of energy conservation measures supplemented by reliance on renewable energy sources such as solar, wind, and biomass. "Hard Path" energy sources such as large-scale hydro, tar-sands, and nuclear would be abandoned as being incompatible with the "soft path" approach.

Even those disagreeing with the basic philosophy of Friends of the Earth should take their positions seriously. In Canada, particularly, their members are among the more rational and thoughtful opponents of nuclear energy. The Canadian branch received funds from the federal government in the early 1980s to conduct a thorough study of the practicality of their ideas, and they produced the report *2025: Soft Energy Paths for Canada.* This report was later issued as a book entitled *Life after Oil.*[16]

The views of Friends of the Earth will be discussed later in the chapter on alternative energy sources. Meanwhile it is only necessary to note that, unlike some other segments of the anti-nuclear establishment, the views of the Canadian branch of Friends are put forward in a thoughtful, nonconfrontational manner and deserve consideration.

THE CANADIAN (AND PROVINCIAL) ENVIRONMENTAL LAW ASSOCIATIONS

CELA and its provincial counterparts are a group of organisations with strong interests in ecological/environmental legislation who often show an anti-nuclear bias. They do not chase headlines but prefer to write briefs

IPPANI

There are always a small number of anti-nuclear activists among the adherents to religious faiths, particularly the Catholic, Jewish, and United Church faiths. Their activities are characterised by a strong advocacy of ethical values and a weak knowledge of nuclear facts.

In Toronto in 1983 a group of these activists representing the three faiths mentioned above (later joined by Anglican and Bahai representatives) planned their own three-week inquiry into nuclear issues. They called the inquiry the Interfaith Program for Public Awareness of Nuclear Issues (IPPANI). They said the inquiry would be the first stage in an education process in which the facts about the nuclear issues would be presented to their congregations.

The inquiry was held before three panels of distinguished Canadians from the Toronto area who were not known to hold strong views on nuclear issues. The three reports from the panels were to be used as the basis for the education program which was to follow.

Each panel met for one week and was presented with briefs and presentations from the supporters of both sides. When the panels' reports were prepared, they showed overwhelming support for the nuclear industry.[17]

The issuance of the reports was delayed for nearly a year while the sponsors wondered what to do with them. The ethical thing to do would be to carry on with their proposed educational program and inform their congregations about the merits of the nuclear industry.

Regrettably, this did not happen, and the whole Interfaith Program for Public Awareness of Nuclear Issues was allowed to slide under the rug.

to the government on issues with which they have concerns. Although they do not have a high visibility as part of the anti-nuclear establishment, their views are listened to with respect.

THE CHURCHES

The Canadian churches have their quotas of members with anti-nuclear views who try to spread their message to the general church membership and outside. The anti-nuclear members of the United Church of Canada are particularly active and have had the support of the Moderator of the Church. The Jewish, Catholic, Mennonite, Anglican, and Lutheran churches also have their quotas of anti-nuclear activists, although in all cases there is no evidence that the church membership at large shares their views.

The church activists usually prefer to give their activities an ecumenical slant by co-operating with each other in organisations such as the Task Force of the Churches on Corporate Responsibility and the Inter-Church Uranium Group. The former had an interest in showing that nuclear waste disposal was unethical, and the latter, based in Saskatchewan, has mounted a prolonged campaign against uranium mining in that province.

LA SOCIÉTÉ POUR VAINCRE LA POLLUTION

This is a Montreal-based environmental group whose activities consist mainly of opposition to the James Bay hydro development, acid rain, and nuclear power. Its criticisms of nuclear power are the same as those of other anti-nuclear organisations. They are believed to have little impact outside their immediate circle of sympathisers.

THE CONCERNED CITIZENS OF MANITOBA

The founder of this group, Walter Robbins, was a resident near AECL's Whiteshell Nuclear Research Establishment in Manitoba when work began in May 1977 on the construction of the Underground Research Laboratory (URL) to investigate the suitability of granite rock for high-level waste disposal. He became convinced that the URL was an incipient waste disposal site and founded the Concerned Citizens group to fight against any high-level waste disposal in Manitoba.[18] Assurances by AECL and the federal government that the URL was not intended as a nuclear waste disposal site did not deter him. Nor did a commonsense appreciation that since most of Canada's waste was being generated in Ontario, an eventual site was most likely to be selected in that province. The CCM has thus conducted a noisy campaign to persuade the federal government not to do something that the government had already said it would not do. The CCM in 1987 reported it had almost zero members.[19]

PHYSICIANS FOR SOCIAL RESPONSIBILITY

This group of M.D.s was formed in 1979 mainly to protest the nuclear arms race, but it has also opposed the use of nuclear power. Its grounds for objecting to both are the health effects that nuclear weapons and nuclear power could have on the population. Considering their medical expertise, the Physicians for Social Responsibility sometimes seem ill-informed on the effects of low-level radiation. They have contributed little to anti-nuclear-power arguments and usually take their cue from the arguments issued by the Big Three. They changed their name to Canadian Physicians for the Prevention of Nuclear War in 1986.

It should be noted that the Canadian Medical Association has endorsed the use of nuclear power as an acceptable method of electricity generation with negligible adverse health effects.

TECHNIQUES OF THE GAME

The anti-nuclear game is played by presenting a continually moving target of inaccurate or misleading information about nuclear energy. A variety of techniques is used to plant this information quicker than it can be uprooted, but always the basic intent is to achieve the first stage of the game, the arousal of fear of nuclear power in an audience. The following list of techniques used to achieve this goal is by no means exhaustive, but it provides some illustrative examples.

INACCURATE STATEMENTS

Some anti-nuclear activists will adopt in a debate any argument which will further their cause. Once an argument has been challenged and shown to be inaccurate or misleading, they will move to another one. However, that will not prevent them from returning to the first statement again in another context. As a result, the same information is presented again and again, and unless a correction is made every time it is delivered, it will eventually be accepted by many people as being true. The most striking feature of the nuclear controversy is the persistent flow of such information. Thanks to constant repetition it floods the public consciousness in much the same way as a dripping tap eventually floods a blocked sink.

A good example of a frequently repeated inaccurate statement is: "Nuclear power reactors can explode like atom bombs." In fact it is impossible for a nuclear reactor to explode like an atom bomb; the laws of physics will not allow it. Yet this inaccuracy has been repeated again and again and has been accepted by many people in many countries. In the early 1980s a poll of populations in countries of the Commission of the European Community showed that a consistent 80 per cent of the people in each country believed this statement may be true, and only 10 per cent believed it to be physically impossible.[20]

The more sophisticated anti-nuclear activists have recently tended to avoid this statement, but they are happy to tell all who listen that one nuclear reactor contains more radioactivity than ten Hiroshima bombs. It does, but they never mention that a reactor is designed to contain radioactivity safely, whereas a bomb is designed to spread it. By mentioning "reactors" and "bombs" in the same sentence, they sometimes manage to perpetuate the fear in the general population that reactors can, in fact, explode like atom bombs.

AVOIDING COMPARISONS

The anti-nuclear establishment tries to isolate the risks of nuclear power from those of other forms of energy generation. It refuses to make comparisons between the risks of energy options, so that the public is given the impression that only nuclear energy has a risk component and that, if nuclear energy were to be abolished, all risks from energy generation could be avoided.

Unfortunately, there is no free lunch. If electricity is not generated by nuclear power, it will be generated by other means, and these other means are almost always more hazardous than nuclear energy systems. (See chapter 8 on risks of energy production.)

There is no totally safe human activity, whether it is operating a car, an electric tooth-brush, or a nuclear reactor. All activities have risks, although some have risks which are vanishingly small. Energy generation systems, including nuclear systems, have very small risks. By ignoring these facts and by refusing to compare the risks of different energy generating systems, the anti-nuclear establishment has succeeded in confusing, and frightening, a large number of people.

SPEAKING OUT

The contrast between the veracity displayed by the nuclear industry and the inaccurate information put out by the anti-nuclear establishment is often recognised but seldom commented upon. An exception to this rule has been provided by John F. Ahearne.

Ahearne was a member of the U.S. Nuclear Regulatory Commission (NRC), a government regulatory agency equivalent to Canada's Atomic Energy Control Board (AECB). It operates differently from the AECB in being much more open to representations from anti-nuclear activists who take advantage of all legal loopholes to delay the issuance of licences for nuclear power plants in the U.S.A. They have been so successful in this that it usually takes twice as long to construct a nuclear plant in the U.S.A. as it does in most other parts of the world. These delays have increased the costs of the plants substantially, and the increased costs are paid by the American public by increased electricity prices.

After he retired from the NRC, Ahearne made some interesting comments in an interview published in the *New York Times*.[21] When discussing the difference between the quality of information provided by the industry representatives, as opposed to that provided by the anti-nuclear groups, he said: "If the utilities say something that is really wrong, they are in deep trouble with us and with their utility commissions . . . . The interest groups really have no responsibility. If they make a misstatement to us, so what? . . . . If they lose their case, they've lost that one. They'll come back and try another one."

Ahearne clearly recognised the nature of the anti-nuclear game. It is a pity he had to wait until after he had left the NRC to publicise this point, but that was really inevitable. A public servant cannot characterise a member of the public as a purveyor of inaccurate information.

Meanwhile, the anti-nuclear establishment will continue to provide inaccurate information and when challenged, ". . . so what? . . . they'll come back and try another one."

REPLACING REASON WITH EMOTION

The campaign against nuclear power is largely concerned with arousing emotions against it, rather than reasoning against it. The anti-nuclear establishment is particularly adept at encouraging fears of the cancer-causing properties of radiation, and it does this by grossly exaggerating the effects of radiation. It also broadcasts exaggerated fears about the possible genetic effects of radiation.

This latter message is sometimes directed to women, who can be expected to be concerned about their offspring. In fact, anti-nuclear issues

---

AN EARLY WARNING

A warning that radiation phobia could be induced in people was made as long ago as 1958.[22]

In that year, the World Health Organisation (WHO) published a report on "Mental Health Aspects of the Peaceful Uses of Atomic Energy," which said: "It is logical to infer that mankind's encounter with a source of energy of such shattering possibilities as atomic power will cause strong psychological reactions and that some of these will probably have to be considered more or less pathological."

The WHO report understated the case. We now know that the reactions of some people to nuclear power are more, rather than less, pathological.

The report goes on to state: "There is indeed evidence that it is exceedingly difficult for many people to keep the productive uses of atomic energy clearly separated in their minds from its destructive possibilities and that this inability contributes to making the whole concept of atomic energy potentially a frightening one."

The potential for fright has now become actual. The arousing of people's fears has been successful.

The WHO report was a warning to the nuclear establishment of what was to come. As a warning, it was a failure. It was also a blueprint for the anti-nuclear establishment on how to attack the nuclear industry. As a blueprint, it was a success.

are considered by some feminists to be "women's issues." That these messages are factually incorrect is apparently immaterial to many anti-nuclear spokespersons. They are used because they are capable of producing strong emotions. As will be seen later, there is no direct evidence of genetic effects in people due to radiation although such effects are theoretically possible.

The attachment of some anti-nuclear activists to solar power as a replacement for nuclear power in Canada is also an emotional rather than a reasonable reaction. Many activists do not understand the technical and economic difficulties associated with solar energy, and probably do not want to. They prefer to regard old sol as a plentiful, benign, cheap, and safe form of energy, even though their views are often not supported by the facts (see chapter 7 on alternative energy sources).

USE OF DISSENTING SCIENTISTS

Among nuclear scientists there is almost 100 per cent agreement that nuclear power is safe enough to warrant its use as one of today's energy options. But as with any other human endeavour, there can never be 100 per cent unanimity. The dissenting scientists are a tiny minority, yet they allow the anti-nuclear establishment to claim that "scientists are divided on the safety of nuclear power." If they mean divided in the ratio of 99 for to 1 against, they may be right, but they carefully refrain from pointing out how small their minority is.[23] However, it is this minority that is often quoted by the media.

PLAYING THE NUMBERS GAME

This is a commonly used technique in the anti-nuclear game. It can be played in several ways, but here we will consider just one, the numbers game as it is applied to risk. For the scientist, risk is a term which can be expressed mathematically as the product of probability of an event happening and the consequences of the event happening. That is,

$$\text{Risk} = \text{Probability} \times \text{Consequences}$$

This equation means that at a constant level of risk the consequences of an accident (e.g., the number of fatalities) can be mathematically increased by decreasing the probability that the accident will happen in the first place. It is obvious that the anti-nuclear establishment can have a field day by using this equation to juggle numbers.

The figures of very high casualties from a nuclear accident involving tens or hundreds of thousands of deaths are derived simply by making the probability of such an accident so small that it is not likely ever to happen. But since this is a mathematical numbers game, it is also true that one cannot assert positively that such an accident could *never* happen. There will always be some minute, residual chance that it could.

The only way the non-scientist can comprehend what is really meant by these large numbers for the consequences of small probability occurrences is to compare them with risks with which he is already familiar. For example, a person living near a nuclear plant is ten times more likely to be killed by lightning than by a nuclear accident. Or, the same person's chance of being killed in a nuclear accident is about the same as being hit by a meteor. Stated in these terms the risks of nuclear energy look ridiculously small, but the anti-nuclear establishment never talks of risk, only of consequences.

When the anti-nuclear establishment cites figures of thousands of possible deaths due to a nuclear accident, it is necessary to ask about the probability of the accident. Then ask how the *risk* compares with those types of accidents we already know about and live with.

MEDIA VERSUS SCIENTISTS

A familiar gambit in the anti-nuclear game is one that starts with "Scientists are divided on . . . ," followed by statements on reactor safety, waste disposal, radiation hazards, etc. Two American sociologists, Stanley Rothman and S. Robert Lichter, decided to find out just how far scientists were divided on the use of nuclear energy. They sent a detailed questionnaire on the subject to a random group of scientists, culled from *American Men and Women of Science*, and published their results.[24]

In answer to a question on whether or not to proceed with nuclear energy, 90 per cent of the *scientists* were in favour of proceeding and 10 per cent were against. The *energy experts* among the group of scientists agreed to proceed with a margin of 95 per cent in favour and 5 per cent against, while a further subset of *nuclear experts* agreed 100 per cent to proceed with nuclear energy.

There is not much evidence in these figures that "Scientists are divided . . . ," and still less that energy experts and nuclear experts are divided.

THE TEN-SECOND INACCURACY

This is one of the most effective weapons in the anti-nuclear game. It is effective because an inaccurate statement which can be delivered in ten seconds often takes up to half an hour of detailed presentation to refute. It is particularly useful in a debate because there is never time to give an adequate refutation before moving on to something else. The use of this technique means that if a public debate is of limited duration it is bound to be loaded against the pro-nuclear advocate from the outset.

One example of this technique was given above: "Nuclear reactors can explode like atomic bombs." Another, which will be dealt with in chapter 4, is: "We don't know what to do with nuclear waste." A third, which is very popular, is: "Plutonium is the most toxic substance known to man." This particular ten-second inaccuracy will also receive full treatment later. Suffice to say that those propagating it appear to have little knowledge of toxicology, physiology, or nuclear physics. They do, however, have a considerable knowledge of psychology, since the inaccuracy remains very effective and persistent no matter how many times the experts refute it. As one plutonium expert bitterly complained at a conference, it was not only necessary for him to understand the physics and chemistry of plutonium, but also the psychology of plutonium.[25]

MANIPULATING THE MEDIA

The accident to the nuclear reactor at Three Mile Island (TMI) in March 1979 marked a turning point in the relationship between the media and the nuclear industry. For the first time the media had a "disaster" story from the industry. The TMI accident was a front-page story for about two weeks, and it set the pattern for sensationalising nuclear events and non-events which has been followed ever since by much of the media.[26]

Although no one was killed by the accident at TMI, it was labelled by the media as a nuclear disaster. Contributing to this view was the anti-nuclear establishment. By feeding the media a continuing stream of "what might happen if" stories, anti-nuclear activists found that they could get their message across to the public on prime-time TV without spending a penny on promotion.

It must be admitted that the media are in something of a quandary concerning nuclear/anti-nuclear stories. Reporters often do not have enough knowledge about the topic to be able to distinguish between a genuine nuclear story and anti-nuclear puffery. As a result, even when a story is favourable to the nuclear industry, the media have been persuaded that it is only fair to give the anti-nuclear side of the story. An anti-nuclear

DOOM

In March 1979 Walter Cronkite (now retired, but then the most senior and respected television journalist in the U.S.A.) appeared on U.S. television and with grave demeanour announced: "Good evening. The world has never known a day quite like today."[27]

He did not announce the beginning of World War Three, or a stock market collapse, or the assassination of a U.S. president.

He announced an accident at a nuclear power station called Three Mile Island—an event which did not kill anybody, seriously injure anybody, or provide significant environmental contamination, but which probably did wonders for Cronkite's Nielsen ratings.

organisation is contacted and is usually able to provide an anti-nuclear quote. The resulting story is then regarded as "balanced," thereby satisfying the media's concept of fairness. The issue of which side is actually stating the truth is not investigated by the reporter.

However, some senior editors in the media are now showing more scepticism about anti-nuclear stories which seem too easily derived. This is particularly true in some parts of the print media. The electronic media so far have not shown awareness of this problem. They appear to accept almost any statements given them by the anti-nuclear establishment.

The above listing of techniques used by the anti-nuclear establishment in the anti-nuclear game is not complete. Other examples will appear later, and any nuclear proponent who has engaged in a dialogue with anti-nuclear activists will be able to produce his own list of techniques which have been used to facilitate the game.

SUZUKI

In November 1987 the CBC presented a typical anti-nuclear television program, as part of David Suzuki's series *The Nature of Things*. The program was called "Problems and Risks of Producing Nuclear Energy." The tone of the background information was strictly doom and gloom from the opening description of the Chernobyl accident to the closing conclusion that ". . . nuclear energy may be both uneconomic and unnecessary."[28]

The program appeared to be fair by including interviews with both pro- and anti-nuclear exponents. However, the antis got to say about twice as much as the pros.

This type of adverse publicity for nuclear energy is worth tens of thousands of promotional dollars to the anti-nuclear establishment, yet it is provided free—in this case by the CBC.

CHAPTER 2

Radiation and Health

The Facts

AN EXAGGERATION OF THE EFFECT OF RADIATION ON HEALTH IS the basic tactic used by the anti-nuclear establishment to frighten the public about the use of nuclear energy. The tactic is intended to convince people that radiation is a uniquely dangerous phenomenon, and that it only arises from nuclear operations.

The fear of radiation is used to develop most other aspects of the anti-nuclear game:

> Nuclear reactors are claimed to be dangerous because in an accident they could release large amounts of radiation.
>
> Nuclear waste is dangerous because, if it escapes into the environment, it could release radiation affecting not only this generation but all generations.
>
> Transportation of nuclear materials is dangerous because a transportation accident could release radiation.
>
> The threat of nuclear terrorism is real because the bombing or sabotage of nuclear facilities will release radiation.

The anti-nuclear establishment has had success in frightening the public about the effects of radiation. In this chapter, the facts about radiation and health will be provided first, followed by the misrepresentations of these facts that are part of the game. It is necessary to have an understanding of the facts in order to appreciate the techniques used in the game.

WHAT IS RADIATION?

Radiation can be emitted with a wide range of energies from low-energy radio waves to high-energy gamma emissions. The most dangerous form of radiation is high-energy radiation. This type of radiation can penetrate matter and produce ions—hence its name of ionising radiation. Ions are normal atoms in which the number of outer electrons has been altered—in this case by ionising radiation. In this book, the term "radiation" will always be used to describe ionising radiation, unless otherwise stated.

Since radiation is an emanation of matter, to understand radiation it is necessary to have a basic understanding of matter. All the material on earth is made up of fundamental building blocks called elements. There are about ninety different elements in our world. Some of them, such as hydrogen, oxygen, uranium, and lead, are familiar to us. Others are less familiar, with names such as praseodymium, hafnium, and tellurium. The atoms of each element are made up of two parts, a central core, or nucleus, containing protons and neutrons, and a number of outer electrons which orbit around the nucleus.

Each element can exist in different forms known as isotopes. All the isotopes of an element have the same number of protons and electrons, but each has a different number of neutrons in the nucleus. As a result, each isotope of an element has a slightly different mass and slightly different physical properties, but all the isotopes of the same element are chemically identical.

Some of the isotopes of an element are stable, while others are unstable. The unstable isotopes will spontaneously change into other isotopes. An unstable isotope is called a radioactive isotope (or radioisotope) because when it changes it emits radiation. The new isotope that it changes into may be stable, in which case no further change takes place. Or the new isotope may also be radioactive, in which case it will again emit radiation and change to a further isotope until eventually a stable isotope is formed.

Some unstable radioisotopes, such as uranium–238, change through about a dozen or so unstable radioactive isotopes before reaching a stable state. Others, such as cobalt–60, change directly to a stable isotope. The number of stable and unstable states in which any particular element can exist is variable depending on the element. Hydrogen, for example, has only two stable isotopes and one unstable radioisotope. The element tin, on the other hand, has ten stable isotopes and twenty-three unstable radioisotopes. The elements uranium and thorium are both unusual in that they have no stable isotopes. All known isotopes of both elements are radioisotopes.

When an unstable isotope (a radioisotope) emits radiation and changes to another (stable or unstable) isotope, it is said to decay. Different radioisotopes have different rates of decay, but for the same radioisotope it is always the same. So far, it has not been possible to devise a means of slowing down or speeding up the rate of decay of this nuclear process, short of bombarding the nucleus to turn it into something else, which of course destroys the original nucleus. The rate of radioactive decay of an unstable nucleus is one of nature's constants.

It has been found that the number of nuclei of a radioisotope which will decay in a given time depends on the number of them that are present, such that half of the unstable nuclei will always decay in the same period of time, no matter how many of them are there to start with. The time taken for half the nuclei to decay is called the half-life of that particular radioactive isotope.

The half-lives of different unstable isotopes vary enormously. Some radioisotopes are very unstable and decay very quickly. Their half-lives are measured in fractions of a second. Some are very stable indeed and decay very slowly, so that their half-lives are measured in billions of years. But whatever the half-life, it is unvaryingly characteristic of a particular radioisotope.

Because of their widely ranging half-lives, it is possible to consider some radioisotopes as less dangerous than others. For example, those with very short half-lives will decay to almost nothing within a few seconds or minutes. Provided their radiation can be shielded from people for this short time (usually not a difficult procedure), they present a minimum hazard.

Similarly, those radioisotopes with half-lives in the hundreds of thousands or even billions of years are decaying so slowly that the amount of radioactivity produced in a few hours is so low that, again, it is not a hazard. For example, the isotope uranium–238 is unstable with a half-life of 4.5 billion years. A small piece of uranium can be held safely in the hand with the expectation of a negligible dose because the number of disintegrations from it will be so small during the handling period.

UNITS OF RADIOACTIVITY

The amount of radioactivity in a sample is measured by the number of nuclei which disintegrate to produce radiation in a fixed time. The current unit of radioactivity is the becquerel (abbreviated Bq), which is one disintegration per second. An older unit of radioactivity is the curie, which was named after Madame Curie, the discoverer of radium. One gram of radium produces 3.7×10^{10} disintegrations per second, and this number was termed the curie. Thus a curie is the same as 3.7×10^{10} Bq.

In this book we will use the older unit of radioactivity, the curie, rather than the new unit, the becquerel. The older unit is better known and less confusing.

UNITS OF RADIATION DOSE

When exposed to a source of radiation, a person receives a radiation dose. The three types of radiation described in the next section do not have the same effect on people, but this can be allowed for in calculating an effective dose. The current unit of effective radiation dose is the sievert (abbreviated Sv). However, in this book an older unit, the rem, will be used. A rem is 0.01 sievert, and for the range of doses we will be considering it will be easier to grasp rems and millirems (one thousandth of a rem) than 0.01 sievert and 0.01 millisievert.

TYPES OF RADIATION

When an atomic nucleus disintegrates, it can give off several types of radiation. In this section, we will confine our interest to the three best-known and most abundant types of radiation, alpha particles, beta particles, and gamma rays.

Alpha particles, compared with the other two, are quite large and heavy. They are also usually ejected from the nucleus with a high energy. When they collide with matter, they transfer this energy to the stopping medium. Because of their size, alpha particles are stopped quite readily. Even a sheet of paper will absorb most of them. This means that when they are outside the human body, alpha particles cause few problems. The slightest shielding is sufficient to protect against them, and even if they do hit the body they are absorbed by the first few millimetres of skin.

However, materials which decay by ejecting alpha particles can enter the body either by being inhaled into the lungs or ingested through the mouth. If this happens, they can be more hazardous. They can settle in a part of the body such as the lungs or the bone, and when they decay the alpha particles are absorbed by the first few millimetres of surrounding tissue. The damage to this tissue can be considerable. Thus alpha particles, when outside the body, may be regarded as posing a minimal health risk, but once inside the body they have a much larger potential for harm. The effects of alpha particles will be discussed in more detail later, particularly the effects of alpha particles inhaled into the lungs.

Beta particles are much smaller than alpha particles and usually carry much less energy. Being smaller, they can penetrate a little more deeply into matter than alpha particles and can in fact penetrate human flesh to a depth of one to two centimetres. However, a sheet of metal only a few millimetres thick can effectively stop all beta particles. Because of their low energy and smaller size, they are much less hazardous than alpha particles if they enter the body, and because they are so readily stopped by shielding material they pose little hazard when they are outside the body. Of the three particles we are considering, beta particles are the least hazardous and they will receive little further mention.

Gamma rays, the third type of radiation, have no mass, but they can carry considerable amounts of energy. High-energy gamma rays can pass right through the human body, and they can be stopped only by several feet of concrete or many inches of lead. Unlike alpha and beta particles, gamma rays can pose a hazard when they are irradiating the body from the outside. They also provide a hazard when they are inside the body. Whereas only a few radioactive materials emit alpha particles in their attempt to return to stability, many radioactive materials emit gamma rays, and most of the radiation dose that people receive from all sources comes from gamma rays.

It should be noted that X-rays are identical to gamma rays. However, they are generated differently. X-rays arise from movements of electrons in the orbits of atoms, whereas gamma rays are emitted from the nucleus at the centre of the atom. X-rays generally lie at the lower end of the energy spectrum, but there is no physical difference between a gamma ray and an X-ray once each has been generated.

SOURCES OF RADIATION

There are two broad categories of radiation to which people can be exposed: naturally occurring radiation and artificially produced radiation.

Naturally occurring radiation arises from radioactivity which is present in our environment. Since the dawn of time all human beings have been conceived and born in a radiation field; they have lived and died in a radiation field. Radiation is a natural part of our environment, as pervasive as the air we breathe and the water we drink. There are two sources of naturally occurring radioactivity: radioactive materials present in the earth; and cosmic radiation from outer space.

In addition to naturally occurring radioactivity there are several sources of artificially produced radioactivity to which we are exposed. The three major sources of this radiation are: radiation used for medical purposes; fall-out from nuclear weapons testing; and radiation from the nuclear power industry. Each of these sources of radiation and the radiation dose they provide to an average person will be discussed in turn.

RADIATION FROM THE EARTH

The earth beneath our feet contains naturally occurring radioactive isotopes. It is believed that they were present when the earth was formed about five billion years ago. Many different types of radioactive isotopes were probably present at that time, but most of them have long since decayed to form stable isotopes. It follows that those which are left must have very long half-lives, comparable in duration to the age of the earth itself. There are very few radioisotopes with half-lives that long. The principal ones, whose half-lives should be compared with the five-billion-year life of the earth are: thorium–232 (half-life 14 billion years); uranium–238 (half-life 4.5 billion years); and potassium–40 (half-life 1.4 billion years).

Uranium–238 and thorium–232 are fairly common radioisotopes found in the earth's crust. They are more abundant than familiar stable elements such as mercury, boron, and cadmium. These two radioisotopes are widely distributed, but their distribution is uneven. In some areas where concentrations are particularly high the radioisotopes are mined. Canada possesses many high concentrations of uranium which have made this country the world's leading uranium producer.

Uranium–238 and thorium–232 are both radioactive isotopes. Each stands at the head of a long radioisotope chain with about a dozen members. It is only after the decay series has progressed through all these radioisotopes that a stable isotope is reached and no further change takes place. Some of the radioisotopes in each series are gamma emitters, and they provide us with an external radiation dose. This dose averages 9 millirems per year for the uranium series and 14 millirems per year for the thorium series.

In addition to the external dose, some of the radioisotopes in each series are found in the food and water we ingest and in the air we breathe. These radioisotopes are taken into our bodies and provide us with internal doses of radiation. Two of these radioisotopes are notable because they provide us with significant internal radiation doses. They are radon–222, which is a member of the uranium decay series, and radon–220, which is a member of the thorium decay series.

Radon is an element with no stable isotopes. Its isotopes, radon–222 and radon–220, are both radioactive, have fairly short half-lives, and decay to a series of other radioisotopes which are known collectively as "radon daughters." Chemically, the element radon is known as an inert gas. It does not react chemically to form compounds, and since it is a gas it can be inhaled into the lungs and then exhaled again without providing a significant radiation dose. However, the radon daughters are solid elements and some are alpha emitters. After being formed by the decay of radon, they can attach themselves to moisture or dust particles in the air, so that when they are inhaled they tend to remain in the lungs.

Radon–222 presents a more significant hazard than radon–220. The former has a half-life of 3.8 days, which is long enough for it to diffuse a considerable distance through solid media before it reaches the atmosphere and decays to produce its daughter radioisotopes. Radon–220, on the other hand, has a half-life of only 55.6 seconds, so that many of its daughters are formed while it is diffusing through the solid media containing it, and its daughters are then absorbed before they reach the atmosphere.

The effect of radon and its daughters on health was recognised long before radon itself was discovered. As early as the sixteenth century it was reported that miners near the Erz Mountains in Europe were "dying from the pestilential air they breathe; sometimes their lungs rot away."[1] Although these were silver mines, there was also a considerable amount of uranium in the ore. When the ore was broken up, the radon was released, and in the confined space of the mine the concentrations of radon daughters could build up considerably.

When uranium mining started on a large scale after the Second World War, the hazards of radon were recognised, and a higher level of ventilation was provided in the uranium mines than was considered necessary in other hard-rock mines. However, it was still not enough, and by the early 1970s there was evidence of increased levels of lung cancer in uranium miners due to radon daughters.[2] Ventilation and work procedures were then improved, and today the hazard to uranium miners from radon daughters is considerably less than other hazards normally associated with working in underground mines.

In the late 1970s measurements were made of radon daughter concentrations in houses. To the surprise of the researchers, some high values were found. Radon from the soil can seep into basements through cracks in walls and through drains. Radon is heavier than air, so that if the basements of houses are not ventilated, comparatively high concentrations can build up. As would be expected, concentrations are dependent on the uranium content of the soil, but they are also dependent on the structural integrity of the house and the degree of ventilation. As a result, adjacent houses can contain widely varying concentrations of radon daughters.

It has been estimated that the radiation dose to the average person from this source of naturally occurring radiation is about 80 millirems per year. Some doses will be lower, but others can be higher than those currently found in uranium mines. The average dose arising from the radon–220 daughters derived from thorium is much less, about 17 millirems per year.

Other members of the uranium and thorium decay series also find their way into our bodies by the ingestion of food and water. However, they provide much less of a radiation dose than radon daughters. Examples of ingested radioisotopes are radium–226 (from the uranium series), which provides an average internal dose of 0.7 millirem per year, and radium–228 (from the thorium series), which provides an average dose of 1.3 millirems per year.

Potassium–40 is a radioisotope of the element potassium, which is the seventh most abundant element in the earth's crust. Potassium is one of the natural minerals found in our bodies, and the concentration of potassium–40 in natural potassium is about 0.1 per cent. Potassium–40 emits both beta particles and gamma rays. It decays directly to a stable isotope, either calcium–40 or argon–40. The gamma rays from potassium in the soil contribute 12 millirems per year to our external radiation dose.

Potassium is much more evenly distributed in nature than uranium or thorium, so that the external field we receive from potassium–40 is more nearly constant. The internal dose we receive from potassium–40 is also fairly constant since our bodies contain a nearly fixed quantity of potassium, amounting to about two grams per kilogram of body weight. This quantity is not quite constant because it varies with age and sex, with adolescent males containing about twice as much as elderly females. Since the amount of potassium–40 in elemental potassium is always the same, the internal radiation dose from this radioisotope received by elderly females will be less than that received by adolescent males. On average we receive an internal radiation dose of about 18 millirems per year from potassium–40.

COSMIC RADIATION

High-energy radiation is continually bombarding the earth from outer space. Some of it is absorbed by the earth's atmosphere, and some of it penetrates to the earth's surface, where it irradiates us externally. The origin of these cosmic rays is not known with certainty, although most of them seem to originate within our galaxy. The sun is known to produce some of this radiation, particularly during periods of solar flares, but the quantity is small. Most of the radiation consists of high-energy protons, with smaller amounts of alpha particles and electrons. The range of energies is broad, but it is believed that the radiation flux has remained fairly constant over the last billion years.

Due to the absorption of cosmic rays by the atmosphere, the strength of the radiation field varies with the altitude above sea level. Thus people living at places one and a half kilometres above sea level, such as Denver, Colorado, will receive twice as much external radiation from cosmic sources as people living at sea level. In Canada the average external radiation dose from cosmic radiation is about 30 millirems per year.

In addition to external radiation doses, cosmic radiation also provides a small internal dose of radiation. The passage of high-energy cosmic radiation through the atmosphere produces small quantities of radioisotopes such as tritium, beryllium–7, carbon–14, and sodium–22, which are then either ingested or inhaled. The resulting internal dose on average is about 1.5 millirems per year.

Table 1 lists all the significant radiation doses received, both internally and externally, as a result of naturally occurring radiation in our environment.

TABLE 1

Average Annual Dose Rates from Environmental Radiation[3]

SOURCE	DOSE RATE (millirems per year)		
	External	Internal	Total
Terrestrial radiation			
Uranium series	9	96	105
(radon–222 contribution)		(80)	
Thorium series	14	19	33
(radon–220 contribution)		(17)	
Potassium–40	12	18	30
Total terrestrial	35	133	168
Cosmic radiation	30	1.5	31.5
Total annual dose	**65**	**135**	**200**

ARTIFICIALLY PRODUCED RADIATION

In addition to radiation exposure from naturally occurring radioactive materials, everyone is exposed to other sources of radiation which have been produced artificially as part of our twentieth-century lifestyle. These sources are numerous, but only those which contribute a significant dose are described below. Some of the minor sources will be mentioned at the end of this section.

Most of the artificially produced sources of radioactivity are used for beneficial purposes, although it is realised that the benefits from one of them, nuclear weapons testing, could be hotly debated. Unfortunately, the benefits derived from the use of radiation cannot always be quantified, whereas the detriment due to radiation can always be assessed fairly accurately. It will be left to the reader to make a qualitative judgement as to whether the benefit is worth the risk in any individual instance.

Medical Applications of Radiation

The medical use of radiation is one area where there can be no doubt about the benefit/risk ratio. The benefits are overwhelming compared with the risks.

The first uses of radiation in medicine occurred shortly after the discovery of X-rays by Roentgen in 1895. The use of diagnostic X-rays has increased considerably since that time, and today it is estimated that about two-thirds of the North American population receive a medical or dental X-ray every year. The amount of radiation received from X-ray examinations is variable. It can be as little as 10 millirems for a dental X-ray or as high as 875 millirems for a barium enema. Averaging the doses from all types of X-ray examination over the whole population gives an annual average dose per person of about 78 millirems.

In addition to X-rays we can also receive radiation from diagnostic radio-pharmaceuticals. These are radioactive chemicals which are swallowed, inhaled, or injected to help determine what is wrong with a particular organ of the body. Different radio-pharmaceuticals concentrate in different parts of the body, and once they are there the radioactive constituent gives off gamma rays which enable the physician to "photograph" the organ to find out what is wrong with it. Sometimes, this type of examination makes surgery unnecessary. When surgery is necessary, it is possible to look at the photograph and make the incision with true surgical precision.

The number of people receiving diagnostic treatment with radio-pharmaceuticals is about one-tenth of those receiving X-rays, but the average dose per treatment is higher. The dose from all radio-pharmaceutical treatments when averaged over the whole population is about 14 millirems. The total average dose from both methods of diagnostic procedure, X-rays and radio-pharmaceuticals, is nearly 100 millirems per year.

The medical profession uses radiation therapeutically to cure diseases such as cancer, as well as diagnostically to find out what is wrong with patients. In therapeutic uses, the radiation doses received by individuals in the treatment of cancer are enormous. They can go as high as 6–7 million millirems. These high doses are necessary to destroy cancer cells, and it is inevitable that despite all attempts to minimise the loss of healthy tissues, some which lie in the path of the radiation beam will also be affected. The seriousness of cancer means that this risk must be accepted by the patient. Since therapeutic radiation doses are given under such special circumstances, they are not included in estimates of the average radiation dose received by the average person.

Radiation from Nuclear Weapons Testing

During the 1950s and 1960s there was extensive testing of nuclear weapons in the atmosphere by the nuclear weapons states. Most of the atmospheric testing ceased after the Limited Test Ban Treaty of 1963, but China and France continue to conduct an occasional atmospheric weapons test.

Each explosion has produced large quantities of radioactive material, much of which has fallen to the earth as debris. A lot of this radioactivity has decayed away, but the amounts that remain consist of the longer-lived radioisotopes and they will be a continuing source of radiation dose for many years to come.

Most of our radiation dose from nuclear weapons testing comes from ingesting radioisotopes which have been incorporated into the food chain. This source is about four times greater than the external radiation dose. The external dose itself is about five times greater than the dose received from inhalation. The average effective dose to people living in the northern hemisphere from nuclear weapons test fall-out is about 4–5 millirems per year.

Radiation from the Nuclear Industry

Radiation from the normal operations of the nuclear industry is included in this section because its alleged hazards are part of what this book is all about. As will be seen, it does not provide a significant radiation dose to people.

In Canada, and in many other countries with nuclear power plants, regulatory authorities insist that nuclear reactors be designed so that the member of the public most likely to be exposed to radiation from the reactor receives no more than 5 millirems of radiation dose per year. The definition of the "most exposed" person is very stringent. It is assumed that this person lives in a house adjacent to the boundary fence of the reactor site. All the drinking water consumed is assumed to come from the water outlet of the reactor. All food consumed is assumed to be grown at the reactor boundary fence. Needless to say, the "most exposed" person is hypothetical and is defined in such a way as to be the worst possible case of radiation exposure from the reactor.

Despite this stringency, the hypothetical "most exposed" person would receive only 2–3 millirems of radiation per year from a typical Canadian nuclear reactor. It is obvious that the radiation dose would decrease as one moved further away from a reactor. For example, at eight kilometres a typical dose would be only 0.1 millirem. Most of the Canadian population live so far from a reactor site that they would receive virtually no radiation dose at all. The radiation dose to the population from uranium mining and waste disposal is also very small.

Miscellaneous Sources of Artificial Radiation

There are a number of other sources of radiation to which we are exposed as a result of our lifestyles and which provide us with smaller radiation doses than we have considered so far. People who live in brick or masonry buildings receive radiation doses of about 7 millirems per year. The source is the naturally occurring radioisotopes which are present in the building materials. Some types of building materials contain more radioactivity than others. For example, Grand Central Station in New York City is a massive granite structure, and the radiation field it provides to people inside is so high that if it were a nuclear facility, it would not be licenced to operate. The best way to avoid getting a radiation dose from your home is to live in a log cabin. Wood has a very low radioactive content.

One source of radiation dose can be avoided by refusing to travel by air. As noted earlier, the dose rate from cosmic radiation increases with altitude. At nine thousand metres, where most jet aircraft fly, a ten-thousand-kilometre return trip from Halifax to Vancouver provides a radiation dose of about 4 millirems. Aircraft flight crews are exposed to higher annual radiation doses (about 160 millirems per year) than most people employed as atomic radiation workers by the nuclear industry.

To reduce radiation exposure even further, it would be advisable to stop watching television. Depending on viewing habits, the tube will provide an annual radiation dose of 0.2–1.5 millirems per year, an average of 0.5 millirem per year per person. There are a number of other sources of artificially produced radiation, but the total dose from all of them is very small, less than 1 millirem per year.

SUMMARY

It is clear that radiation is an unavoidable component of our lives, whether it originates from our natural environment or is artificially produced. The average annual dose rates from all the sources described above are listed in Table 2.[4]

TABLE 2
Average Annual Dose Rates from Miscellaneous Sources

SOURCE OF RADIATION	AVERAGE EFFECTIVE ANNUAL DOSE (millirems per year)
Terrestrial radiation	168
Cosmic radiation	32
Medical diagnosis: X-rays	78
Medical diagnosis: radio-pharmaceuticals	14
Nuclear weapons testing	5
Brick and masonry buildings	7
Airline travel (10,000 kilometres)	4
Television	0.5
Nuclear power reactors	much less than 1
	Total (rounded) 310

A number of facts in this Table should be noted. The absolutely unavoidable radiation dose to which we are all exposed as a result of terrestrial and cosmic radiation in our environment is, on average, 200 millirems per year. The average annual dose received from radiation from the nuclear industry is much less than 1 millirem per year. It should also be noted that the radiation doses listed above are averages spread across the population. In many parts of the world there are large populations which receive doses much larger, or smaller, than the average.

A frequently used example is the city of Denver in Colorado. Denver is situated about one and a half kilometres above sea level, so that the external cosmic radiation dose in Denver is twice what it is in sea-level cities such as New York or Miami; that is, 60 millirems per year rather than 30 millirems per year. In addition, the geological formations around Denver contain much more radioactive materials than the geological formations on which New York and Miami are built. As a result, the external terrestrial radiation dose in Denver is also twice what it is in the other two cities; again, about 60 millirems per year rather than 30 millirems per year. Thus Denverites are exposed annually to 60 millirems more radiation dose than the occupants of the other two cities.

Wider disparities can be found in other parts of the world. In some parts of Brazil, India, and Iran the radiation dose from environmental radiation can rise as high as 600–1,000 millirems per year because of high concentrations of uranium or thorium in the soil. It is worth anticipating the next section to note that no evidence of harm to the populations in these areas has been found which can be ascribed to the effects of these high radiation doses.

THE EFFECTS OF RADIATION

More is known about the beneficial and harmful effects of radiation than almost any other toxic material. The beneficial effects are demonstrated daily in hospitals around the world. The harmful effects have been demonstrated comparatively rarely, despite having been the object of intensive study since the end of the Second World War.

There is good information about the effects of *high* levels of radiation on people, but despite the best efforts of thousands of scientists working in scores of laboratories in dozens of countries we still have not detected any harmful effects from the exposure of people to *low* levels of radiation. Because of the efforts which have been devoted to trying to detect it, the lack of evidence of harm to people from low levels of radiation is very significant. It means that any effect, *if there is one*, is so small that it has not yet proved to be measurable.

The effects of radiation on body tissues are due to the formation of ion pairs, free radicals, and ionised molecules. These chemical species damage chromosomes and enzymes, impair and prevent cell reproduction, and generally disrupt the normal functioning of the cells.[5] Radiation is not unique in this respect. Certain viruses and many chemicals and drugs also disrupt the normal functioning of cells. Human cells have a remarkable capacity for restoring themselves after they have been damaged by any of these radiation, chemical, or viral agents. If this were not so, the human species would have died out long ago.

Nonetheless, if the damage caused to cells is large enough, it can result in serious harm to the organism. In the event of extreme harm, death will ensue. We have good knowledge of the levels of radiation which are required to cause serious harm to people. The best evidence comes from studying the survivors of the two atomic bomb explosions on Hiroshima and Nagasaki in 1945. These two explosions killed many tens of thousands of people, but many more tens of thousands survived. The health of the survivors has been carefully followed for more than forty years, and it has provided us with the best evidence we have of the effects of high levels of radiation on human health.

Other information has come from examining patients who received very large doses of X-rays to alleviate an arthritic condition known as ankylosing spondylitis between 1935 and 1955. By 1955 the harmful effects of large doses of X-rays had been recognised by the medical profession, and this form of treatment was discontinued. The condition of these patients has been followed since 1955.

Radiation exposures of patients during other medical treatments, all since discontinued, have added to our knowledge of the effects of high levels of radiation. Additional evidence has been obtained from radium dial painters, who absorbed large quantities of radium while licking their paint brushes to provide a fine point; from uranium miners who inhaled large quantities of radon daughters during their work; and from doctors and technicians who were exposed to large doses of X-rays while treating patients. All these groups were exposed to high levels of radiation in their occupations, and these exposures have now ceased. However, these unfortunate occurrences have been examined in detail to provide us with evidence of the effects of high levels of radiation.

The effect of *very* high levels of radiation is death. Estimates from the atom bomb survivors show that a radiation dose of 500–600 rems (500,000–600,000 millirems) delivered over a short period will result in death for about half the exposed population. At radiation dose levels of over 1,000 rems, most people will die.

These estimates from studies of the Japanese atom-bomb survivors were confirmed by the Soviet experience at Chernobyl. About two hundred reactor-station workers and fire-fighters were exposed to very large radiation doses during their efforts to contain the results of the accident. These workers were examined by Soviet authorities, and Table 3 describes their experience.[6]

At very high doses, above 1,000 rems, death is expected within hours or days. There is widespread destruction of cells in the body, especially those of the central nervous system. It is this impairment which usually leads to death. At doses between 600 and 1,000 rems complications due to gastrointestinal injury dominate the clinical picture. Survival can depend

TABLE 3
Effects of Very High Levels of Radiation at Chernobyl

RADIATION DOSE (rems)	NUMBER AFFECTED	NUMBER DECEASED
600–1600	22	21
400–600	23	7
200–400	53	1
100–200	105	0
Totals	203	29

on the general health of the patient, with healthy young adults showing the best chances of survival.

At 400–600 rems most complications are due to the destruction of the blood and blood-forming tissues. Acute radiation syndrome occurs with nausea, vomiting, and loss of hair. Below 400 rems the damage to blood and blood-forming tissues decreases rapidly as does the acute radiation syndrome. Between 50 and 200 rems a few patients may develop mild dizziness and nausea, but their recovery is likely to be complete. Between 10 and 50 rems some reduction of lymphocytes in the blood can be detected, but an irradiation dose below 10 rems produces no clinically observable effects.

The observations on the effects of high levels of radiation dose, described above, all refer to effects which will be produced within hours or days of the radiation dose. Below 600 rems the chances of recovery from acute effects increases rapidly. However, it is known from long-term studies of people exposed to high levels of radiation that they are more susceptible to contracting some forms of cancer.

The damage inflicted on cells by radiation does not always cause death of the cell. Cells may be injured and then repair themselves by well-known mechanisms. However, the repair may not be perfect. In some cells a defective repair can cause the cell to proliferate more rapidly than it would normally. These cells are a site of cancer, a disease caused by rapidly proliferating cells. Cancers can take a long time to show themselves. Leukemia, a form of cancer of the blood, can express itself in about two years. Other solid cancers take about ten years, or as long as thirty years to become apparent.

Unfortunately for diagnostic detectives, cancers produced by radiation are no different from cancers produced by many of the other materials to which we are exposed. It is not possible to pin-point any cancer as arising from a particular cancer-causing agent such as radiation. It is only possible to express statistically the chances that a cancer has been caused by radiation. This statistically expressed effect applies to people who received high levels of radiation, recovered from the acute symptoms, and then one or more decades later become afflicted with cancer. Studies of these people allow us to estimate the statistical relationship between radiation dose and the risk of developing cancer.

From the highly irradiated groups of people who have been studied, it is estimated that approximately one fatal cancer will be developed in a population exposed to 10,000 person rems.[7] The term "person rem" is defined by multiplying the number of people in an exposed population by the average radiation dose they have received. Thus, if 100 people are each exposed to 100 rems of radiation, the population dose of this group is 10,000 person rems (100 persons multiplied by 100 rems), and one extra fatal cancer will be expected in these 100 people. However, it is not possible to predict which individual person will contract the cancer. It could be any one of the 100 exposed population.

This type of statistical calculation does not apply to very highly irradiated individuals. It has already been noted that if 10 people are each exposed to 1,000 rems (which also gives a population dose of 10,000 person rems), most of the 10 people will die.

The risk of contracting cancer from exposure to high levels of radiation (where "high" can be defined roughly as being between 10 and 500 rems) is now well established experimentally. What has not been established is a relationship between low levels of radiation (i.e., less than 10 rems) and the risk of cancer. It is possible that at some low level of radiation dose, below 10 rems, the damage to cells caused by radiation will be repaired in such a way that the chances of any of the cells becoming cancerous is virtually nil. But it is not *known* whether this is true.[8]

As a result, radiation health specialists have assumed since the mid-1950s that any level of radiation can cause a cancer and that there is no threshold level for radiation effects. This means that there is no safe level of radiation; that the only safe level of radiation is assumed to be zero radiation. It must be emphasised that the assumption that there is no threshold below which radiation exposure is safe for people *is an assumption only*. There is no evidence that the assumption is correct. It has been adopted by experts because it is considered to be a safe assumption, which means it is more likely to exaggerate the effects of low levels of radiation rather than underestimate them.

Knowing from our irradiated populations the risk of cancer at high levels of radiation, and assuming that zero risk is only obtained at zero radiation dose, it is possible to make reasonable estimates of cancer risk from intermediate and low levels of radiation. This is done by assuming that the risk is linearly proportional to the dose from high dose levels down to zero dose. A relationship of this type is assumed by experts all the world over to provide a conservative estimation of the effects of low levels of radiation. It illustrates what is known as the linear, no-threshold hypothesis of the relationship between radiation dose and risk of cancer.

It is possible that the effect of 1 rem of radiation on people could be zero. Certainly it would not be possible to measure its effect experimentally. In order to have a 50 per cent chance of detecting the carcinogenic effect of 1 rem of radiation with a 95 per cent confidence limit, it would be necessary to compare about 100 million irradiated persons with a control, non-irradiated population of a similar size for a period of several decades. This type of experiment with people cannot, of course, be carried out.[9]

However, the size of the sample (100 million) needed to detect the effects of 1 rem (1,000 millirems) of radiation should be noted. This vast sample is necessary because the effect to be measured is so small, even from this relatively large radiation dose. To detect the effects of smaller doses would require correspondingly larger experimental populations.

It was noted earlier that the effect of radiation on cells caused damage which could be repaired by the cell but which could leave it permanently damaged and prone to cancerous proliferation. If the cell that is damaged is one of the reproductive cells, it is also possible for the damaged cell to pass on genetic changes to offspring. If it does this, the changes will almost certainly be deleterious, and the genetic change will appear as a defect in the progeny.

Genetic changes due to radiation have been detected in single cells and animals, but they have not yet been detected in people. Even the survivors of the Japanese nuclear weapons explosions, who have shown that high levels of radiation can produce cancer, have not shown that the same levels of radiation can produce detectable genetic effects.[10]

Nonetheless, since genetic defects can be produced in animals, it is prudent to assume that they can also be produced in people. Based on animal experiments, it has been concluded that genetic defects will be produced at about half the rate of fatal cancers. It is assumed that an exposure of a population of twenty thousand persons to 1 rem of radiation dose will result in the production of one genetic defect in the offspring of that population.

Having seen that the two major effects of high levels of radiation are the induction of cancer and the possible production of genetic malfunctions in offspring, it is of interest to assess the possible effects of background radiation on the health of the population. Natural background radiation exposes each of us to an average radiation dose of 200 millirems per year (i.e., 0.2 rem). The collective exposure of a population of one million people will then be 200,000 person rems (one million people times 0.2 rem). For cancer induction we have noted that the linear, no-threshold hypothesis postulates that an exposure of about 10,000 person rems will lead to one fatal cancer. So among our one million population, we can expect background radiation to produce twenty extra cancer deaths per year.

If a life expectancy of seventy years is assumed, then each year 14,000 of our one million population will be expected to die. Of these, we can expect that about 20 per cent will die of cancer. (Cancer, heart disease, and stroke are currently the leading causes of death in our population.) Thus 2,800 people will be expected to die of cancer, and, of these, 20 deaths may be due to natural radiation–induced cancer, less than 1 per cent.

Similarly, background radiation will produce about 10 serious genetic effects per year in our population of 14,000 births. At present, about 10 per cent of births are accompanied by genetic defects; that is, about 1,400 per year. The effect of natural background radiation will again be expected to contribute less than 1 per cent to the number of serious genetic defects in this population.

These calculations assume that the linear no-threshold hypothesis is correct. If it is *not* correct and if there is a threshold level for radiation effects, the number of excess cancers and genetic effects could well be zero. It would be more accurate, scientifically, to describe the excess in both cases as "between 0 and 1 per cent." However, the hypothesis has been used so widely and for so long that radiation health experts have often forgotten it is only a hypothesis and not an experimentally demonstrated fact. Thus the effects of low levels of radiation are routinely stated in explicit numbers, and the possibility that there may be zero effect is usually neglected—even by the experts.

THE REGULATION OF RADIATION

In this section, the growing realisation of the effects of radiation on health and the setting of standards for protecting workers and the public will be described from a historical perspective. This history will give some additional insights into how the assessments and the standards evolved as new scientific facts were discovered.[11] Since the exploitation of nuclear fission during the Second World War changed scientific thinking about the possible effects of radiation on people, it is convenient to divide the historical survey into two parts, pre-war and post-war.

THE PRE-WAR PERIOD: 1895–1940

In 1895 the German physicist Wilhelm Roentgen discovered invisible rays that could pass through substances which were opaque to ordinary light. This was considered an extraordinary phenomenon at that time, and Roentgen tentatively dubbed his discovery X-rays, a name that has since been adopted universally.

About three years later Marie Curie in Paris first isolated two radio-active elements from pitchblende. One she named polonium, after her native Poland, and the other, which became more widely used than polonium, she called radium.

For the next forty years the two major sources of ionising radiation were the electrically generated X-rays of Roentgen and radiation from the naturally occurring radioactive materials isolated by Madame Curie. Both were subjected to considerable scientific scrutiny, particularly with respect to the reactions of their radiations with other substances.

X-rays were more widely used than the radiation from radium since for many years the latter was scarce due to the difficulty and expense of extracting radium from its ores. X-rays, on the other hand, could be gener-ated cheaply and quickly with a modest amount of scientific equipment. Most of the discussion of the first fifty years of ionising radiation will be confined to experience gained with X-rays.

The discovery of this invisible radiation immediately captured the interest of the medical profession. It could pass through the body and, in conjunction with a photographic plate, could produce an image of internal bones and organs. Many X-ray machines were constructed and used, and it was not long before unusual biological effects were reported from those in close daily contact with them. Before the end of the nine-teenth century, instances of eye and skin irritation had been reported, but for a while there was a reluctance to believe that X-rays were the cause.

However, with increasing use it soon became abundantly clear that X-ray exposure, if too frequent or intensive, could produce untoward bio-logical effects. One American physicist went so far as to expose the little finger of his left hand to an X-ray tube for half an hour each day. He found that the finger swelled, stiffened, reddened, and then blistered. There could be little doubt as to the cause.

Experiments were carried out with small animals, and they showed that radiation damage was not necessarily confined to the skin. Large doses could cause damage to internal organs and result in death. It was also shown that irradiation of pregnant animals could cause abortions. One response to these perceived radiation hazards was the use of protective equipment such as goggles, gloves, and lead aprons by X-ray machine operators. This was accompanied by attempts to shield the operators from the direct and scattered radiation of the machines.

Until the mid-1920s recommendations concerned with reducing the radiation exposures of X-ray workers did not mention what level of exposure might be acceptable. This was not surprising since the physical and chemical methods used to measure radiation dose at that time were inadequate. Clinical dosimetry was sometimes defined in terms of a biological unit, the Threshold Erythema Dose (TED). It was well known by experiment and by clinical experience that a single dose of X-radiation could cause a slight reddening of the skin (erythema), similar to the effects of a mild sunburn.

The TED came to be defined as a single dose of radiation which would produce an erythema on the forearm of 80 per cent of the people tested within seven to ten days of exposure.[12] This dose could be defined in terms of the operating parameters of the X-ray machine, such as the current of the X-ray tube, the distance from the tube, and the time of exposure. Other doses could then be defined as fractions or multiples of the TED.

The accuracy involved in this method of measurement was very poor because of biological factors involved in the reaction of the skin to radiation (e.g., degree of pigmentation, amount of hair cover), and errors of 200 or 300 per cent between different observers were common. Even the same observer would not expect to repeat his results within a 25 or sometimes a 50 per cent margin of error.

Despite this, the first recommendation for a "safe" level of radiation exposure was made in 1925 based on the TED unit. The German radiologist A. Mutscheller observed that a dose of one TED spread over a month had no observable ill effects on the operator of an X-ray machine, and he recommended that a tolerance dose of 1/100th of a TED per month was a safe dose for radiation workers.[13]

There are a number of interesting facets to this first attempt to describe "safe" radiation levels. Firstly, the dose limit was intended to apply to radiation workers, those clinicians and technicians who would be working year-round exposed to radiation as part of their job. Establishing a dose for the members of the public (in this case individual patients) was not considered necessary since only a small number of people received a limited number of exposures to the radiation during the course of a diagnosis or treatment, and, as a result, their risk was small by comparison with that of radiation workers. This situation continued for many years, and it was not necessary to introduce recommended dose limits for the general population until the mid-1950s.

A second facet was that this exposure limit was based on the lack of observed, short-term effects. One TED delivered over a month produced no observable effect, and exposure to 1/100th of a TED in a month should therefore certainly be a safe level of exposure. Implicit in this approach is the concept that there is a threshold level of radiation below which no damage would be sustained. As Mutscheller put it: ". . . for in order to be able to calculate the thickness of the protective shield there must be known the dose which an operator can, for a prolonged period of time, tolerate without suffering injury." This tolerance dose is the threshold below which damage does not occur, and from observations on the health of operators who had worked with radiation for many years without apparent ill effects, it would have seemed obvious at that time that there was a safe threshold level of radiation.

Thirdly, those advocating the recommended dose limits, and those accepting them, were exercising a *judgement* on what should be a safe level of exposure. There was no information, either from experiment or observation, that the proposed level had any deleterious effects on radiation workers. In the absence of such information, judgement must be applied in deciding what should be a dose limit. Based on the lack of observed effects, it could have been proposed that a level of 1/10th of a TED, or 1/1000th of a TED, would be a safe level. But a judgement was made that the former could possibly be too high for safety and the latter could be so low as to prevent widespread clinical use of X-rays.

This question of judgement in the setting of exposure limits would recur every time new limits were recommended. Limits have always been set which are below the level of any observed effects of radiation, and this has caused problems in explaining exposure limits to the public. As the American L.S.Taylor put it in 1978, "So what we have today is a large array of philosophy [of radiation protection] built on observing nothing. Sometimes this causes troubles. I'll tell you it sure is hard to explain that to a Congressman."[14]

The measurement of radiation doses with improved accuracy had to await the development of the small ionisation chamber. This instrument uses the ionising ability of X-rays to ionise a small volume of air which then becomes an electrical conductor. The greater dose of X-rays the larger the charge which can be produced by the saturation current. The definition of a unit of radiation dose based on this phenomenon was established formally in 1928 and was called, appropriately enough, the roentgen.

In 1928 the International Committee on X-Ray and Radium Protection was formed as a result of recommendations made at the second International Congress of Radiology meeting in Stockholm. This committee was later to be renamed the International Commission on Radiological Protection (ICRP). In July 1934 the ICRP recommended a tolerance dose of X-rays of 0.2 roentgen per day. A similar exposure limit was adopted later by the ICRP for exposure to radium radiation.[15]

Although data on the biological effects of radiation continued to accumulate after the publication of the ICRP report in 1934, no further recommendations for whole-body radiation exposures were made before the beginning of the Second World War. The war effectively terminated the activities of the ICRP for the duration of hostilities, but it also increased enormously the volume of research on the biological effects of radiation.

THE POST-WAR PERIOD: 1940 TO THE PRESENT

Up to the outbreak of the Second World War, exposures to ionising radiation had been largely confined to workers in the medical profession. The discovery of nuclear fission at the end of 1938 and its rapid exploitation during the war led to the construction of nuclear reactors and to the manufacture of artificially produced radioisotopes which had widespread applications outside the medical profession.

The manufacturing and research industries soon began using radioisotopes for a variety of activities, and the transportation industry was involved in moving them from the point of production to the point of use. The personnel employed in these industries, as well as the personnel employed directly in the rapidly expanding nuclear industry, considerably widened the spectrum of population who could be exposed to the hazard of radiation. As will be seen later, radiation hazards were extended to cover the entire world population in the 1950s with the advent of atmospheric nuclear weapons testing programs, and an additional potential hazard to local populations developed in the 1960s and 1970s with the increasing use of nuclear power.

One of the early problems addressed after the war was the question of the units of radiation measure. It was noted in the previous section that the first measurement unit, the threshold erythema dose (TED) unit, had been supplanted by the roentgen, which expressed the capability of radiation to produce ionised particles in air. This unit was used until after the war when it became evident that a unit which would describe the effect of radiation on living organisms through the amount of energy absorbed in tissue would be a more appropriate measure of the biological effects of radiation. In 1951 the International Commission on Radiation Units recommended the adoption of a unit of radiation absorbed dose, the rad. The rad was defined as an absorbed dose of 100 ergs per gram. The roentgen and the rad were sufficiently equivalent for X-rays and gamma radiation that they could be used interchangeably by those involved in radiation dose measurements.[16]

However, it was known that the biological effects of different types of radiation on tissue cannot be defined solely in terms of the energy deposited in the tissue. Gamma rays, alpha particles, and neutrons, for example, all produce different intensities of biological effects in the cells through which they pass. In addition, different types of tissues have different sensitivities to the same type of radiation.

It was evident that a new term was needed to describe these different effects, and the adoption of a further unit was proposed, the roentgen equivalent man (rem), which is the dose of ionising radiation *equivalent in biological effect* to a dose of one rad of X-rays or gamma radiation. The rem is thus intended to take into account the quality factors (QF) of different types of radiation, such that the dose in rem = dose in rad × QF. By definition, the QF for X-rays and gamma radiation is unity, and currently accepted values for neutrons and alpha particles for radiation protection purposes are 10 and 20 respectively. It should be noted that neutrons are seldom encountered outside the nuclear industry.

By the end of the Second World War, knowledge of the carcinogenic effects of radiation was increasing rapidly, and leukemia had already been recognised as an occupational disease of those who worked with radiation and radioactive substances. A survey of the incidence of leukemia in radiologists over a fifteen-year period (1925–1940) had shown it to be ten times as great as the incidence in non-radiological physicians over the same period.[17] The radiation doses which led to the induction of these leukemias were not known, but judging from the working conditions at that time they were thought to be not less than 1 rem per day and frequently of the order of 5 rems per day. These levels gave annual dose rates of 250–1,250 rems per year.

Experiments had also been carried out with animals to see whether the damaging effects of radiation on reproductive cells would cause hereditary defects in offspring by gene mutations. As early as 1927 H. Muller reported that not only did such effects occur in fruit flies, but there was a strict proportionality between the radiation dose and the number of mutations produced. The mutations were predominantly harmful, but they were also found to be usually recessive so that they would only be propagated as a result of in-breeding.[18] By 1945 limited data on mice suggested that gene mutation in mammals was produced less readily than in fruit flies.

There was clearly a lot of new evidence to be considered in the formulation of radiation exposure standards, and in the mid-1940s the ICRP was reconstituted and began to consider the new evidence prior to formulating new recommendations for radiation exposure limits. A report by the ICRP published in 1951 recommended that the maximum permissible level of radiation to the blood-forming organs, the gonads, and the lenses of the eye be 0.3 rem per week and 0.6 rem per week for the skin.[19] The former was less than the previous level of 0.2 roentgen per day for the whole-body exposure recommended before the war, and the reduction was due partly to the increased knowledge concerning the long-term carcinogenic effects of ionising radiation and partly to concern over the increasing number of people being exposed.

One result of a better understanding of the effects of radiation was the specification in the recommendations of certain critical organs which were known to be specially susceptible to radiation damage and which were likely to receive the highest dose. Other parts of the body were known to be less liable to damage; for example, the maximum recommended dose to the extremities of the body, the hands and forearms, feet and ankles, was 1.5 rems per week.

An important extension, made by the ICRP in a further report in 1957, was the addition of limits for those who were not exposed occupationally. The ICRP recommended that the levels of radiation where large numbers of people were involved should be one-tenth of the levels for occupationally exposed persons.

By the mid-1950s there was an accumulation of events which prompted further examination of permissible dose limits. One was public concern over nuclear weapons testing. The first thermonuclear device had been exploded by the U.S.A. in 1952, and the quantity of fall-out debris from that test had been underestimated. It was evident that, in the future, every new thermonuclear test (the U.S.S.R. started in 1953) would significantly increase the radioactive burden on people and the environment. A second concern was the rapidly increasing use of artificially produced radioisotopes in medical diagnosis and therapy. In this connection the first two commercially produced cobalt–60 therapy machines went into operation in Canada in 1951, and they were an instant success.

The U.S. National Academy of Sciences set up a committee to examine the *Biological Effects of Atomic Radiation* (BEAR Committee), which reviewed the increasing literature on the subject and reported in 1956.[20] A sub-committee on genetic effects provided a basic input into the final BEAR report, and, on the basis of the evidence then available, it was concluded that all radiation exposures should be assumed cumulative, that there was no recovery of genetic cells damaged by radiation, and that there was essentially a linear, no-threshold relationship between radiation dose and the probability of biological damage.

The exposure recommendations of the BEAR Committee limited the lifetime exposures of radiation workers to 5 rems per year, a reduction from the 0.3 rem per week or 15 rems per year limit which had been introduced by the ICRP. This exposure limit was also adopted by the ICRP two years later. The limiting exposure was to be applied to critical organs: the gonads, the blood-forming organs, and the lens of the eye in the case of the ICRP; and the whole body, head and trunk, and active blood-forming organs in the case of the BEAR Committee. The ICRP also limited the skin dose to 30 rems per year and 15 rems per year to all other organs. It should be noted that the changes in the whole-body dose limit were influenced primarily by genetic considerations, although there was also concern about long-term cancer risks.

Both organisations adopted the principle that the permissible dose to individuals in the general population should not exceed one-tenth of the dose to radiation workers, that is, 0.5 rem per year. This was the *maximum* exposure, and the ICRP recommended that an *average* exposure to the gonads should not exceed 5 rems from conception up to age thirty years, an exposure of 0.17 rem per year averaged over the whole population.

The maximum values for whole-body exposure of 5 rems per year for radiation workers and 0.5 rem per year for the general population have been examined several times by the ICRP since they were first introduced in the 1950s. No substantial changes have been introduced to these maximum exposure levels, but the ICRP now recommends that more attention be paid to the dose levels to individual organs in the body.[21] The ICRP also recommends that the average exposure of a population should not exceed 0.1 rem (100 millirems) per year.

Several national and international bodies have conducted periodic assessments of the effects of radiation by examining all the relevant literature. Two of these, the BEAR Committee in the U.S.A. and the international organisation, the ICRP, have been mentioned already. The BEAR Committee was re-named the BEIR Committee (*Biological Effects of Ionising Radiation*) in the early 1970s and has issued comprehensive reports in 1972, 1976, and 1980. These reports are assessments only and make no recommendations for exposure levels. The ICRP maintains an ongoing review of the effects of radiation and has issued over thirty reports since 1959. Many of them make recommendations on exposure levels for various organs to different types of radiation.

A third group which assesses radiation effects was set up by the United Nations in 1955. It is called the United Nations Scientific Committee on the Effects of Atomic Radiation (UNSCEAR), and it was set up as a result of world-wide concern about the effects of radioactive fall-out from atmospheric nuclear weapons testing. This committee has reported yearly to the General Assembly of the United Nations and at irregular intervals has published more comprehensive reports. Eight of these substantive reports have now been issued, the last in 1982. UNSCEAR assesses radiation effects only; it does not make recommendations for exposure limits.

Several hundred of the world's top scientists have been involved in producing the reports for the organisations described above. Their published views have not been identical, but they are sufficiently in agreement that there can be considerable confidence that the broad outlines of the effects of radiation on health have been firmly established. There are a few dissenting scientists, and the views of some of these will be examined later in this chapter.

THE REGULATION OF RADIATION IN CANADA

During the Second World War, Canada entered into an agreement with the U.S.A. and the U.K. to build a natural uranium, heavy-water reactor for the production of plutonium as part of the Allied war effort. A group of Canadian, U.K., and foreign scientists was assembled at makeshift laboratories in Montreal to undertake this task.

One important factor to be considered in the construction of the reactor was how to ensure that the operators, and anyone else coming into contact with the radioactive materials it would produce, would be protected from the hazards of radiation. To this end, J. S. Mitchell, a British radiologist working with the Montreal group, prepared a memorandum in 1945 on *Some Aspects of the Biological Action of Radiation*, which reviewed the field.[22] He suggested that ". . . every effort should be made within the Canadian and United Kingdom project to ensure that a radiation exposure value of 0.05 roentgen per day is never exceeded." This was the first distinctively Canadian recommendation for a tolerance dose level. The 0.05 roentgen per day meant an exposure of 0.3 roentgen per week (a six-day working week was normal at that time) and 15 rems per year. This level was subsequently recommended by the ICRP in 1951.

In 1946 the government of Canada passed the Atomic Energy Control Act, which created the Atomic Energy Control Board with a mandate to "make provision for the control and supervision of the development, application and use of atomic energy."[23] At that time the Board had a small staff of two to three persons, so that it was not in a position to provide an original evaluation of radiation hazards. As a consequence, it followed the recommendations made by the ICRP.

The AECB was not even in a position at that time to provide for inspection and surveillance to ensure that recommendations for radiation exposure were followed, and for this service it relied on the federal Department of National Health and Welfare assisted, as appropriate, by the provincial departments of Health and Labour. Even though health matters are a provincial responsibility in Canada, the federal Department of Health and Welfare played a lead role at this time because provincial departments did not have the expertise to assess and apply radiation standards.[24]

The AECB published regulations for the control of atomic energy in 1947,[25] but the only mention of radiation protection occurred in Section 402, which stated that ". . . every person dealing in any prescribed substance or prescribed equipment shall in relation thereto take all reasonable and proper precautions for the protection of persons and property against injury or damage . . . ."

By the mid-1950s it was apparent that a more comprehensive statement of radiation protection was needed, and in May 1957 the AECB and the Department of National Health and Welfare began to prepare a draft of a new section on health and safety precautions which could be incorporated into the atomic energy control regulations. This was intended to provide uniform minimum requirements for all the provinces with the understanding that within such minimum requirements an individual province could enact its own regulations to meet special local conditions. In October 1959 the draft was approved by the Dominion Council of Health, and the health and safety precautions section was incorporated as Part VI of the Revised Atomic Energy Control Regulations issued in 1960.

Appendix B of the new regulations specified maximum permissible doses of ionising radiation for atomic energy workers as follows:

1. for whole body, blood-forming organs,
   gonads, and eyes: 5 rems per year
2. for skin of the whole body: 30 rems per year
3. for hands and forearms, feet, and ankles: 75 rems per year

These limits were changed in 1974 when a revision of the regulations gave a different breakdown of dose in terms of critical organs as follows:

1. for whole body, gonads, and bone
   marrow: 5 rems per year
2. for bone, skin, and thyroid: 30 rems per year
3. any tissue of hands, forearms, feet, and
   ankles: 75 rems per year
4. other single organs or tissues: 15 rems per year

In all cases, exposure of any other person was one-tenth the exposure limits prescribed for atomic radiation workers.

While specifying maximum exposure limits, the AECB has also adopted a principle recommended by the ICRP that all radiation exposures should be As Low As Reasonably Achievable, economic and social factors being taken into account—the so-called ALARA principle. This principle of radiation protection is a necessary consequence of the no-threshold hypothesis. If radiation effects are dependent upon dose, such that only at zero dose is there zero effect, then clearly all radiation doses should be kept as low as reasonably achievable.

An example of the ALARA principle in action, which will be discussed in more detail later, is the AECB decision that the most exposed person to radiation from a nuclear power reactor should only receive 1 per cent of the maximum permitted exposure. As noted above, the maximum exposure for a member of the public is 500 millirems (0.5 rem), so that nuclear reactors are designed to give the most exposed person a dose of less than 5 millirems.

DISSENTING VIEWS: THE LOW-LEVEL RADIATION CONTROVERSY

By using the linear, no-threshold hypothesis to plot a graph from high radiation levels, where the risk is known, to low levels of radiation, where the risk is not known, the theoretical risk of cancer to a population is found to be about one cancer death per 10,000 person rems of radiation exposure (see ref. 7). There have been some studies of the relationship between radiation exposure and cancer which purport to show that the risk of cancer is higher than generally accepted. The more significant of these studies are mentioned below.

A study by Mancuso, Stewart, and Kneale of occupationally exposed workers at the Hanford plant in the U.S.A. reported dose-related excess cancers among the workers at a much higher rate than would be expected.[26] This study has been widely criticised for inadequate dosimetry and for being distinctly lacking in statistical power; that is, the numbers of cases are too small in many instances to be statistically significant. It has also been pointed out that if the figures for cancer risk from radiation predicted by this study are correct, natural background radiation would produce more cancers than are currently observed in the population.

A study by Najarian and Colton of employees at the Portsmouth Naval Shipyards who had worked on nuclear powered ships was first published in the *Boston Globe* newspaper.[27] The story that twenty-two deaths from leukemia were found among these employees where only five were expected made headlines. A follow-up study by the National Centre for Disease Control in the U.S.A. concluded there was no evidence for health effects among the shipyard workers, and Najarian withdrew most of his claims at a Congressional hearing. He was chided at the hearing for unduly alarming the families of the shipyard workers.

John Gofman has written a book *Radiation and Human Health* in which he claims that the current assessment of cancer risk from radiation is about thirty times too low.[28] That is, there will be thirty cancer deaths for each population exposure of 10,000 person rems, rather than one fatality. He arrives at this conclusion by selecting two particular studies of breast cancer from the literature and one study of skin cancer in children irradiated for ringworm of the scalp. The studies conducted on the atomic bomb survivors are all dismissed by Gofman. The results from the limited number of studies are combined with a method of projecting future radiogenic cancers which assumes they increase sharply ten years after exposure, peak after forty years, and decline to zero only after seventy years. These assumptions enable Gofman to predict a cancer risk far higher than the current consensus of experts. Needless to say, the experts who regularly examine all the evidence do not agree with Gofman's conclusions.

Dr. Rosalie Bertell apparently believes that current estimates of risk of cancer from radiation are about ten times too low. This view is put forward at length in a *Handbook for Estimating Health Effects from Exposure to Ionising Radiation*.[29] The 1984 version of this book was presented as evidence at the Sizewell B inquiry in the U.K. The inquiry had been called to examine evidence on whether a nuclear reactor should be constructed at Sizewell in England. Dr. Bertell gave evidence that international bodies of experts such as the ICRP had underestimated the risks of radiation-induced cancers. As will be noted later, Dr. Bertell's evidence was not accepted by the inquiry commission.

THE PLUTONIUM MYTH

Plutonium is an element which does not occur naturally but which can be manufactured by bombarding uranium–238 with neutrons in a nuclear reactor. The radioisotope plutonium–239 has the longest half-life of all the plutonium isotopes, twenty-four thousand years. It is also an alpha emitter. These two properties have been combined to create the plutonium myth. The long half-life ensures that any plutonium escaping into the environment will be around for a very long time. The fact that it is an alpha emitter means that any plutonium taken into the body by ingestion or inhalation could be potentially harmful.

Most scientists who have studied the effects of plutonium on people agree that the risk from ingestion is low. The toxic effect of ingested plutonium has been compared with the toxic effect of caffeine, an active ingredient in coffee. The real potential for the toxicity of plutonium resides in the possibility that a particle of the material lodged in the lung will cause lung cancer. It is this effect which has given rise to the inaccurate statement that "plutonium is the most toxic substance known to man."

The high-energy alpha particles emitted by plutonium have a limited range in the body, but they deposit large amounts of energy in the thin layer of cells which stops them. A small particle of plutonium lodged in the lung will provide an intense radiation field to the cells in its immediate vicinity, and this radiation may cause some of the cells to become cancerous and thus initiate a lung cancer.

The origin of the myth about plutonium toxicity can be placed in 1968, when an American, Donald Geesaman, calculated the size of a plutonium particle which would probably deliver enough energy to the lung cells in its vicinity to initiate a cancer.[30] He concluded that a particle one-millionth of a metre in diameter and containing 0.23 picocuries of plutonium would be sufficient. (A picocurie is a trillionth of a curie.) The weight of such a particle would be only 4×10^{-12} gram, so that one gram of plutonium could cause about 3×10^{11} lung cancer deaths. Geesaman's theory of the effect of a plutonium particle in the lung became known as the "hot particle theory." From it, the myth that plutonium is the most toxic substance known to man was born.

Geesaman's theory attracted a lot of criticism. The most telling concerned his assumption that a plutonium particle in the lung would stay in one place and irradiate only the immediately adjacent tissue. It is generally agreed that particles entering the lung will move over the lung surface in the mucus which bathes the walls of the lung. The radiation field from the plutonium will then be spread out to involve about one kilogram of lung tissue rather than a few micrograms. It has been sarcastically suggested that the only way to ensure that a particle of plutonium stays in one place in the lung is to use sub-microscopic techniques to surgically implant it.

The arguments about the "hot particle" theory continued during the first half of the 1970s, but they have since dropped out of sight. The vast majority of experts in the field believe that the theory is wrong. In addition to the theoretical grounds on which the theory is believed to be incorrect, there are three pieces of practical evidence against it which, while not being conclusive, are strongly indicative.

The first is the fact that about three tonnes (i.e., three million grams) of plutonium have been dumped into our environment from the atmospheric weapons tests conducted in the 1950s and early 1960s. According to the "hot particle" theory, this is enough for about 10^{18} lung cancer doses. The world population is about 5×10^9, so that every man, woman, and child on earth has been exposed to enough plutonium in the environment to kill them more than one hundred million times over. The fact that we have not succumbed to this "most toxic substance known to man" should give pause for thought.

The second piece of evidence is that we know from experiments conducted in New York, that New Yorkers inhaled a total of 43 picocuries of plutonium from fall-out between 1954 and 1975. This is nearly two hundred times the amount that has been claimed to produce a lung cancer. Since New Yorkers seem to be surviving, this fact too gives reason to question the "hot particle" theory.

The third piece of evidence concerns twenty-six plutonium workers who had worked with plutonium during the Second World War and who were selected for follow-up studies in the 1950s because they had received high exposures to plutonium during their work. Estimates of depositions in these subjects, almost entirely due to inhalation, were between 6,000 and 80,000 picocuries. As noted above, the "hot particle" theory predicts a fatal cancer will be caused by 0.23 picocuries of plutonium. There have been no lung cancers among this group. In fact the study shows no evidence suggesting that any adverse health effects have resulted from thirty-two years of exposure to internally deposited plutonium.[31]

Practical evidence, such as the three instances given above, contradict the theoretical predictions of the "hot particle" theory. As a result, there is little controversy over the theory today. It is widely ignored by the experts. But not by the anti-nuclear establishment.

IS RADIATION NECESSARY FOR HEALTH?

Before closing this part of the chapter on the facts concerning radiation and health, it is necessary to mention a topic which has received increasing attention in recent years and which has become very controversial. This is the topic of radiation hormesis.[32] Hormesis is an effect that is well known in nature, but it has only recently been related to radiation. It describes the observed phenomenon that small quantities of some substances are essential to the health of organisms, whereas large quantities of these same substances can be toxic to those organisms. For example, small quantities of a number of elements such as copper, cadmium, zinc, and selenium are all known to be essential elements for the proper functioning of the human body. However, it is equally well known that large amounts of these same elements taken into the body can have very harmful effects. A similar effect has been suggested for radiation, and it has been named radiation hormesis.[33]

Many people have become so frightened of even small amounts of radiation that the idea that radiation may be good for them in small quantities will likely be heretical. But it must be remembered that all living cells have been created in a radiation field, and those cells which have evolved a better system for adapting to the effects of low-level radiation will have much better chances of survival than those which have not. From this concept it is only a small step to assume that cells may have developed an actual need for radiation in order to be able to function properly.

In support of this assumption it should be noted that plant cells have developed the process of photosynthesis using radiation from the sun. Without this process there would be no plants. Is it possible that later developing cells such as those found in the animal kingdom have adapted themselves to extract energy from the ionising radiation in their environment in order to be able to function properly?

A body of research literature on radiation hormesis has already been developed, most of it tending to confirm the existence of the phenomenon. Best known are the stimulating effects of low levels of radiation on the germination of seeds and the growth of plants. Other beneficial effects have been reported in both plants and animals, including improved fertility, increased lifespan, prevention of tumours, and an improved immune response system leading to resistance to infection.

Some interesting experiments have been carried out on a primitive single-cell life form found in water known as paramecium. The growth rate of paramecia in our normal radiation environment has been compared with the growth rate of paramecia placed inside a lead box to shield the cells from terrestrial and cosmic radiation. The control cells were also placed in a box, but this box had thin walls which would allow the passage of natural radiation. Other parameters such as light, air confinement, composition of medium, and temperature were maintained the same for both the control and the experimental samples. Over a period of ninety days there was a decrease in the rate of growth of the shielded paramecia compared with the controls. To confirm that the effect was due to the absence of radiation, a small radioactive source giving a radiation dose similar to natural radiation was placed inside the shielded box. The growth rate of the shielded paramecia then reverted to that observed with the controls.[34]

Other experiments have been conducted in which small animals such as mice, rats, and guinea pigs have been exposed to radiation. In most cases their lifespans have been shortened, which is the expected result. However, at certain low levels of radiation it has been found that the animals have lived significantly longer (about 20 per cent on average) than non-irradiated animals. This effect has been well established, but it remains to be seen whether it can be translated from small animals to people.

Research work on radiation hormesis is continuing, and it will be followed closely by those interested in the effects of radiation on health. Any results showing that radiation hormesis is a genuine effect will be strongly attacked by the anti-nuclear establishment.

Meanwhile, the most that can be said is that the present body of knowledge on radiation hormesis is indicative. It is a long way from being definitive. The scientific community will be rightly cautious in assessing any future evidence. The difficulty of collecting experimental evidence directly relating to people may well leave the proof or disproof of radiation hormesis as a tantalising conundrum for many years to come.

The Game

As noted at the beginning of this chapter, an induced fear of low-level radiation is basic to most aspects of the anti-nuclear game. As a result, the supposed hazards of low levels of radiation have been repeated constantly by the anti-nuclear establishment until, as Professor Bernard Cohen, professor of physics at the University of Pittsburgh, has described it, the public has been driven insane over fear of radiation.[35] Cohen uses the word *insane* purposefully since one of its definitions is loss of contact with reality.

One possible consequence of inducing insanity, and one that is never mentioned by the anti-nuclear establishment, is the harm it might do to the public. For example, Energy Probe sent out one of its periodic fund-raising letters in which the topic was the hazards of low levels of radiation. The letter was franked with the statement "Radiation Attacks the Young and the Unborn First."

It would be interesting to find out how many parents were driven "insane" by this statement, and whether their actions were influenced by it. Were any of them driven so "insane" that they refused medical radiation diagnosis or treatment for their children, and what were the possible adverse outcomes of this refusal? Of similar interest is whether consideration of such possible outcomes crossed the minds of those at Energy Probe who decided to frank their letters with this pernicious slogan.

The number of people directly involved in exaggerating the hazards of low-level radiation is very small. In Canada the principal activist in this field is Dr. Rosalie Bertell, who works through the International Institute for Concern with Public Health (IICPH). Other anti-nuclear organisations in Canada usually take their cue from Dr. Bertell, and from similar members of the anti-nuclear establishment in the U.S.A.

Although other organisations in Canada seldom make original contributions to the subject, they have produced their own literature, even if it must be considered somewhat derivative. Examples of literature from the three major anti-nuclear organisations will be presented below.

The U.S.A. has a few more anti–nuclear-radiation "experts" than Canada, but even there the total number is small. The best-known are Dr. John Gofman, Dr. Karl Morgan, Dr. Carl Johnson, and Dr. Ernest Sternglass. The doyen of this group is Dr. John Gofman. He had a distin-

A MAJOR HAZARD OF RADIATION

The accident at Three Mile Island (TMI) was a media event. Every-one "knows" it was a nuclear catastrophe, but few people realise that no one was killed at TMI and no one was injured.

The Kemeny Commission, set up by President Carter to investigate TMI, made one interesting observation in its report.[36] Noting the lack of fatalities and injuries, it concluded that the major adverse health effect of TMI was the stress caused by the fear of radiation, rather than the effects of radiation itself.

This fear was caused by the inaccurate information on the effects of low-level radiation given to the public, via the media, by members of the anti-nuclear establishment.

We can safely conclude that such inaccurate information is more of a hazard to our health than low-level radiation.

guished scientific career at the University of California before he became interested in the effects of radiation on health.

Gofman has written a book, *Radiation and Human Health*, which is a comprehensive and generally accurate description of most of the evidence on the effects of low-level radiation on the health of people. However, by selecting parts of this evidence and ignoring other parts, Gofman has come to the conclusion that the currently accepted values for the effects of low-level radiation are too low by a factor of about 30. Gofman's views on radiation are as widely disputed in the U.S.A. as Bertell's are in Canada. However, that does not prevent the rest of the anti-nuclear establishment in both countries from quoting these two authors to the exclusion of the majority view.

INTERNATIONAL INSTITUTE OF CONCERN FOR PUBLIC HEALTH (IICPH)

Dr. Bertell is the founder of the Institute. Her major contribution to the subject of radiation and health is a book called *Handbook for Estimating Health Effects from Exposure to Ionising Radiation* (1984; 2nd ed., 1986).

HOW SAT?

Dr. Ernest Sternglass of the University of Pittsburgh School of Public Health has published many papers about the effects of low levels of radiation on people, principally its effects on children. Many of his papers have been rejected as unscientific by organisations of scientists such as the BEIR Committee in the U.S.A.

In 1984 he held a press conference to proclaim his latest findings. According to Sternglass the atom bomb tests carried out by the U.S.A. in Nevada during 1966–68 had affected the brains of the children conceived at that time. This was reflected in decreased test scores in the Scholastic Aptitude Test (SAT) between 1983 and 1984 in those states downwind from the Nevada test site. Sternglass cited seven states downwind from Nevada whose average SAT scores had dropped by 1 to 11 points between 1983 and 1984. The winds from Nevada are mainly from the southwest.

One reporter at the press conference noted that Washington State was one of the seven mentioned by Sternglass.[37] Washington is northwest of Nevada, and therefore is not in the path of the prevailing winds.

This aroused the reporter's suspicions, and he then gathered information on neighbouring states which had not been mentioned by Sternglass. He found that the Wyoming SAT score (not mentioned by Sternglass) had *increased* 12 points between 1983 and 1984. Wyoming is closer to the Nevada test site than North Dakota (minus 11 points) mentioned by Sternglass. Also Kansas (+ 13) is closer than Iowa (− 4), and Arkansas (+ 3) closer than Alabama (− 4). It was apparent that Sternglass had simply selected those states which fitted his hypothesis and ignored those which did not.

This unscientific approach is common within the anti-nuclear establishment. It explains why their "results" are delivered to the press and not to peer-refereed scientific journals. The journals would not accept such scientific nonsense, but the press can often be relied upon to give a platform to stories promising disaster or threat of disaster. Unless, as in this case, a journalist decides to do some investigating himself.

The 1984 version was presented as evidence to the Sizewell B inquiry in England.[39] This inquiry was set up under a distinguished lawyer, Sir Frank Layfield, Q.C., to inquire into whether a nuclear power reactor should be constructed at Sizewell. Dr. Bertell went to the inquiry to give evidence on behalf of the "Stop Sizewell B Association." Her *Handbook* was a major part of the evidence to support her contention that the risks of low-level radiation had been significantly underestimated.

Bertell was examined at length on the contents of her book, and she appears to have been unsuccessful in persuading the inquiry towards her viewpoint. In his final report, Sir Frank Layfield made the following comments on Dr. Bertell's evidence:[40]

— "Bertell was selective in her choice of data."
— "She repeatedly used the largest reported incidence of cancer."
— "Bertell acknowledged that her evidence was marred by basic errors. These errors included:
  (a) incorrect quotation of data,
  (b) confusing the incidence of fatal and non-fatal cancers,
  (c) multiplying by the same correcting factor twice to give a figure for cancer deaths that was 35 times too large."

Sir Frank Layfield concluded that "Bertell's recommendations for changes to safety criteria for normal operation of nuclear power stations were based on a misunderstanding of the existing criteria, as well as an estimate of the risk of fatal cancer from radiation that was not supported by evidence."

It should be noted that the majority of Canadian experts in the field of radiation protection support the views of national and international bodies on the effects of low-level radiation. Like Sir Frank Layfield, they do not accept the views of Dr. Bertell. In order for Dr. Bertell's views on the hazards of radiation to be accepted, it is necessary for the views of the three major bodies who carry out independent assessments of radiation effects to be discredited. Bertell has made continuing efforts to achieve this goal by casting various types of aspersions on the ICRP, UNSCEAR, and BEIR.

For example, according to Bertell,

> the International Institute for Concern for Public Health has documented the fact that the ICRP, the recommending body Canada relies on for radiation standards, has been dominated by physicists and medical administrators, most of whom headed their countries' nuclear research or regulatory programs and, to a lesser degree, medical radiologists. None of the foremost world authorities in the field of radiation epidemiology; Dr. Alice Stewart . . . Dr. Victor Archer and Dr. Joseph Wagonner . . .

A LEGAL BROADSIDE

The U.S.A. is a very litigious country, and so it is not surprising that there have been many lawsuits in the U.S.A. over the effects of radiation on people.

No cause and effect relationship can be established between a low-level radiation dose and a cancer. On the other hand such a relationship *may* be possible, so that responsibility for damage cannot be denied outright by a defendant. All a lawyer needs in a case like this is a good "expert" who can produce a case on technical grounds that radiation *might* have caused the cancer.

Professor Karl Morgan and Dr. John Gofman are two of the best-known radiation "experts" on the U.S.A. legal circuits and pillars of the U.S. anti-nuclear establishment. Between them they have served as plaintiff's expert witnesses on several radiation-related cases.

One case involved four workers at a plant which refurbished aircraft instruments, some of which had radium-painted luminous

Drs. R. Seltser and P. E. Sartwell . . . Dr. B. Modan and L. H. Hempleman . . . R. A. Conard . . . W. M. Court Brown and Sir David Doll . . . and scores of other researchers of international repute. [*sic*][41]

These statements are misleading and inaccurate. They are also typical of the repeated attempts that Bertell has made to discredit the International Commission on Radiological Protection (ICRP). The ICRP works through a main committee and four working committees. The selection of members for these committees is based on their relevant experience with regard to an appropriate balance of expertise rather than nationality. Although not all eminent epidemiologists could work on the ICRP committees, the list above is inaccurate. Drs. Modan and Doll have both served on Committee 1 (Radiation Effects). Drs. Court Brown and Doll have both assisted in preparing reports for the ICRP. Drs. Stewart, Seltser, Sartwell, markings. Radium and its decay product, radon gas, can cause cancer, so that when the four workers, late in life, contracted the disease they sued everyone in sight. Twenty of the defendants settled out of court for $1.6 million. The twenty-first, the U.S. government, decided to fight.

The case was heard by a U.S. District Court judge in Kansas, Judge Patrick F. Kelly. Initially, Kelly was sceptical of the government's case. But over a period of ten months he informed himself of rems, microcuries, gamma rays, and alpha particles, and when he delivered his judgement it was devastating.[38]

Morgan and Gofman he characterised as partisan and unfair. Gofman, he said, is an alarmist, whose testimony was not based on medical facts.

Kelly dismissed the cases with prejudice and assessed costs against the plaintiffs.

and Conard have all had their work refereed in ICRP reports.[42]

Similar statements condemning the independence and objectivity of the ICRP were made by Bertell to the Sizewell B inquiry mentioned earlier. In the final report, Sir Frank Layfield responded to her charges that the ICRP was self-constituted and had vested interests by saying, "In view of the nature of the rest of her evidence, I do not give serious weight to her criticisms."

Bertell has also attacked the integrity of the members of UNSCEAR. For example: "UNSCEAR, which is composed of 'official representatives of scientific advisors of national delegations' to the United Nations is biased by the politics of self-interest"; and ". . . I believe that the health hazards [of radiation] are underestimated systematically [by UNSCEAR] . . . ."[43] These statements are inaccurate.

UNSCEAR is the United Nations Scientific Committee on the Effects of Atomic Radiation. The committee periodically reports to the UN on the effects of atomic radiation. It is composed of distinguished radiation health specialists from many countries, some of which have nuclear programs and some of which do not. It is absurd to suggest that these experts would for any reason unanimously agree to misrepresent the effects of radiation on people or that their views should be biased either in favour of or against the health effects of radiation. There is no evidence whatsoever that UNSCEAR has "underestimated systematically" the health effects of radiation. There is no reason to believe that its members are "biased by the politics of self-interest."

The third major committee which describes the effects of radiation on people, the BEIR Committee of the U.S.A., has also been commented upon by Bertell: "The BEIR Committees are heavily staffed with personnel from U.S. Government nuclear research laboratories such as Oak Ridge and Brookhaven, and with researchers from the atomic bomb research centres at Hiroshima and Nagasaki."[44] This statement is inaccurate.

The most recent report (1980) from the U.S. National Research Council's Committee on the Biological Effects of Ionising Radiation (BEIR Committee) lists twenty-three members, three from Oak Ridge, and two from Brookhaven. Hardly "heavily staffed" with representatives from these

---

EXPERTS

A few days after the Chernobyl accident, the CBC program *The Journal* devoted itself to an account of the accident and its ramifications. To comment on the health effects to be expected from Chernobyl, *The Journal* editors selected two people, one Canadian and one American, but both in the anti-nuclear minority as far as views on the health effects of radiation are concerned. The interviewees were Dr. Rosalie Bertell and Dr. Carl Johnson.

There are hundreds of recognised experts on radiation and health in Canada and the U.S.A. who would have been readily available for an interview by the CBC. Yet the CBC sought out two of the small minority of dissenters, one from each country, in order to give their versions to the public of the health effects of low-level radiation from Chernobyl.

The CBC did not inform the public that these two individuals held minority opinions on this subject or suggest that their opinions might be unnecessarily alarmist.

two laboratories. None of the committee members lists atom bomb research centres at Hiroshima and Nagasaki as an affiliation. However, thirteen of them are affiliated with distinguished universities from Harvard University in the East to the University of California in the West.

Dr. Bertell has also written a more general book on the hazards of the nuclear industry, entitled *No Immediate Danger? Prognosis for a Radioactive Earth*. The sub-title of the book reveals much about her attitude towards radiation. She ignores the fact that the earth is naturally radioactive to a considerable extent. The book, needless to say, is an attack on the nuclear industry. According to the author, the radioactive emissions from the nuclear industry are polluting the earth and poisoning its people. The term "omnicide" is used to describe this process.

The book begins with a graphic story of a boy named Jimmy dying of leukemia.[45] According to Bertell, leukemia is related to exposure to benzene, microwave radiation, X-rays, and nuclear fission products. She goes on to say, "These in turn are part of the strategies for national growth and development, as well as advances in the art of war. Energy mix and a weapon strategy inseparably involve human consequences in terms of increased incidence of leukemia, other cancers, neonatal and infant mortality, mental retardation, congenital malformations, genetic diseases and general health problems."[46] In this early paragraph, she presents the viewpoint she will adopt throughout the rest of the book. She believes that nuclear power and nuclear war are inextricably combined in national strategies for growth and development. The consequence of these strategies, according to her, is an increase in many of the ills that flesh is heir to, due to increased radiation levels in the environment.

Unfortunately, the facts do not support this thesis. Microwaves, X-rays, and nuclear fission products have been used in increasing abundance since the end of the Second World War. Ever since these items were introduced, the incidence of most diseases has *decreased*, not increased. People are healthier, living longer, infant death rates are down, etc. These improvements in health of the last forty years have occurred during a time of increased use of radiation for many purposes, such as nuclear power generation and medical diagnostic and therapeutic procedures. The facts contradict Bertell's basic thesis so completely that one might almost be tempted to claim that low levels of radiation are good for you. Certainly this statement can be more readily supported by the evidence than the opposite. However, there is no direct evidence to support such a claim.

The use of Jimmy's story by Bertell is followed by others. One such is the story of Ted Lombard, who worked on the wartime Manhattan Project in the U.S.A. and whose children developed a variety of illnesses.[47] Ted too developed various ailments, the most serious of which appeared

AN UNEXPECTED RESULT FROM HIROSHIMA AND NAGASAKI

The two atomic bombs dropped on Hiroshima and Nagasaki in 1945 killed thousands of people. However, many more thousands survived even though they had been exposed to very high levels of radiation. This group of survivors has since been extensively studied to find out the effects of high levels of radiation on people. They have been compared with the normal population of Japan, which did not receive any radiation from the nuclear explosions. As expected, the irradiated survivors are dying of cancer more frequently than the unirradiated control population.

But the statistics also show they are dying less frequently of all other diseases, particularly heart disease. In fact, if the age-related increased deaths from cancer are balanced against the decreased age-related deaths from all other diseases, the Hiroshima and Nagasaki survivors are healthier than the average Japanese population.

This is an astonishing result.

It is difficult to believe that high levels of radiation increase the incidence of cancer but decrease the incidence of everything else; so the explanation must lie elsewhere. Most probably it lies in the fact that the Hiroshima and Nagasaki survivors have been studied as a special group. They have had more frequent medical check-ups than the average Japanese, and these would have provided earlier diagnosis and treatment of all diseases. They are also probably more aware of good health habits such as proper diet and proper exercise. This improved health care and health consciousness could be made readily available to all people without excessive expense.

It may seem remarkable that the absence of these simple measures should have a more profound effect on health than the hazards from very high levels of radiation. But this unexpected result does serve to put the effects of so-called "lethal radiation" into perspective. Even high levels of radiation are less lethal than an absence from one's lifestyle of medical check-ups, bran muffins, and a brisk walk.

to be lung fibrosis. Bertell, without setting out the evidence, ascribes all these ailments in the Lombard family to the fact that Ted worked with radioactive materials on the Manhattan Project. However, Ted was a moderate smoker. This could account for his lung fibrosis, and from the viewpoint of an anti-smoking advocate it could be said to cause all his family's other ailments as well.

One final story of this type, which is mentioned in Bertell's book and frequently appears in her writing and speeches, is a description of "jellyfish babies." During the late 1950s and early 1960s, the Marshall Islands in the South Pacific were the site of nuclear weapons tests carried out by the U.S.A. The population of the islands was evacuated before the tests began, but some islanders were nonetheless accidentally contaminated with fall-out from the bombs. Bertell's story relates to some of the offspring of the Marshallese women. "Women in the Marshalls have described their babies as 'a bunch of grapes . . . or a jellyfish baby. . . . the heart beats for 2 to 12 hours and then they die.' In the case of a blighted embryo, the uterus can fill with cystic grape-like structures varying in size from microscopic to 3 centimetres in diameter."[48]

Bertell appears to assume that these blighted births are caused by radiation, although there is no evidence for this assumption. When she tells this story, there are a number of points which she does not mention. The condition described is known medically as a hydatidiform mole. These moles are well known to the medical profession. They were known long before radiation came to be used on a large scale. They occur naturally in one in two thousand births. Most interestingly, they occur much more frequently in the Orient, especially in China, the Philippines, and Malaysia, where the frequency rate is four times greater than for other areas of the world.[49] Since these facts may, to some extent, dilute the effectiveness of the story about jellyfish babies, it is understandable why they are never mentioned.

One aspect of radiation and health to which Bertell draws attention in her book, and which she has repeated many times, is the lack of statistical information relating to health effects and the need for data collection so that epidemiological studies can be conducted. Bertell says, "Inadequate collection of information on public health by governments makes it difficult for scientists concerned about radiation exposure levels to document changes in public health. The problem is not that they are poor scientists, but that they do not have access to detailed information, since governments have failed to collect it."[50] What Bertell apparently would like to see is a massive collection of health (illness) data for all regional populations, so that it would then be possible to relate all illnesses to *possible* exposures to radiation.

This uni-causal approach to disease, where the cause is radiation, has long been espoused by Bertell. But proclaiming radiation as the one explanation for all illnesses is as unwise as espousing spinal misalignment or improper diet as the cause of all ill-health. The only disease which has been proven to have been caused by radiation is cancer, and, as noted earlier, an experimental population of 100 million people would be required to assess the cancer-causing effect of 1 rem (1,000 millirems) of radiation. The average person's exposure to radiation from the nuclear industry is so much less than even 1 millirem per year that it is not easily measurable. There are not enough people in the world to be able to conduct an experiment to assess the effect of this level of radiation from the nuclear industry.

Even if the assessments of Bertell (or Gofman) are assumed to be correct, and the effects of low levels of radiation are one order (or one and a half orders) of magnitude greater than the consensus of expert opinion, it will still not be possible to measure the effect of radiation from the nuclear industry using epidemiological techniques.

The fact that the world's population has always lived in a natural radiation environment is largely ignored in Bertell's book. This results in a one-sided account of the potential risks from natural and man-made radiation. In addition, Bertell has her own definitions of these two sources of radiation which are neither used nor accepted by the majority of experts in this field.

For example, she says that ". . . 'natural background radiation' has been used for all radioactive particles not man-made . . . in the fission reactor. Blasted out of the ground with dynamite . . . these natural radioactive chemicals have been enabled more easily to enter the body . . . . Although in a sense they are 'natural,' they are not in their natural state."[51] She appears to be saying that uranium mining residues are considered part of natural background radiation. They are not. Mine tailings are always considered to be part of technologically enhanced radiation.

Also, Bertell believes that ". . . last year's pollution from a reactor becomes 'background' if it persists in the environment longer than a year . . . ."[52] This belief is erroneous. Some assessments of radiation dose from nuclear reactors extend into the future for one hundred million years (see the next section on Energy Probe).

Bertell's concept that last year's technologically enhanced radiation (e.g., from nuclear reactors) becomes part of this year's assessment of naturally occurring background radiation is not only erroneous, it is irrelevant. Nowhere in her book does Bertell provide figures for comparative levels of radiation dose from both sources, as are provided in the first part of this chapter. The unavoidable average natural background radiation dose from radioactive materials already in our environment (and which have been in our environment since the world began) is about 200 millirems per year. The additional average radiation dose from the nuclear industry is less than 0.1 millirem per year.

Even if there were no decay of this reactor-produced radioactivity and even if none of it were removed from access to people by being absorbed into our environment (e.g., into the oceans), the additional annual radiation dose to people from the operations of the nuclear industry is completely trivial compared with natural background radiation. Bertell's case for claiming unacceptable hazards from the nuclear industry relies entirely on ignoring this comparison between natural and technologically enhanced radiation. The reader is invited to flip back to Table 2 to refresh his memory on the numbers.

EXPLOSIONS

When describing what happens when a particle of radiation enters the body, Dr. Bertell likes to compare it with a "little explosion" going off in the body. She then carefully explains that each of these "little explosions" can cause a cancer to start.

This description of the hazards of radiation is likely to sound very frightening to a person not familiar with the subject.

What she neglects to mention is the number of "little explosions" going off in our bodies all the time as a result of natural radiation in our environment.

We are being zapped by these "little explosions" at the rate of thirty thousand every second, or about two million per minute for every minute of our lives.

Before leaving Bertell's book, it should be noted that it contains several factual inaccuracies. Two examples citing incidents familiar to Canadian readers will be mentioned.

On page 170, the following account of the NRX accident is given: "On 13 December 1950, the first major nuclear generator accident took place at the NRX reactor at Chalk River, about 150 miles north-west of Ottawa, Canada. A hydrogen explosion occurred, killing one man and seriously contaminating five others."[53] There are three inaccuracies in this account.

(1) The accident occurred on December 12, 1952, not December 13, 1950. (2) No one was killed. (3) No one was "seriously contaminated."

On page 171, a brief description of the NRU reactor accident in 1958 is more accurate, but after mentioning that more than six hundred people were required for the clean-up, Bertell goes on to state, ". . . the Canadian government failed to do a follow-up study on the men to find out what their actual experience was."[54] This statement is inaccurate. A report entitled *Follow-up of AECL Employees Involved in the Decontamination of NRU in 1958* (AECL–7901) was published in September 1982 (Bertell's book was published in 1985). A similar report on NRX was published in July 1982 (AECL–7760). Both reports showed that those involved in the clean-up operations had suffered no ill-effects.

In addition to her two books, Bertell's reputation as a radiation expert rests on her published papers. As noted earlier, it is believed that her last major contribution to the refereed literature was made in 1977. It was an article entitled "X-Ray Exposure and Premature Aging."[55] The assumption is made in the paper that the biological changes which occur when humans are exposed to ionising radiation from medical X-rays are comparable to those occurring through the natural aging process. By using data from the Tri-State Leukemia Survey, Bertell purports to show that a one-rad skin dose exposure to the trunk is comparable to one year of natural aging.

As noted earlier, the Tri-State Leukemia Survey is widely believed to have been a flawed study (even by Dr. John Gofman), so that its results are not reliable for estimating radiation effects. As a result, Dr. Bertell's paper has been widely ignored. For example, the 1982 UNSCEAR report devoted a section of about sixty pages to the topic of "Radiation Induced Life-Shortening." The section is supported by 355 references, but Dr. Bertell's paper is not mentioned. A smaller section entitled "Aging" also appears in the 1980 BEIR report. Again, her paper is not mentioned. Both BEIR and UNSCEAR agree that there is no reliable evidence that radiation causes aging, a conclusion diametrically opposed to the conclusion in Dr. Bertell's paper.

Another major paper by Bertell, to which she often refers, is "Environmental Influence on Survival of Low Birth Weight Infants in Wisconsin, 1963–1975." This is a more recent paper published in her own journal, *International Perspectives on Public Health*.[56] The State of Wisconsin keeps good records on low birth-weight infants. A local anti-nuclear group, League Against Nuclear Dangers (LAND), asked Dr. Bertell to study the health effects of radiation from nuclear power plants in or near Wisconsin in order to provide them with ammunition to use against the local nuclear utilities. Bertell examined the records of mortality of low birth-weight infants and the records of routine gaseous radioactive emissions from the local nuclear plants and concluded that there was a correlation between the two. She claimed that in the years when nuclear reactors released radio-activity, the excess mortality rate in regions downwind from the reactors increased compared with control areas. Three areas downwind from nuclear reactors were examined and compared with three control areas.

A number of criticisms can be made of this paper. (1) The incidence of low birth-weight infants and their mortality rate can be influenced by a large number of well-known factors. Radiation is not considered to be one of these factors. (2) Bertell presents no evidence to show that low levels of radiation can cause the death of low birth-weight infants. (3) She presents no evidence to show that the radiation from the nuclear reactors gave any radiation dose at all to the mothers or the infants. (4) In one "affected" region, the nuclear reactors are on the shore of Lake Michigan downwind from the population. Apart from a reference to "lake-effect," Bertell does not explain how a population could have been irradiated by gaseous emissions from a reactor which is downwind of the population. (5) Another reactor is located in Minnesota one hundred and thirty kilometres away from the nearest part of the "affected" region in Wisconsin. Any radiation from gaseous emissions would be so dispersed by the time it had travelled one hundred and thirty kilometres it would no longer be measurable. (Its initial value at the reactor boundary fence would give a radiation dose of less than 5 millirems per year.) (6) In one region, her figures appear to show that the excess infant death rate decreases as the quantity of radioactivity released increases. This is the opposite of the result she is claiming to show. This paper shows the danger of being trapped into a uni-causal theory of illness. It can result in a forced fit of two unrelated events which do not necessarily have a connection.

A light-weight example of this way of thinking is apparent from the following pair of hypothetical facts: In 1894 clergymen's stipends in the U.K. increased by 20 per cent; in 1895 imports of rum into the U.K. increased by 20 per cent. The obvious deduction from these two facts is almost certainly wrong—no matter what the statistical correlation.

ENERGY PROBE

Energy Probe's major contribution to the issue of radiation and health is a book called *Radiation Alert,* by David Poch.[57] The cover blurb states, "Sources of radiation are part of everyday life—here's how you can minimize the risk." Taken at face value, this book could be a commendable endeavour to explain to people the minimal risks presented by low levels of radiation compared with the risks from most other activities encountered in everyday life. However, the book is not written in this manner. Its tone seems designed to alert the public to radiation hazards which are so small that a sensible person could safely ignore them.

The objectivity of the book is questionable from the outset because of the selection of an expert opinion on the hazards of radiation: ". . . because we [sic] are impressed with Dr. John Gofman's methodological rigour and clarity and his independence from vested interests, this book relies on Gofman's estimates for cancer risks due to high energy radiation."[58] It would have been interesting if the book had stated what was wrong with the consensus view of the hazards of radiation accepted by 99 per cent of the professionals in this field. Why was their view deficient in "methodological rigour and clarity"? Was the fact that Gofman's assessment of risk makes radiation appear to be thirty times more dangerous than it really is a factor in his selection as an expert?

Judging by the triviality of some of the radiation exposures listed in the book, the author needs all the help he can get in trying to persuade the public that some of his sources of radiation are truly hazardous. Some of the radiation exposures cited are so small that no attempt at all is made to provide any dose rate or risk level. For example, when describing the alleged hazards of fluorescent lights, the book says that ". . . women who work under fluorescent lights were twice as likely to develop malignant melanomas [a potentially fatal form of skin cancer]."[59] The normal risk of this type of skin cancer is small, and it is usually curable. The absurdity of worrying about running even twice that level of risk from exposure to fluorescent lights is obvious. However, women are left to worry about the "likelihood" of getting "fatal cancer" from this source of radiation.

For the benefit of parents who are likely to worry about their children, the book gratuitously adds: ". . . hyperactivity in young children may be one effect of fluorescent lighting."[60] Again, the probability implied in the word "may" was not defined. If it had been, it would probably have been so close to zero that it would have reduced the effectiveness of the statement in raising anxiety in parents.

According to the book, mantle lamps ". . . add a potentially serious radiation source to the otherwise comforting country setting."[61] It quotes a value of about 0.3–2.3 millirems of radiation dose per year from radioactive thorium in the mantle. The book does not mention that the possibility of getting cancer from this "potentially serious" source is about the same as getting cancer from benzopyrene by eating one charcoal-broiled steak every month.

Tritium-based painted dials on watches are also invoked to arouse concern. "Individual internal whole-body user doses of beta radiation have been measured at between 0.06 and 0.33 millirems per year. The collective dose to wearers in the U.S.A. has been estimated at 3,275–18,012 person rems per year."[62] Using Gofman's magical malignancy multiplier, these data lead to a calculation of twelve to sixty-seven cancer deaths in the U.S.A. per year from the use of these dials. The book does not mention that a radiation dose of 0.1 millirem per year is about as likely to cause cancer as eating a single peanut butter sandwich per year (because of the cancer-causing properties of aflatoxin B in five grams of peanut butter).

The most extensively treated source of radiation in the book is the nuclear power industry. In this long section, Poch repeats in large measure the standard complaints of the anti-nuclear establishment against nuclear power.

The section starts off with the following statement: "Even without the military use of nuclear technology, President Dwight D. Eisenhower's 'peaceful atom' is wreaking havoc on us and on our descendants."[63] This statement is erroneous.

As will be seen in chapter 8 on the risks of nuclear power, nuclear power is a safer source of energy than any other except for natural gas. It is safer than solar energy and much safer than its only realistic alternative, coal. Chapter 9 on the benefits of nuclear energy shows that the "peaceful atom" in terms of lives saved due to safe nuclear power and the benefits of nuclear energy in medicine, industry, agriculture, etc. is an enormous boon to this generation and future generations. The benefits of nuclear energy so far outweigh the risks that the statement cannot be taken seriously.

According to *Radiation Alert*, "the risk to the public from nuclear power is an imposed risk; it is not voluntarily assumed."[64] This statement is inaccurate. Decisions to employ nuclear power are made by provincial governments. Decisions to license nuclear power reactors are made by the federal government. Both levels of government consist of representatives elected by the public. To state that there is an imposed risk from nuclear power, as if the nuclear industry were in some way outside the direct control of governments, is misleading. The anti-nuclear establishment appears to refuse to accept the fact that Canada is a democratic country governed by elected parliaments.

Another misleading statement from the book is: "The benefit provided by nuclear power, i.e. electricity, is one that can be obtained by other means which do not have these kinds of [radiation] drawbacks."[65] Other energy sources may not have the drawbacks of small emissions of radioactivity, but they do have other drawbacks, environmental, economic, safety, etc., which leave them at a disadvantage compared with nuclear power. See chapter 7 on alternative energy sources.

PRECAUTIONS

It is worthwhile asking the question whether the anti-nuclear activists' fear of radiation is genuine or whether it is just part of their game, which creates fear among the general public.

Those with a genuine fear of low levels of radiation can take a number of steps to reduce their exposure by simple alterations of lifestyle. Some of these alterations are listed below, together with the approximate reduction in radiation dose in millirems (mrem) they can be expected to achieve during a year.

— Live in a wooden house rather than in a brick house (7 mrem).

— Install good ventilation in the house to remove radon (80 mrem).

— Avoid air travel. One return trip between Halifax and Vancouver gives 4 mrem.

— Do not live or work in high-rise buildings. A forty-five metre increase in altitude (about twelve stories) gives 1 mrem.

— If married, sleep in separate beds. Mutual irradiation is then reduced (4 mrem).

— Do not breast-feed or cuddle babies for prolonged periods, because of parental radiation of the child (1 mrem).

— Do not watch television (1 mrem).

— To lessen the chances of genetic effects appearing in future generations, all men and women of reproductive age should wear lead-lined jock-straps or lead-lined corsets respectively (50 mrem to the gonads).

To test the sincerity of anti-nuclear activists who proclaim the hazards of low-level radiation, ask them how many of these simple precautions they use regularly to reduce their annual radiation dose.

Chances are that they will use none of them.

The book also says: "It [plutonium–239] is considered to be one of the most toxic substances known to man"[66]; and "Plutonium is one of the most hazardous substances on earth."[67] As pointed out earlier in this chapter, there is an anti-nuclear myth about the toxicity of plutonium which does not correspond with the facts. In the two statements above, the book is trying to perpetuate the myth.

In an attempt to bury this particular myth, an American pro-nuclear advocate, Professor Bernard Cohen, has offered to eat as much plutonium as an anti-nuclear advocate will eat caffeine (as found in coffee). He has not yet found an anti-nuclear advocate to take up the challenge, perhaps because he insists that the event be televised. The anti-nuclear establishment would not want to see one of its favourite myths destroyed on network television.

In a section on releases of radioactivity from the nuclear industry and the associated radiation doses to the public, the book quotes some apparently scary figures on what the effects may be in terms of cancer deaths. UNSCEAR has produced some speculative figures (which it recommends should not be used for decision-making purposes—a stricture not mentioned by Poch) on the possible radiation dose received by the public as a result of generating one gigawatt-year of electricity. Using these figures, and estimating there were 55.5 gigawatts of nuclear electricity produced in 1979 in the U.S.A. and Canada, the book calculates that ". . . we have sentenced roughly 2,222 people to premature death due to cancer from that one year of nuclear power generation in North America."[68]

The statement that 2,222 people will be killed *in the future* due to this one year of nuclear power generation sounds scary until we inquire how far into the future? The book refers to "millennia," but a reading of the UNSCEAR report shows it to be, not thousands of years, but *one hundred million years*. If the 2,222 deaths are averaged over this period, then the average death rate amounts to 0.00002 deaths per year. In fact, even this death rate is unlikely. It makes uncertain assumptions about the risks from very low levels of radiation; it assumes a steady state for the world's population for the next one hundred million years; and it assumes that there will be no cure for cancer over that period.

Radiation Alert provides us with examples of most of the techniques of the anti-nuclear game mentioned in the Introduction to this book. They include: inaccurate and misleading statements (the comments on the "peaceful atom"); avoiding comparisons (of radiation effects with other common low-level risks like eating steaks or peanut butter); replacing reason with emotion (by exaggerating the risks of radiation—particularly to offspring); use of dissenting scientists (John Gofman—a minority viewpoint—is used as an authoritative source while the consensus views of the other

99.9 per cent of experts is ignored); playing the numbers game (a death rate of 0.00002 persons per year is put forward as an unacceptable risk); and the ten-second inaccuracy (see the statements on plutonium). It should be noted that other examples of the game appearing in *Radiation Alert* will be found in later chapters of this book.

CANADIAN COALITION FOR NUCLEAR RESPONSIBILITY (CCNR)

The CCNR has published little on the effects of radiation on health. Its major work is a report first written by Gordon Edwards in 1978 on the problem of radon gas in buildings entitled "Estimating Lung Cancers; or, It's Perfectly Safe, but Don't Breathe Too Deeply."[69] Despite its title this work is meant to be taken seriously.

The evidence presented in the report purports to show that the risk of contracting lung cancer from radon gas is greater at low levels of radiation exposure than it is at high levels. In other words there is an increasing risk with decreasing dose. It provides an estimate of the increased risk and claims that radon gas in buildings could provide "a whopping 31 per cent increase" in the natural lung cancer death rate for Ontario males.[70]

Because no direct evidence has been accumulated that radon in buildings causes lung cancer, the report bases its estimate on three sets of data from other sources which show the induction of lung cancer by radiation. Two of these derive from experience with uranium miners in the Colorado Plateau area of the U.S.A. and in Czechoslovakia. The third set of data has been obtained from survivors of the Hiroshima atom bomb explosion.

The most significant evidence was provided by the Czechoslovak uranium miners in a paper written by Svec, Kunz, and Placek.[71] Their data relating the incidence of lung cancer to exposure to radon daughters showed that the risk factor for the lowest exposure group was twice the average for all the other groups. This would confirm the thesis that lower exposures carry higher risk factors.

What was not mentioned in the CCNR report was a statement in the Czech paper that the excess cancer deaths are non-significant at the 5 per cent level for the two lowest exposure groups; that is, the number of cases in these two groups is too small to allow any statistically reliable conclusions to be drawn from them. When using the Czechoslovak figures to prove its case, the CCNR report did not warn its readers of the low level of confidence which the authors themselves placed in the key data at low radiation levels which were critical to its thesis. It should also be noted that the Czech authors said that their data showed a linear relationship between dose and risk. The report's thesis was that such a relationship was not linear, but it does not cite the contradictory statement of the Czech authors.

Another omission was apparent in the treatment of the Colorado Plateau data. A set of 1971 results[72] was quoted in which the risk factor was clearly larger for the lowest exposure level than for higher levels. What was not mentioned in the Edwards report was a revision and updating of the 1971 data published by the same authors in 1973.[73] This data showed that the risk factor for the lowest exposure level was now negative, a result which clearly contradicted the thesis that risk factors increased at lower exposure levels.

MISCELLANEOUS EXAMPLES OF THE GAME

The major works of the major members of the anti-nuclear establishment clearly show how the anti-nuclear game works with respect to the subject of radiation and health. However, although these works give direction to the anti-nuclear game, its ultimate effectiveness depends on the widespread repetition of misleading or inaccurate information by the anti-nuclear establishment, which is then transmitted by the media to an unsuspecting public. It is possible to obtain further insights into the anti-nuclear game by examining lesser works and lesser authors. Listed below is a collection of quotable quotes, with comments, from both the major and minor members of the anti-nuclear establishment.

". . . they've never found a threshold [for radiation]. So at every level that has been tested, there has been an effect" (Rosalie Bertell, IICPH).[74]

This statement is inaccurate.

No effect of radiation on people has been detected below a dose level of about 10,000 millirems, although studies have been carried out on populations exposed to this, and lower, levels of radiation. In some of these studies which have been carried out on workers in the nuclear industry, it appears that the exposed population is healthier than the non-exposed population. This is probably not due to the effects of radiation but to what is known as the "healthy worker" effect. This effect simply takes account of the obvious fact that a working population is healthier than a general population because it does not contain sick people.

However, because an effect has not been detected it does not necessarily mean that there is no effect. It is for this reason that radiation health experts assume there may be effects even if they are not detected. While it is true to say that an effect of radiation is *assumed* down to every low level, it is inaccurate to say (as Bertell does) that an effect has been *found* at every low level.

"Tritium toxicity has been systematically under-estimated by the ICRP. . . . Perhaps this is because it is so difficult to extract tritium from nuclear plant effluence" (Rosalie Bertell, IICPH).[75]

Both statements are inaccurate.

Scientific consensus would indicate that Bertell has overestimated tritium toxicity, not that the ICRP has underestimated it.[76] It is not difficult to extract tritium from nuclear plant effluence. Ontario Hydro has a plant to do this at its Darlington generating station.

"As a result of an estimated annual release of 3,800 curies of carbon–14 in the year 1986, hundreds or thousands of people world-wide would contract cancer (the estimate depends on the risk factor used). These cases will occur over thousands of years to come; they represent human suffering, not only to people in the immediate area" (Rosalie Bertell, IICPH).[77]

These statements are misleading.

They are another example of number juggling, used to make something extremely safe appear to be extremely dangerous.[78] According to Bertell, 3,800 curies of carbon–14 were released from the Pickering and Bruce nuclear stations in Canada in 1986. Carbon–14 has a long half-life, 5,730 years, so that it will eventually spread all over the world and give everyone a minuscule dose of radiation before it decays away. By adding up these minuscule doses to a world population of ten billion people over a period of ten thousand years, a significant population dose can be obtained—enough to cause a maximum of 590 cancers (according to the ICRP) or a maximum of 7,200 cancers (according to Gofman). Even if Gofman's maximum figures are accepted, the average death rate over ten thousand years is less than one death per year. This one death occurs in a population of ten billion, about one to two billion of whom will die of cancer from other causes during their lifetimes.

When looked at in this light, nuclear power appears so safe that its use becomes almost mandatory. But that is not the impression gained from the anti-nuclear establishment when they make statements about "hundreds or thousands of cancers" over "thousands of years."

It is also worth remembering that carbon–14 occurs as a natural constituent of our environment. It is formed by the action of cosmic radiation on nitrogen. There are about 280 million curies of it in the environment. This figure should be compared with the 3,800 curies mentioned by Bertell. It is also worth noting that the 280 million curies in our environment give us all an annual radiation dose of about 1 millirem per year. Is it any wonder that experts in the field believe that the dose from the 3,800 curies is trivial?

One final point about carbon–14. The quantity of it in our environment has gone up slightly since the end of the Second World War. Nuclear weapons testing has added about 5 per cent, and nuclear power reactors have added about 1 per cent, to the amount found naturally. But the radiation dose we receive from carbon–14 has stayed the same during this period.

The reason for this is quite simple. Our bodies contain a fixed amount of carbon according to our weight. The ratio of radioactive carbon to non-radioactive carbon is also fixed at any one time. Because the amount of radio-carbon has increased slightly over the last forty years, it would be expected that the radiation dose due to carbon–14 would have also increased. This has not happened. Thanks to the massive burning of fossil fuel which has occurred during the last forty years, the quantity of stable carbon in our environment has also increased, and the ratio of radioactive carbon to stable carbon has remained approximately the same. This phenomenon is known as the Seuss effect, where the credit goes to a scientist not a children's writer.

"Focus on cancers, fatal and non-fatal, has diverted attention from other effects of exposure to ionising radiation, especially as it relates to reproduction, although this has been given lip service since 1950" (Rosalie Bertell, IICPH).[80]

This statement is misleading.

There has probably been less attention paid to the reproductive and genetic effects of radiation than to its cancer-causing effects, but this is not surprising since *no genetic effects of ionising radiation on people have*

CHEERS

One way in which radioactive materials can enter the body is through drinking liquids.

For those who are interested in reducing their radioactive intake while drinking, the Table below provides some typical radioactivity concentrations per litre for a number of liquids.[79]

TYPE OF LIQUID	RADIOACTIVITY LEVEL (picocuries per litre)
Typical nuclear power plant waste-water discharge	less than 10
Domestic tap water	20
River water	10–100
4 per cent beer	130
Ocean water	350
Whiskey	1,200
Milk	1,400
Salad oil	4,900

After perusing this list, one might expect the members of the anti-nuclear establishment to immediately start drinking beer for breakfast instead of milk.

Unless, of course, they happen to live near a nuclear reactor, in which case they have an even better choice . . . .

yet been detected even at very high levels of radiation exposure. Nonetheless, more than lip service has been paid to genetic effects in all BEIR and UNSCEAR reports since 1950, and also in ICRP publications. Direct evidence from experiments with mice is extrapolated to human scale, and it is generally considered to be a safe assumption that the risk of hereditary defects in people caused by radiation is about half the risk of fatal cancers.

A large number of chemicals are mutagenic and so are a number of viruses. Radiation is a minor mutagen compared with many others, but it is the one to which the anti-nuclear establishment draws attention at every available opportunity.

To put the genetic risk from radiation into a comparative context, it can be compared with the risk of Down's syndrome (mongolism). A woman's risk of bearing a child with Down's syndrome increases with her age and the age of the father. It has been calculated that if all electricity in the U.S.A. were nuclear generated, the maximum increased risk of Down's syndrome to the typical American woman due to radiation would be the same as if she and her husband had delayed conception by 2.6 days. (At minimum there would, of course, be no risk of Down's syndrome from radiation.)

"It is unfortunate to have to point out that future generations are unlikely to thank us for regulating exposures of their ancestors to mutagenic radiation as if those future generations do not count" (David Poch, Energy Probe).[81]

This statement is misleading.

The claims by the anti-nuclear establishment that radiation from the nuclear industry is impacting adversely on future generations are made repeatedly, but they are without justification. About 10 per cent of all new-born children show some evidence of genetic defects. There are several thousand known mutagens in our environment which can cause these defects. One of these mutagens is radiation.

There is no difference between the effects on people of naturally occurring radiation and radiation from the nuclear industry. The average amount of radiation dose from the nuclear industry is less than 0.1 millirem per year. The average amount from naturally occurring radiation is about 200 millirems per year (see Table 1). The latter figure is highly variable, with some parts of the world experiencing radiation doses several hundred millirems higher than the average. The children of people living in these areas do not have an increased number of genetic defects due to this increased radiation dose.

The concept that radiation doses, even as high as several hundred millirems per year, can have a deleterious effect on human health over the long term is erroneous. Anthropologists believe that the first human appeared on earth about five million years ago. Since that time the human gene pool, which we all share, has been irradiated with a dose of about *one thousand million millirems*. This massive radiation dose may well have produced some genetic defects, but if they were harmful to the development of the human race the law of natural selection would have ensured that they would not survive. They would have been bred out of the human gene pool.

The myth of two-headed monsters produced by radiation is one that is assiduously cultivated by some members of the anti-nuclear establishment, but its expression should be left to the makers of B-grade movies. It has no basis in fact.

WITCHCRAFT

Thomas Connolly, writing in *Nuclear News*,[82] quoted the following from an article appearing in the editorial pages of the *Los Angeles Times*: "TMI Unit 1 had opened two years earlier, and Lee suspected that radioactive emissions might be causing some of the 'strange goings on' widely reported by local animal owners: deformed chicks hatching, duck eggs not hatching at all, whole litters of stillborn kittens, cows and goats with reproductive problems."

Connolly then compared these statements with a description of things in England three hundred years ago: "For more than a year, the families of Cromwell and Throgmorton continued to persecute her, and to assert that her imps afflicted them with pains and fits, turned the milk sour in their pans, and prevented their cows and ewes from bearing."

It would appear that belief in witchcraft is not dead in our modern society. The anti-nuclear establishment believes that the cause of our misfortunes has simply changed from "imps" to "radiation."

"So much of what we are exposed to now [i.e., radon] is coming from uranium mining which has occurred since 1945" (Rosalie Bertell, IICPH).[83]

This statement is inaccurate.

The concentration of radon at a distance of one kilometre from a mine is so low that it is not detectable, and very few people live within one kilometre of a uranium mine. The radiation dose we receive from radon originates from naturally occurring deposits of uranium found in the soil. The radon diffuses into houses through basement drains or through cracks in basement walls, giving an average dose to the population of about 80 millirems per year (see Table 1). The statement above is a good example of how to confuse artificially enhanced radiation with naturally occurring radiation.

CHAPTER 3

Nuclear Power Reactors

The Facts

THERE ARE TWO METHODS OF PRODUCING ELECTRICITY ECONOMically and in large quantities. One uses hydro power; and the other uses thermal power.

Hydro power utilises the energy of falling water to rotate a turbine which in turn rotates a generator producing electricity. Ontario Hydro first produced electricity from falling water early in this century by using the drop in water level at Niagara Falls. Other provinces in Canada and many other countries have exploited hydro power.

Generally, the production of electricity by means of hydro power is cheaper than by other means, but only if large-scale hydro sources are available. One reason for the economy of hydro power is that the "fuel" is essentially free. It will be pointed out in a later chapter that hydro power is the only economical source of solar energy.

Thermal power utilises the energy in high pressure steam to rotate the turbine which rotates the generator. The turbines and generators which produce electricity from thermal power are similar to those used to produce electricity from hydro power. The main difference is in the propulsive medium for the turbine: falling water in one case, high pressure steam in the other.

Thermal plants can generate steam by burning coal, oil, gas, wood, garbage, or anything else that is combustible. Steam can also be raised by using the energy derived from splitting uranium atoms. The only major difference between a nuclear power station and other thermal power stations is that nuclear fission energy rather than other fuels is used to boil water and produce steam. The rest of the plant—the turbines, generators, condensers, etc.—is similar for all thermal generating stations.

THE DISCOVERY OF NUCLEAR FISSION

The discovery of nuclear fission was made by accident about fifty years ago. It has since led to the production of weapons of mass destruction and to the production of many mass benefits. One of its benefits is the production of nuclear generated electricity. In order to understand the contrasting results flowing from the discovery of nuclear fission, it is necessary to follow its development since it was first observed in 1939.[1]

The neutron, discovered in 1932, is a small uncharged particle found in the nuclei of nearly all atoms (the only exception is hydrogen). Small quantities of neutrons could be produced for experimental purposes by mixing radium with a light element such as beryllium. The alpha particles from the radium bombard the nuclei of the beryllium atoms and release neutrons.

After 1932, neutrons were used to bombard many different types of elements. Some of them became radioactive, and when the radioactivity decayed a new element was produced. Thus the age-old dream of being able to transmute matter was finally achieved, even though the transmuted elements were similar to the original elements in mass, and the quantities of new elements produced were incredibly small.

In 1939 two German scientists, Hahn and Strassman, were engaged in some experiments in which the element uranium was bombarded with neutrons. They expected some of the uranium atoms to be transmuted to another element which would resemble radium. To separate this new "radium," which would only be present in minute quantities, they dissolved the uranium and added some soluble barium to the solution. Barium is chemically similar to radium, and they hoped that by subsequently separating the barium from the uranium the new radium would be carried along with it. Sure enough, when they separated the barium, the radioactivity that had been produced in the uranium stayed with the barium. They then set about separating the new radium from the barium, but this they were unable to do. Reluctantly, they were forced to the conclusion that what they thought might be a new species of radium was in fact a previously unknown species of barium.

This was an astonishing result. Prior to this discovery, all transmuted elements had had mass numbers close to the original elements. That was why they expected to get a species of radium from the uranium. Instead, they had obtained a species of barium, which is about half the mass of uranium.

Before publishing their results,[2] Hahn and Strassman wrote to an ex-colleague, Lise Meitner, who had been driven out of Germany by the Nazi's Jewish pogrom. Meitner talked over the discovery with her nephew, Otto Frisch, and they came to the conclusion on theoretical grounds that a neutron striking a uranium nucleus could in fact cause it to break into two nearly equal fragments.[3] If it did this, an enormous amount of energy would be produced, about two hundred thousand electron volts for each atom that was fissioned. This energy would be mainly carried by the two fission fragments, and it would cause them to fly apart. Frisch soon obtained experimental evidence confirming the existence of the fission fragments.

The world of nuclear physics was set on its ear. The amount of energy produced by fissioning the nucleus of a uranium atom was enormously greater than that involved in any chemical reaction. If it could be harnessed, the world would have a new and very powerful source of energy.

It was quickly realised that this energy could be harnessed if one or more neutrons were expelled from the uranium nucleus during each fission. If only one neutron were expelled, it would be possible theoretically to obtain a chain reaction since that neutron could fission another uranium atom, which would produce another neutron to fission another uranium atom, until all the uranium was used up. However, it was also realised that in practice more than one neutron on average would have to be released to achieve a chain reaction because inevitably some neutrons would be lost to the system by being absorbed by atoms other than uranium or by simply escaping from the system.

It was soon found that neutrons were indeed released during the fission process, and shortly afterwards a first estimate of three neutrons per fission was made.[4] This was a good figure for a first estimate. Today, we know that on average about 2.5 neutrons are released per fission.

It was also known at that time that uranium consisted of two isotopes. One has a mass of 235 units (uranium–235), and the other has a mass of 238 units (uranium–238). It was unlikely that both responded equally to the fissioning process, and it was found quite readily that uranium–235 was the fissionable isotope and that uranium–238 fissioned hardly at all.[5] This was unfortunate since uranium consists of only 0.7 per cent uranium–235. The other 99.3 per cent is uranium–238. This means that the fissionable isotope is accompanied by a large mass of unfissionable uranium which could interfere with the fission reaction by absorbing some of those valuable neutrons necessary to keep a chain reaction going.

It was now necessary to find out whether a chain reaction could be sustained using natural uranium, or whether it would be necessary to increase the proportion of uranium–235 by artificial means before a chain reaction could occur. Researchers realised that part of the answer to this question might lie in the properties of the neutron. When fission occurs, the neutrons are expelled from the nucleus with a very high velocity. It was found that slow neutrons were much more effective as fissioning agents than fast neutrons.

How then could the speed of the neutrons be moderated? The best way would be to allow them to bounce off the nuclei of other atoms rather like demented billiard balls. Each collision would decrease the energy of the neutrons. However, there was one important provision about the nuclei involved in the collision process. They must have a very small tendency to capture neutrons; otherwise too many neutrons would be removed from the system, and the chain reaction could not be sustained.

It was quickly found that there were three candidates for a medium which could be used to moderate the speed of neutrons. Two of them are familiar, ordinary water and graphite (a pure form of carbon). The third medium is heavy water, which is less familiar. Heavy water is similar to ordinary water, but the two hydrogen atoms are replaced by two deuterium atoms. Deuterium is an isotope of hydrogen. It has a neutron in its nucleus and has twice the mass of hydrogen.

The most readily available of these moderating materials is ordinary water, but unfortunately its absorptive properties for neutrons were found to be just too great for it to sustain a chain reaction using natural uranium.[6] The second most readily available moderator was graphite, and this material was found to be suitable. In fact, the first ever sustained nuclear chain reaction was achieved in a graphite-moderated reactor containing natural uranium built by Enrico Fermi in Chicago in 1942.

The third moderator, heavy water, was at that time a chemical oddity. The only place which had produced any considerable quantity of it was a fertiliser plant in Norway, which had produced it as a by-product. The company had hoped to sell it, but no one had found a use for it, until the advent of nuclear fission. The Norwegian company had a stock of 180 kilograms of heavy water, and early in the Second World War this stock was bought by the French government. When France was overrun by Germany, the heavy water was smuggled to England and eventually found its way to Canada.

The discovery of uranium fission occurred just before the beginning of the Second World War, and so it is not surprising that much of the early investigational work into the fission process was directed towards turning fission energy into an uncontrolled explosive energy source rather than into the controlled release of energy for peaceful purposes. As mentioned above, the unwanted uranium–238 isotope could dampen a chain reaction by absorbing too many neutrons. But supposing the uranium–235 could be enriched in proportion to the uranium–238, so that virtually pure (i.e., more than 90 per cent) uranium–235 could be produced, would a chain reaction then be possible in uranium–235 with fast neutrons? Such a reaction would spread through a mass of uranium–235 with lightning rapidity, and a violent explosion would result. A certain minimum mass of nearly pure uranium–235 would be required for this reaction. Below this mass too many neutrons would be lost from the surface of the uranium, so that a chain reaction could not occur. A theoretical calculation showed that a few kilograms of nearly pure uranium–235 would be sufficient.[7]

The Second World War was now well underway, and the U.S.A. undertook a massive and expensive effort to separate uranium–235 from natural uranium. It succeeded, and the resulting effect on the Japanese city of Hiroshima was devastating. But meanwhile, it was found that the supposedly useless uranium–238 isotope was a valuable source of another fissionable isotope. When bombarded with neutrons, uranium–238 is transmuted to plutonium–239. This isotope is fissionable in the same way as uranium–235. By the end of the war enough plutonium–239 had been produced to charge the second bomb dropped on Japan at Nagasaki.

THE PRODUCTION OF NUCLEAR POWER

With the two nuclear explosions in Japan, the Second World War came to an end, and the peaceful development era of nuclear energy began. For a few countries this development meant a continuation of wartime activities, such as the development of nuclear weapons. Some countries with aspirations to major-league status in a continuingly unstable world decided to acquire nuclear weapons. They were the U.S.S.R. (first nuclear explosion in 1949), the U.K. (1952), France (1960), and China (1966). Together with the U.S.A., these countries are now collectively designated as Nuclear Weapons States. All of these countries, in parallel with their nuclear weapons development, decided to proceed with nuclear power development. In this they were joined by other countries without nuclear weapons ambitions such as Canada.[8]

First off the mark in the development of nuclear power was the U.S.A. Shortly after the war, a nuclear propulsion unit for submarines was developed for the U.S. Navy. It used enriched uranium fuel and ordinary water under pressure to produce high temperature steam. This unit was adapted to produce one of the first land-based nuclear power reactors, the 60-megawatt reactor at Shippingport, which went into operation in 1957.[9] The U.S.A. was able to proceed via this route because it had mastered the art of enriching uranium during the war. By enriching its nuclear power fuel to just over 3 per cent uranium–235 (instead of 0.7 per cent uranium–235 in natural uranium), this system was able to overcome the slight neutron absorbing capability of ordinary water and sustain a continuous chain reaction using water as a moderator.

The U.K., France, and the U.S.S.R. did not at first have enrichment capabilities, and thus they elected to build graphite moderated reactors fuelled with natural uranium. These reactors were used to obviate the need for an enrichment process for uranium by producing plutonium for weapons production. However, in order to provide a degree of "peacefulness" to the projects, some of these reactors were also designed to produce nuclear electricity by using the carbon dioxide cooling gas to raise steam to generate electricity.[10]

The gas-cooled, graphite-moderated, natural uranium reactors were not very efficient, but they served their purpose in getting the U.K., France, and the U.S.S.R. into the business of providing nuclear weapons material and electricity quickly. Meanwhile, each country went ahead with the development of a uranium enrichment process.

In the early 1960s, when commitments to large nuclear electricity generating programs were being made, these countries pursued individual paths. The U.S.A. continued with its program of using natural water and enriched uranium to build larger individual plants. One variation success-fully developed in the U.S.A. used the high pressure steam from the reac-tor to drive the turbine directly. This is the boiling water reactor (BWR) produced by General Electric.

The U.S. company Westinghouse developed the original design in which the steam from the reactor was used to produce further steam in a secondary circuit, and this steam was then used to drive the turbine. There were some safety advantages in separating reactor-produced steam from the turbine-propelling steam, but there was also the disadvantage of extra complications in the process. In any event, more Westinghouse-type pressurised water reactors (PWR) have been built than the BWRs offered by General Electric.

When the French decided to embark on an ambitious nuclear elec-tricity program, they recognised the disadvantages of their graphite-moderated, gas-cooled concept developed earlier. These reactors were phys-ically large because of the bulky nature of graphite. This led to massive containment structures and poor heat density characteristics. The French swallowed their pride in their indigenous reactor and imported the Westinghouse PWR design.[11] They have since developed this basic design to produce one of the world's most successful nuclear power reactor programs. France produces about 70 per cent of its electricity from nuclear power.

It took the U.K. longer to drop the graphite-moderated, gas-cooled reactor system. It developed an advanced gas reactor (AGR),[12] which involved a lot of engineering problems, and finally in 1987 the U.K. also switched to the PWR for its future reactor needs.

The U.S.S.R. also persevered with graphite as a moderator but used water as a cooling medium instead of gas in their RMBK series. The Cher-nobyl reactor was one of this series. Following the reactor accident at Cher-nobyl, the U.S.S.R. announced that it would build no more RMBKs but will switch entirely to a PWR design which it had developed in parallel with the RMBK.

In this encapsulated history of the development of nuclear power in various countries, it should be apparent that one material used in the early nuclear experiments with fission is missing—heavy water. It has been noted that the U.S.A. used light water for moderating its nuclear power reactors from the outset, while other countries initially used graphite before transferring to light water. The only country which developed a successful nuclear power reactor program using heavy water and natural uranium was Canada.

In a way, Canada was forced into this decision because this country did not develop an enrichment capability for uranium in order to manufacture nuclear weapons. Without a weapons enrichment program, Canada had to decide whether to enrich uranium to get extra uranium–235 or to enrich water to get concentrated deuterium from ordinary water.

The ratio of deuterium to hydrogen in ordinary water is about 130–160 parts per million.[13] Assuming that all the deuterium can be separated from ordinary water, it would be necessary to process about seven thousand tonnes of ordinary water to get one tonne of heavy water. In practice only about 20 per cent of the available deuterium could be extracted. It was evident that deuterium production would not be easy, but it still looked simple compared with uranium–235 enrichment.

Canada's choice of reactor system was also influenced by that 180 kilograms of Norwegian heavy water which had been brought to Canada in 1942 by a group of French scientists. Canada learned a lot about heavy water and its potential as a reactor moderator. In 1944 the wartime Joint Committee of the U.S.A., U.K., and Canada decided that Canada's best contribution to the nuclear war effort would be the construction of a heavy water–moderated research reactor which could be used to produce plutonium. The U.S.A. was already building a graphite-moderated reactor at Hanford, Washington, for this purpose.

The research reactor that Canada created in 1947, the NRX reactor, was the most successful reactor built at that time and for many years afterwards. It had a large core volume, so that several experiments could be accommodated at one time. It also had the highest neutron flux of any reactor of that period. The NRX reactor also gave Canadian scientists a considerable amount of experience in using heavy water as a moderator.

As a result, when Canada decided to enter the nuclear power field in the early 1950s, its choice of a basic type of reactor was almost a foregone conclusion. It would use natural uranium as fuel and heavy water as moderator. This was not only a practical solution; it was also, scientifically speaking, the most elegant solution because of the neutron economy obtained by using heavy water.[14]

THE CANADIAN NUCLEAR POWER PROGRAM

In 1953 the Canadian government approved a proposal by Atomic Energy of Canada Limited (AECL) to design and construct a small, 20-megawatt, prototype nuclear power reactor.[15] At that time it was not known whether nuclear energy could be harnessed for electricity production or, if it could, what problems would be involved. It made sense to start with the design of a small reactor.

The first design called for the reactor core to be housed inside a thick-walled, steel pressure vessel. This was similar to the PWR concept which was being developed in the U.S.A. However, Canada did not have the industrial capacity to fabricate such a vessel, and so an order was placed with a firm in Scotland.

By the mid-1950s a new alloy had been discovered in the U.S.A., and tested in the NRX reactor in Canada. This alloy promised to revolutionise reactor design. The material was an alloy of zirconium named, appropriately enough, zircaloy. It was mechanically strong, corrosion-resistant and, above all, it absorbed very few neutrons. With the advent of zircaloy, AECL scientists decided to forego the pressure vessel type of construction and place the fuel rods in individual zircaloy pressure tubes. A collection of these tubes in a steel container would constitute the core of the reactor.

By placing bundles of fuel rods end to end in a horizontal zircaloy pressure tube, it was now possible to add another refinement to Canada's reactor. By pushing new fuel bundles into one end of a tube and extracting used fuel bundles from the other end, it was possible to refuel the reactor without shutting it down. The PWRs, which use a massive pressure vessel with walls over twenty centimetres thick to contain the reactor core, can only be refuelled by shutting down the reactor and removing the top from the vessel to insert new fuel. This is a lengthy process occupying several weeks each year during which the reactor is not in operation. The Canadian system of refuelling while the reactor is running is more efficient—and more elegant.

Canada's prototype reactor, the Nuclear Power Demonstration (NPD) reactor, was built on the Ottawa River at Rolphton, a few kilometres upstream from Chalk River. It set the stage for the unique Canadian reactor designs which were to follow. It was fuelled by natural uranium (not by enriched uranium), moderated and cooled by heavy water (not by ordinary water), used zircaloy pressure tubes (not a steel pressure vessel), and could be refuelled on load (without shutting the reactor down). The *chutzpah* of Canadian scientists and engineers is something to marvel at in retrospect. Where the rest of the world (the U.S.A., and later France, the U.K., and the U.S.S.R.) went one way, Canada went another.

The NPD reactor was a success. It was followed by a larger prototype, the 200-megawatt Douglas Point reactor built on the shore of Lake Huron, and then by full-scale reactors at Pickering, Bruce, and Darlington in Ontario, at Gentilly in Quebec, and at Point Lepreau in New Brunswick. Domestic construction was accompanied by foreign sales to India, Pakistan, Argentina, Korea, and Romania.[16]

THE SAFETY OF NUCLEAR POWER REACTORS

From the first discovery of nuclear fission, scientists and engineers have been aware of the hazards which could arise from the careless use of nuclear energy. Enormous quantities of energy are involved in the splitting of the atom, and the radioactive properties of the fragments produced by fission make them potentially hazardous. As a result, extraordinary safety measures have always been taken in the handling of nuclear reactor materials. The scientists and engineers who work closer to nuclear energy than other people are no different from the rest of us in wanting to preserve their own health and safety.

The first nuclear reactor accident of any significance anywhere occurred in Canada at the NRX research reactor in 1952. The cause of the accident was complex. It started with an operator error compounded by partial equipment failures due to inadequate maintenance of the shut-off rods, followed by the failure of hoses carrying cooling water which were subjected to pressures for which they had not been designed. Although the resulting accident severely damaged the reactor, no one was killed or injured by it.[17]

The whole core of the reactor had to be replaced. The cost was considerable, but the NRX accident did provide practical experience in dismantling and reassembling an operational nuclear reactor, and even more importantly it provided experience on how to prevent future reactor accidents.

One of the lessons learned from the NRX accident was that the *number* of safety devices present in a reactor system is not as important as the *quality* of the devices. In NRX many safety features had been incorporated, and the sheer number could have given rise to unwarranted complacency. As Dr. George C. Laurence, a past-president of the Atomic Energy Control Board (AECB), expressed it many years later: "It was like piling every available object against a door to brace it against some menace from outside, when a well designed lock or cross-bar would have served the purpose better."[18]

Under the guidance of Dr. Laurence a series of principles for reactor safety was developed and adopted by the AECB, as part of its philosophy for deciding safety questions before issuing a licence to operate a nuclear power reactor. It was noted after the NRX accident that some parts of one safety system were common to another, so that when the common element failed, both systems failed. As a result, the AECB recognised that all safety systems must be independent of each other, so that this type of cross-linked failure could not occur.

In addition, no safety device can be considered 100 per cent reliable or 100 per cent independent. As part of the design phase, designers had provided assessments of the reliability and independence of their safety systems. During subsequent operation of the reactor the AECB insisted that these assessments be frequently checked against actual operating performance, so that the design calculations would either be verified or, if design weaknesses became apparent, they could be rectified. The AECB emphasised the responsibility of the operators as well as the designers to ensure that the actual performance of the plant fulfilled the good intentions of the designers.

The principle of defence-in-depth for reactor safety was also adopted in Canada. In the Canadian context this involved distinguishing three separate sectors of the reactor plant: the *process equipment* which fulfilled the function of producing nuclear energy and using it as required; the *protective devices* which were designed to prevent a failure of the process equipment becoming so serious that fission products could escape from the fuel; and the *containment system* which would confine the fission products within the reactor building if there were a simultaneous failure of the process equipment and their protective devices. Each of these sectors is required to be as functionally independent of the other two as possible.

In assessing the risks from an accident to a nearby population, the AECB first considered the radiation exposure that might result from a malfunction of the process equipment that was *not* accompanied by a failure of the protective equipment. Such malfunctions may be so frequent (i.e., about once every ten years) that they must be considered part of "normal" operations; hence the exposure limits prescribed must also be "normal" dose limits. Accordingly, the AECB set the limits of annual exposure from normal operations and the worst single process failure at 500 millirems (whole body) to any individual member of the public.

For any malfunction of the process equipment that *was* accompanied by a failure of the protective devices or by failure of the containment, the exposure of an individual should be limited to 25 rems to the whole body. The value of 25 rems was adopted by the AECB because it is the dose level below which no damage is readily observable and above which the International Commission on Radiological Protection recommends that the exposed person be examined by a physician.

It was necessary not only to specify the limits of exposures resulting from these two types of malfunction but also to specify how frequently they should be allowed to occur. It was recognised that even with high quality design, construction, and operational targets for all process equipment systems, the total of the individual frequencies of all serious process failures might be as high as one per three years on average. It was therefore decided that protective devices should be tested at a frequency which would demonstrate that the unavailability of protection was less than one one-thousandth of the time. Thus the probability of having a serious process equipment failure occurring simultaneously with the failure of a protective system should be less than one three-thousandth per year.

The third line of defence in the event of an accident was the containment of a reactor, and it was decided that this too should have as a design target a demonstrated unavailability of less than one one-thousandth of the time. In the design of a reactor the failure of a process system alone and the failure of a process system coincident with a protective or containment system failure were both considered as credible accidents, although the estimated average frequency of the latter would be no more than one in a thousand reactor years of operation.

The chance of an occurrence of a triple simultaneous failure of process system, protective system, and containment was about one in a million. This was considered to be so improbable that useful estimates of its frequency could not be derived and hence the consequences of a triple failure were not calculated in safety analyses.

The design philosophy just described was first applied to the construction of the Pickering Nuclear Station on the outskirts of Toronto. The problem of containment effectiveness for the reactor system was a difficult one. It was eventually solved by the design of an additional large concrete building adjacent to, and connected with, the reactors. This building would be maintained at low pressure, so that in the event of a release of hot coolant from the reactor core, there would be no build-up of pressure inside the reactor containment building. The air, steam, and fission products would be sucked into the vacuum building, where a sprinkler system would ensure that there would not be any sustained pressures above atmospheric throughout the containment system.[19]

In the design of the CANDU 600 reactor the vacuum building was replaced by installing a sprinkler system in the roof of the containment building. The system would condense the steam generated by a serious accident and thus keep the pressure inside the containment building below the design level.

A further development occurred in safety philosophy during the early stages of the design of the Bruce reactor. It was pointed out by the designers that a runaway accident which would result from the failure of both a process system and the protective shut-down system would have such unpredictable consequences that it was not reasonable at an early stage of design to demonstrate by analysis a containment system which would cover all eventualities. Instead, the designers proposed the addition of a second shut-down system in the reactor, different in design and completely independent of the first. This proposal would render a runaway accident so improbable that a containment system capable of coping with a runaway accident would not be necessary. This approach was accepted by the AECB, and the new criteria for reactor licensing were published in 1972.[20]

The evolution and application of safety criteria in Canada's reactors has not been a static function. This has led to some claims that because newer reactors had improved safety devices, the older reactors are in some way "unsafe." This is not so. In fact, it has been argued by some industry experts that some safety measures are an unnecessary waste of money. This sort of argument between experts can be expected to continue. Since there can never be absolute safety in any human endeavour, including reactor design, there will always be reasonable arguments about how safe is safe enough.

It is interesting to note that right from the early years a basic difference was apparent between the American and Canadian approaches to reactor safety. The Canadian approach started by specifying a maximum exposure of the public at the reactor boundary and then worked back through the containment and the protective devices to the fuel at the core of the process system. In the U.S.A. the principle of defence-in-depth was also adopted, but the regulatory body set out to achieve it by means of elaborate codes, procedures, and regulations which specified the operating conditions and components in the reactor systems and then estimated what radiation limits would be present at the boundary as a result of a malfunction. The Canadian approach may be characterised as going outside-in and the American approach inside-out.

There was, and still is, little enthusiasm in Canada for the American approach because it is felt that by specifying in detail the design rules for the reactor, the designer would have restricted latitude to apply his skills, and also that there would be limited incentive for those skills to be applied to producing safe designs. In Canada, the designer was provided with a set of boundary requirements, and it was up to him to develop a design proposal which would meet them to the AECB's satisfaction. This proposal would be presented to the AECB staff, who would assess it, point out any deficiencies, and discuss with the designer what modifications were required. The whole process became a learning experience for both the designers and the regulators, and the give-and-take of engineering discussions yielded benefits to both sides.[21]

MELT-DOWN

The most serious accident which can occur in a nuclear reactor is a melt-down. This type of accident would happen if the coolant surrounding the uranium fuel were lost and the fuel temperature rose to a point at which the uranium melted and released its radioactive content.

A melt-down is *not* the same as a nuclear explosion. An accident to the fuel in a nuclear reactor could never cause a nuclear explosion. This is true for the natural uranium fuel used in a CANDU reactor and for the enriched fuel used in light-water reactors. In both cases the laws of physics dictate that a nuclear explosion cannot occur.

A melt-down, on the other hand, is a credible accident which could occur in a nuclear reactor. Its possibility has been recognised since reactors were first designed and built. As a result, measures to prevent a melt-down occurring, and to mitigate its effects if it did occur, have been designed and built into every nuclear power reactor.

Most reactors are cooled by water, either heavy water or light water. If the water flow were lost, by a break in the cooling water pipe for example, the nuclear reaction would stop, but there would be enough heat generated in the fuel by the decay of the radioactive materials in the uranium fuel to cause the uranium to melt. When this happens, a fraction of the radioactive materials in the fuel could be expelled and provide a potentially dangerous situation.

Getting the uranium to melt so that it will release its radioactive content is not easy. The temperature of the fuel must be raised to about 2,800 degrees centigrade. However, there is enough heat generated by the decay of the radioactive materials in the fuel that within a few hours, without any cooling, the temperature of uranium could rise high enough for it to melt.

What would happen to the molten mass of fuel in the event of a melt-down is a subject of conjecture. It is probable that the uranium would melt its way through the core containment vessel, and the molten mass would reach the thick concrete floor of the reactor building. Its fate would then be uncertain. It has been suggested that it could melt its way through the concrete, then into the ground under the reactor.

If it kept on going, macabre humour suggests that it could melt its way through the earth and come out in China—hence the "China Syndrome." This scenario, suggested in the film of the same name, should be taken with a large grain of salt. The decay heat generated in the fuel is decreasing rapidly, and the thermal capacity of the barriers to the movement of the molten fuel is increasing rapidly. The fuel may not even penetrate the concrete base of the reactor, and if it does, the thermal capacity of the earth beneath the reactor is almost infinite.

If a melt-down occurs, the reactor will almost certainly be irretrievably damaged, and the financial loss would likely be one or more billions of dollars. In addition, the radioactive materials released from the molten fuel would be available to cause damage to the population nearby. It is not surprising that considerable precautions are taken to ensure that a melt-down will not occur and that if one did occur, the radioactive materials would be confined within the reactor building.

The first precautions are taken in the design and fabrication of the cooling system. Reliable pumps for water circulation are used. If these pumps fail, back-up pumps are waiting on standby. Reliable piping, rigorously inspected during construction and during maintenance shut-down periods, is employed.

If, despite these precautions, there is a failure of the coolant system, a second coolant system is brought into operation. This emergency core-cooling system (ECCS) is independent of the primary core-cooling system. Before a melt-down occurs, it would be necessary for the primary cooling system to suffer a devastating fracture releasing all its water. This unlikely event would then have to be followed by a similar failure of the ECCS, which would be equally unlikely. The possibility of these two unlikely events happening almost simultaneously is very, very unlikely indeed.

But suppose the near-impossible did happen and a melt-down occurred. What would be the effect on a population living near the reactor? The answer is, very little.

Each reactor core is situated inside a thick reinforced concrete containment building. The function of the building is described by its name; it contains any radioactive materials released as a result of a melt-down. The containment building is designed to be strong enough to withstand the steam pressures which will build up as a result of the hot core reacting with the spilled water from the two cooling systems within the building and also the pressures of non-condensible gases produced by a reaction between the fuel and the concrete. In the current CANDU system, if the pressures get too high, they can be relieved either by discharge into a large vacuum building connected to the containment building or by a sprinkler system which will send cool water into the containment building to condense the steam.

Before any substantial amounts of harmful radioactive materials can get into the environment, the containment system must be breached. There are a number of ways in which this could happen: (1) a violent increase in steam pressure caused by the hot reactor core contacting a large volume of water; (2) a hydrogen explosion caused when high-temperature zirconium contacts water and releases hydrogen; (3) the containment doors being left open accidentally; (4) a fully loaded jumbo jet crashing into the reactor building just after the core melt-down has occurred. None of these events is very likely. Some nuclear engineers think that the most likely may well be the crashing jumbo jet.

If it is assumed that everything has gone wrong and that a melt-down has occurred, the consequences to the local population will now depend on how much radioactive material is released and on the prevailing meteorological conditions. As will be noted below, the amount of radioactive material likely to be released is the subject of some doubt, but it is likely to be considerably less than assumed in currently accepted studies.

Meteorological conditions are important because they will determine

the distribution of the radioactive plume. The worst meteorological condition would be the existence of an inversion layer in the vicinity of the
reactor site combined with a light wind. An inversion layer is a fairly
uncommon meteorological event in which a layer of warm air is suspended
above a layer of cooler air adjacent to the earth's surface. This combination would prevent the radioactive plume from rising into the air and dis-
persing. Instead, the plume would remain close to the ground. A light wind
would be necessary to move the plume. Zero wind would leave the plume
suspended above the reactor, and a strong wind would break up the inversion layer. The direction of this light wind would have to be towards the
nearest major population centre for maximum effect.

A final factor to be considered in describing the effects of a major melt-
down is the question of evacuation of the population. A melt-down would
normally be a slow process lasting over a period of many hours or even
days. A maximum effect would only be obtained if there were no attempt
to evacuate the population located downwind from the reactor site.

The sequence of events in a severe nuclear accident starts with a major
failure of the core cooling system and ends with a decision to evacuate
a neighbouring population. This sequence is called a scenario, and if it
followed through all the steps described above it could be called a "worst-
case" scenario. This, however, is really a misnomer. No matter how bad
are the theoretical consequences of an accident, they can always be made
worse by the use of a little imagination. For example, the loss of electricity from the power station could be factored into the scenario, and assumptions could be made about tragic deaths due to this cause. Or the number
of traffic accident deaths due to a pell-mell evacuation could also be factored in. Suffice to say, no "worst-case" scenario exists. Any scenario can
be made worse by using more imagination.

Nonetheless it is important to assess what might be the *consequences*
of an arbitrarily described worst-case accident. It is just as important to
assess the *probability* that such an accident would happen. Taken together,
the probability and the consequences of an accident can be used to define
the *risk*. As mentioned earlier, the risk arising from an accident is defined
as the product of the consequences and the probability; that is,

$$\text{Risk} = \text{Consequences} \times \text{Probability}$$

This simple mathematical expression conveys what is known intuitively
about accidents. For a given risk of an accident, the higher the consequences
the less likely it is that an accident will happen. Conversely, an accident
with low consequences will occur more frequently.

It is necessary to distinguish clearly between the *risk* of an accident
and the *consequences* of an accident. The anti-nuclear establishment often

insists on considering only the consequences of an accident, and if the consequences are large they then claim that this justifies their belief that reactors should be banned. This view is clearly indefensible. If the probability of an accident with large consequences is very low, then the risk can also be very low. When comparing the hazards of several related activities (such as various methods of generating electricity), the only way to make a fair comparison is to compare risks—not consequences.

It is easier to estimate the consequences of a nuclear power reactor accident than to estimate the probability that an accident will occur. The consequences are estimated by calculating the amount of radioactive inventory in the reactor which will be released, and then calculating the effect of that radioactivity on the nearby population.

The first assessments of the consequences of a reactor accident were contained in a safety study performed by Brookhaven National Laboratory for the United States Atomic Energy Commission (USAEC), published in 1957 (WASH–740).[22] A range of accidents was considered, and the worst occurrence under extremely pessimistic conditions was postulated to kill 3,400 and injure 43,000. The results of this "worst-case" scenario were widely publicised and contributed to a growing public mistrust of nuclear power.

An update of WASH–740 prepared by Brookhaven in 1964 was not published. Neither study had considered the probability of the accidents whose consequences were being described. As noted above, without a consideration of both probability and consequences, the risk to the public resulting from a reactor accident cannot be properly assessed. Since the figures from WASH–740 had been misinterpreted and improperly used by the antinuclear establishment in the U.S.A., the USAEC decided that any further reactor safety study should include estimates of both probabilities and consequences.

Such a study was begun in 1972 and completed in 1975 by Professor Norman Rasmussen of MIT. It was an exhaustive study contained in eight volumes (WASH–1400). Although parts of it have been criticised, it remains a benchmark study.[23]

The "worst-case" scenario described in WASH–1400 made assumptions similar to those described above. It was assumed that the cooling water to the reactor core was interrupted (e.g., by a pipe break) and that this was followed by an interruption in the flow of emergency core-cooling water. Without adequate cooling, the radioactive decay heat would cause the temperature of the core to rise. Eventually the temperature could rise high enough to melt the uranium oxide fuel, and a large fraction of the radioactive products in the core could be released. The reactor pressure vessel and then the reactor containment building were assumed to fail, providing a pathway for the release of radioactive products to the atmosphere. It was next assumed that the radioactive plume was held close to the ground by the presence of an inversion layer and that a light wind was blowing towards the nearest large centre of population.

At the time the study was prepared, it was not known what fraction of the radioactive inventory in the core could escape to form the radioactive plume. As a result, pessimistic assumptions were made in WASH–1400. For example, since iodine is a volatile element, it was assumed that 70 per cent of the iodine–131 inventory would escape. Less volatile elements such as cesium, rubidium, tellurium, antimony, and ruthenium were assumed to contribute 40 per cent of their core inventory to the plume.

The early fatalities and illnesses resulting from such an accident were estimated as 3,300 and 45,000 respectively, similar to those predicted in WASH–740. However, the probability of such an accident occurring would be one in a billion per reactor year of operation. To put this risk into perspective, Rasmussen pointed out that the *risk* of death to the average American from such a severe reactor accident was about the same as the *risk* of death from a falling meteorite.

This did not prevent special interest groups from again widely publicising the maximum consequence figures without mentioning probabilities. In particular, the possibility of a core melt-down was often described in conjunction with the consequences of a "worst-case" accident. This made it appear that *any* melt-down would result in "worst-case" consequences. This is not so. As pointed out by Rasmussen, the most probable consequences of a core melt-down are zero fatalities and minimal damage outside the reactor because the containment would limit the release of any radioactive material.

PRACTICAL EXPERIENCE OF NUCLEAR POWER REACTOR ACCIDENTS

In about four thousand reactor years of operating experience world-wide, there have been only two significant nuclear power reactor accidents: the one at Three Mile Island (TMI) in the U.S.A. and the one at Chernobyl in the U.S.S.R.

The TMI accident occurred in 1979 to a pressurised light-water reactor. It did not kill or injure anyone,[24] but the reactor was destroyed. The accident began with the malfunctioning of a piece of equipment and was compounded by operator errors. The reactor fuel lost its cooling water and there was a partial melt-down of the reactor core. However, the reactor containment was not impaired, and it performed its design function in keeping most of the radioactive material inside the reactor building.

The safety lessons learned from TMI have since been applied to other reactors, both light-water and heavy-water. As a result, currently operating reactors are safer now than they were before TMI occurred. This means that the *probability* of an accident has now been even further decreased, thus reducing the *risk* of the type of accident described by Rasmussen in WASH–1400.

In addition, TMI caused scientists and engineers to look more closely at the *consequences* of reactor accidents, particularly the amount of radioactivity which would be released by a severe accident, the so-called "source term." For example, out of a core inventory of about 14 million curies of iodine–131 in TMI, only about 20 curies escaped from the containment. Although the TMI core suffered only a partial melt-down, considerably more iodine–131 would have been expected to escape. The Rasmussen report asssumed that 70 per cent of the iodine (10 million curies) would escape following a complete core melt-down and failure of the containment.

After the TMI accident, research programs were begun in several countries, notably the U.S.A., the U.K., Germany, and Canada, to obtain more accurate estimates of the source term under various accident conditions. This work is still continuing, but so far there seems to be a consensus that all existing source terms are too high by a factor of at least ten and in some cases are too high by a factor of one thousand.

The reduction in the source term means that the estimates of the *consequences* of severe accidents should be reduced. This too will reduce the *risk* from a severe accident even further. Although current source term estimates are likely to be reduced in the future, there is some reluctance on the part of researchers, and more so on the part of regulators, to propose definitive reductions until all the research has been completed. The certain outcry from the anti-nuclear establishment, particularly in the U.S.A., which will result from any proposed reductions means that any changes must be thoroughly documented before they are proposed.

The accident at the Chernobyl–4 reactor in the U.S.S.R. involved a reactor of the RMBK series. As noted earlier, these reactors are moderated by graphite and cooled by light water. They are of the direct cycle type, in which the steam produced by the fissioning uranium is used directly to power the turbines without an intervening stage of heat exchangers.

Ironically, the Chernobyl accident occurred during an experiment to improve the safety of the reactor system. If the steam from the reactor to the turbine generators were suddenly cut off for any reason, the RMBK reactors, in common with most other reactors, have a number of diesel-driven generators on standby which will produce electrical power to operate essential equipment. However, it takes some time, about thirty seconds, for the diesels to kick in and get up to full power. Although a delay of this duration is not critical, the experiment was designed to find out whether the spinning inertia of the large turbo-generators would continue to produce electricity long enough to bridge the gap.

During the previous year, the Chernobyl–4 reactor had performed flawlessly. It was the pride of the Soviet reactor program and also of its operating crew. It was due to be shut down at the end of April 1986 for routine maintenance. If the experiment were not completed at that time, it could not be attempted again for another year.

As with all nuclear reactors, the RMBK is fitted with a mixture of control and safety devices to ensure that it does not get out of control. For various reasons most of these were disconnected as the experiment progressed. Eventually the reactor was put into a position of operating at low power without enough control systems available to maintain its stability. At low power the RMBK design is particularly unstable, in much the same way that an aircraft is unstable at low speeds—it tends to stall and crash.[25] At 1:23:40 on April 29, 1986, Chernobyl–4 stalled and crashed.

An effort to regain control by shutting the reactor down came too late. The safety rods would take six seconds to become effective, but within four seconds the power rose to what was later calculated to be one hundred times full power. The heat developed by this power surge caused the fuel to break into small hot fragments which rapidly turned the water into steam. The first explosion was a steam explosion, followed a few seconds later by a hydrogen explosion. The explosions tore the top off the reactor building, exposing the core. Parts of the walls collapsed, and incandescent particles started thirty fires in neighbouring buildings. The graphite moderator caught fire and smouldered for ten days until it was quenched by pumping liquid nitrogen into the base of the reactor building.

Two reactor operators were killed immediately by the explosions. The fire-fighters who quickly arrived on the scene were exposed to massive doses of radiation. About two hundred were hospitalised, and twenty-nine subsequently died.

The graphite fire wafted radioactive particles a thousand metres into the air, where they were dispersed by the prevailing winds. The day after the accident the population near the Chernobyl site began to be evacuated. Over the next few days 135,000 people from a radius of about thirty kilometres around the site were moved away. The average radiation dose received by these evacuees was about 12 rems, which will nearly double the naturally occurring radiation dose they will receive during their lifetime. The number of fatal cancers predicted for this population is between zero and two hundred. Arrangements have been made to keep them under surveillance as a check on the current method of predicting cancers from low levels of radiation. In the first two years after the accident, no abnormal genetic effects have appeared in the offspring of this population.[26]

Wind-borne radioactive contamination affected other parts of the U.S.S.R. and Europe, and minute traces were detected in the U.S.A. and Canada. The combined population of these areas is very large, so that even though individual doses from the radiation were low, the calculational method mentioned in the previous chapter enables thousands or tens of thousands of future cancers to be predicted. However, if the average radiation dose received by the population of Europe and the U.S.S.R. is compared with the annual background radiation dose to which they are exposed, then it is possible to say that for these populations the year 1986 had fifty-eight weeks.

The other three reactors at the Chernobyl site are now operating again, but Chernobyl–4 has been enclosed in a concrete sarcophagus and will remain there for the indefinite future.

Four months after the accident, Soviet nuclear scientists and engineers met with their peers from the rest of the world in Vienna and explained what had happened at Chernobyl. Their openness in disclosing details of the accident was an early example of Glasnost in action. According to the Soviets there had been six separate contraventions of procedures by the reactor operators during the experiment. If any one of these had not been perpetrated, the accident would not have happened. Since the accident, the U.S.S.R. has changed its regulatory procedures and operating instructions. It has also improved some of the control and safety devices in its RMBK reactors.

The major interest for the Western nuclear experts attending the Vienna meeting was to upgrade their own operations in the light of Soviet experience at Chernobyl.[27] The Canadian Atomic Energy Control Board sent two senior experts to the meeting. In their report they concluded that the differences in the regulatory and operating procedures as well as the differences in the design of the CANDU and RMBK reactors did not reveal any significant new information that could affect current safety requirements for CANDU reactors. All important aspects of the accident and its causes had been considered already by the AECB in its licensing process.[28]

The Chernobyl accident with its thirty-one deaths has been the world's worst nuclear accident by far. It is also safe to say that it will not be the world's last nuclear accident. However, despite Chernobyl nuclear energy is still one of the safest means of practical, large-scale electricity production.

CANADIAN REACTOR SAFETY ASSESSMENTS

As noted earlier, the Canadian approach to the assessment of reactor safety is not the same as the approach used in the U.S.A. In addition, the CANDU reactor is of a quite different design from the American light-water reactor

(LWR). As a result, the American analyses, such as that conducted by Rasmussen, although indicative of what could happen to a CANDU reactor, do not provide entirely satisfactory descriptions of possible accident sequences and consequences in the CANDU.

There are two design differences between the CANDU and LWR which have major safety implications. The first is the use of a vacuum building on all multi-unit CANDU stations. Only small amounts of harmful radioactive materials can escape during an accident unless the reactor containment building is breached. For example, at Three Mile Island the containment was not breached and only about 20 curies of iodine–131 escaped to the environment. The most likely cause of rupture would be pressure build-up by steam formed by heavy water contacting hot fuel. To safeguard the integrity of the containment, the CANDU design includes a separate large concrete building which is maintained at a low pressure and which is connected to the containment building. This vacuum building will accommodate any excess pressure generated by steam in the containment building. The vacuum building is also fitted with a spray system which will condense the steam and thus assist in maintaining a low pressure during an accident.[29]

The second difference is the large quantity of water (heavy water) in the CANDU core compared with a LWR core. In some accident sequences this large volume of water will keep the CANDU core cooler for a longer period, thus reducing the chances of radioactive materials being released from the core.

Detailed studies have shown that there are virtually no conceivable circumstances in which a core melt-down could occur in a CANDU reactor.[30] It can be appreciated that these assessments are so radical that supporting studies will be required before they can be accepted by the licensing authorities. Nonetheless, they do indicate that it would be very difficult to obtain a melt-down in a CANDU reactor.

Many accident analyses have been carried out on the CANDU reactor system, including analyses which involve a loss of coolant followed by a loss of emergency core cooling. These analyses show that core melt-downs and accidents involving total failure of shutdown are extremely low probability events. Even if a low probability event occurs (e.g., an event with a frequency as low as one chance in a million that it will occur during any year), the off-site consequences resulting from such an event would be very small.

The most recent (1988) independent examination of reactor safety in Canada was carried out as part of the Ontario Nuclear Safety review. This review was commissioned by the Ontario government following the Chernobyl accident. The commissioner was Dr. F. Kenneth Hare, professor emeritus in geography at the University of Toronto, advised by a panel of distinguished Canadians. To assist the commissioner a large number of technical reports were commissioned from consultants, some of whom (e.g., Norman Rubin and Rosalie Bertell) were members of the anti-nuclear establishment.

Before publication, the final report was vetted by a panel of reviewers appointed by the Royal Society of Canada. The panel found that the review of reactor safety documented in the report had been performed with competence and thoroughness and that the recommendations made and opinions expressed by the commissioner were soundly based and adequately supported. In the report the commissioner concluded: "The Ontario Hydro reactors are being operated safely and at high standards of technical performance. No significant adverse impact has been detected in either the work-force or the public. The risk of accidents serious enough to affect the public adversely can never be zero, but is very remote."[31]

The views on CANDU reactor safety expressed by Professor Hare are accepted by all the experts in Canada who have examined the scientific evidence. These experts include nuclear scientists and engineers at Ontario Hydro, Atomic Energy of Canada Limited, and the Atomic Energy Control Board, as well as those in universities and in industry. It is important to realise that these views have not been challenged *on a technical or scientific basis* by the anti-nuclear establishment.

THE NUCLEAR LIABILITY ACT

There has never been a serious nuclear reactor accident in Canada. In the unlikely event that such an accident should occur, the government of Canada has passed the Nuclear Liability Act to provide a means of compensating Canadians (and neighbouring Americans) in the case of claims resulting from personal injury and property damage.

Since its implementation in 1976, there has not been a single claim made under the Nuclear Liability Act.

The Nuclear Liability Act has its counterpart in similar acts in other nations. It is based on the concept of absolute liability of the nuclear plant operator, who is responsible for third-party damages, no matter what the cause of the accident giving rise to the damages. A claimant does not have to prove negligence on the part of the operator, only that damage has been suffered. Such an approach avoids long delays in the processing of claims which could result from legal proceedings to determine responsibility and liability for the incident giving rise to the damages. There is a limit of $75 million on the liability of the operator for each designated nuclear installation. There are also time limits under which it is possible to bring claims under the Act.

The $75 million coverage is provided by a consortium of private sector insurance companies (the Nuclear Insurance Association of Canada) to whom the reactor operators pay the annual premiums. However, if the claims are in excess of $75 million, the Act allows the government to set up a Nuclear Damage Claims Commission which will address such claims and which may recommend their compensation from the Consolidated Revenue Fund. This is similar to the type of action which a government would normally expect to take in the event of any emergency situation.

The Act also protects suppliers of fuel and components used in nuclear power plants by channelling all third-party liability to the operator. Because of the Act, the public is not able to sue a parts supplier in respect of his liability arising from the accident; only the operator of the reactor can be sued.

As will be seen in the second part of this chapter, this provision exempting suppliers from legal action by third parties has aroused the ire of the anti-nuclear establishment. The absolute liability of the operator and the dollar and time limitations to that absolute liability were designed by the government to create a liability regime which would fairly and effectively serve the interests of both the potential claimant and the nuclear plant operator. However, this legislation was drafted in the late 1960s, and it is probably time to reassess some of its terms, such as the $75 million limit on insurance coverage. Such a review has been underway by the Government of Canada for the last several years.

The Game

The supposed hazards of nuclear power plants are constantly put before the public by the anti-nuclear establishment. The worst exaggeration is that nuclear reactors can explode like atom bombs. They cannot.

Even without explosions, nuclear reactors can suffer the "dreaded melt-down." According to anti-nuclear mythology, every melt-down will lead to hundreds of thousands of casualties and billions of dollars of damages to the environment. This mythology is unfounded. The facts are that there is only a remote possibility of a melt-down occurring, and that if one were to occur the most probable result would be zero casualties and minimal damage to the environment.

The quotations below, taken from the utterances of members of the anti-nuclear establishment, will give a flavour of the anti-nuclear game as it is played with nuclear power reactors. Many of the techniques of the game will be recognised as the same as those described previously.

> "A 1982 study done . . . by the Sandia National Laboratory found that the worst-case consequences for a LWR accident could be as many as 102,000 first-year fatalities . . . and as much as $314 billion in property damage" (Norman Rubin, Energy Probe).[32]

> ". . . a couple of hundred thousand people might die if the wind is blowing the wrong way . . ." (Norman Rubin, Energy Probe).[33]

> "According to a U.S. government study done by Sandia National Laboratories in 1982 . . . over 140,000 people could die" (David Poch, Energy Probe).[34]

These statements are misleading.

They are made frequently by Energy Probe staff. The casualty figures for a nuclear accident, described by them as between one and two hundred thousand, have been taken from a Sandia (U.S.A.) siting study which estimated the consequences of a "worst-case" scenario at a number of reactor sites in the U.S.A. The statements made by Energy Probe staff when quoting this study are misleading for a number of reasons.

(1) They do not mention the probability of the accident, only the consequences, and therefore people reading the statements from Energy Probe have no idea of the risk. The probability of such a worst-case accident is given in the study as 1 in 1 billion years of reactor operation. Even *if* such an accident occurred, the average death rate over the billion year period would be only 0.0001 deaths per calendar year (one death every ten thousand years), and one could hardly have a safer electricity-generating system than that.

The Sandia study was widely publicised by the anti-nuclear establishment in the U.S.A. when it first came out. It was accompanied by the inevitable calls for closure of all the nuclear industry on the grounds of extreme danger. A member of the U.S. Nuclear Regulatory Commission held a press conference to put the risk into perspective. He pointed out it was the same as the risk of two jumbo jets colliding over the Super Bowl, falling on the spectators, and killing one hundred thousand of them. Any reasonable person would dismiss such a risk as being too small to consider. Certainly the threat of a risk of this magnitude would not stop anyone from flying in a jumbo jet or from going to the Super Bowl.

(2) The Sandia study uses "old" estimates for the release of radioactivity similar to those used by Rasmussen. It is now known that these values are much too high. A reduction in source-term estimates would lead to a corresponding reduction in casualty estimates.

(3) The study deliberately uses extremely adverse conditions to derive a "worst-case" scenario. For example, it assumes nobody beyond sixteen kilometres from the reactor would be evacuated or take protective action for twenty-four hours after the accident. If this evacuation assumption is changed from sixteen kilometres to forty kilometres (as was the case in the Rasmussen report), *the number of deaths in the worst-case scenario drops from 102,000 to zero.*

(4) There is no comparison of the risk of nuclear power with the risks from alternative energy sources. As will be described in the chapter on risks of energy production, Inhaber (Canada) and Holdren (U.S.A.) have independently concluded that the risks from nuclear power (including the risks of catastrophic accidents) are much less than the risks from coal- or oil-generated electricity and are also less than the risks from solar energy.

Energy Probe's insistence that only the consequences of nuclear accidents should be mentioned and not risks could generate needless anxiety in members of the public on this and other safety issues. There are many industries for which "worst-case" scenarios can be derived which project thousands of casualties, such as hydro power, food processing, rail and road transport, chemical production, and oil refining. It is not reasonable to suggest that all these industries should be closed down, regardless of the actual risks they pose, simply because imaginative but highly improbable accident scenarios involving thousands of casualties can be derived.

(5) The anti-nuclear establishment in Canada always quotes American reports for worst-case scenario figures, despite the fact that American light-water reactors are different from Canadian heavy-water reactors. The risks from a severe CANDU reactor accident are quoted in the first half of this chapter. They show that it is unlikely there will be any casualties. These risk figures are never mentioned by the Canadian anti-nuclear establishment.

"According to a recent study done for the U.S. Nuclear Regulatory Commission (NRC), up to 100,000 people could be killed *within one year if the worst reactor accident occurred . . . . Another recent study, also for the NRC, concludes that a catastrophic accident could occur on average* once every eight years*" (emphases in the original; Margaret Laurence, Energy Probe).*[36]

The conjunction of these statements is misleading.

They appear in an Energy Probe fund-raising letter signed by the late Margaret Laurence. The "catastrophic accident" of the second statement refers to a reactor accident in which *no* deaths would occur. As J.A.L. Robertson of Atomic Energy of Canada Limited stated in an open reply to Margaret Laurence's statements:

> To scare people by putting these two statements together without any proper explanation is completely unethical, in my view. Several other studies, including one by the American Medical Association, conclude that generating electricity from nuclear energy, including the effects of accidents, is much safer than generating it from coal and oil. That is why we believe that nuclear energy is actually saving lives.[37]

If Margaret Laurence had thought about the statements quoted above, would she have really believed that any government would license for operation a facility which would kill one hundred thousand of the population on average every eight years? Any government condoning such a reckless action would soon find itself out of favour with the electorate.

"[The Ontario Nuclear Safety Review] . . . wrongly concludes . . . [CANDU reactors] are safe" (Norman Rubin, Energy Probe).[38]

This statement is inaccurate.

THREE MILE ISLAND

It is claimed by pro-nuclear advocates that the accident at Unit 2 of the Three Mile Island nuclear generating station in 1979 did not kill anyone.

They are only half right.

The worst radioactive exposures resulting from the accident were provided by about 20 curies of iodine–131. This in itself was not enough to kill anyone.

But the institutional panic caused by the accident at Unit 2 also caused the shut-down of Unit 1. For a long time after the accident this unit continued to be shut down while regulatory authorities agonised over whether it should be allowed to re-start. When the decision was finally made that Unit 1 was safe to operate, legal challenges to its start-up were mounted, and by the time the courts had decided Unit 1 was safe, about five years had elapsed.

During the time it was down, Unit 1 would have generated about four gigawatt-years of electricity. Instead, this electricity was provided by coal-fired electrical generating plants.

It is estimated that the atmospheric pollution produced by generating a gigawatt-year of electricity from coal results in about twenty-six deaths, most of them elderly people or those with lung ailments.[35] The four gigawatt-years of lost nuclear production from Unit 1 were therefore responsible for about one hundred deaths.

The members of the U.S. anti-nuclear establishment who delayed the opening of Unit 1 through court challenges claimed they were doing so on the grounds of safety.

In the name of safety they were possibly responsible for the deaths of one hundred people.

The Ontario Nuclear Safety Review under Professor Kenneth Hare made a very detailed study of the safety of CANDU reactors. Information was gathered from many sources, American as well as Canadian. Energy Probe submitted four briefs to the review on various safety aspects of CANDU reactors and received $35,000 for its trouble. Other anti-nuclear sources were also funded, so that they could provide their best information to the review. Having considered all the information, Professor Hare concluded that Ontario's CANDU reactors are acceptably safe. Energy Probe has not published any detailed technical criticism of the Ontario Nuclear Safety Review to support its view that this conclusion is wrong.

"After Bhopal and Three Mile Island, people are realising a little more what hazard is about . . ." (Norman Rubin, Energy Probe).[39]

This statement is misleading.

By juxtaposing the Bhopal accident, in which releases from a chemical plant in India killed two thousand people, with the Three Mile Island accident, which did not kill anybody, Rubin would appear to be confusing people over "what hazard is about" rather than helping them realise the true nature of hazards.

This attempt to connect nuclear power to the latest disaster story is a typical technique in the game as played by Energy Probe. Another example occurred when the inquiry into the Challenger disaster pin-pointed an O-ring seal as the cause of the accident. Energy Probe quickly got media exposure for statements that nuclear reactors also used O-rings, implying that a disaster similar to that suffered by the Challenger could happen to a nuclear reactor. In fact there is no relationship between the hazards of using O-rings in the Challenger and their use in nuclear reactors.

"One thing that all the Commissions and Select Committees have agreed on is that catastrophic accidents can *happen in our CANDU reactors"* *(Norman Rubin, Energy Probe).*[40]

This statement is misleading.

BRAINWASHING

If you want to know how brainwashed you may have been, ask
yourself if you have heard of Gajurat. You almost certainly have
not. Then ask yourself if you have heard of Three Mile Island
(TMI). You almost certainly have.

TMI involved an accident in 1979 to a nuclear power reactor
generating electricity. No one was killed or injured.

Gajurat involved an accident in 1979 to a hydro dam used for
generating electricity. The death toll was 1,500 people.

TMI is in the U.S.A. and Gajurat is in India. But local interest can
hardly explain the difference in media coverage between the two
events.

So, if you want to know how brainwashed you may have
been . . . .

(1) It is a truism that any accident *can* happen. No human activity
can be considered to be absolutely safe. If the human race had denied itself
any activity which involved the risk of an accident, it would not have
evolved from the Stone Age. The real question to be addressed is the *risk*
of an accident, which includes the probability that the accident *can* happen
as well as the magnitude of its *consequences* if it does happen. This question
is usually avoided by Energy Probe.
    (2) The "Commissions and Select Committees" referred to by Rubin
are the Royal Commission on Electric Power Planning and the Ontario
Select Committee on Hydro Affairs. Although both have agreed that catastrophic accidents *can* happen, they have also both agreed that the *risks*
are sufficiently low that CANDU reactors should be allowed to operate.

"The catastrophic accident at the Chernobyl nuclear generating station
released as much long-lasting radioactive poison into the Earth's environment as all the nuclear bombs ever exploded . . ." (Norman Rubin,
Energy Probe).[41]

This statement is inaccurate.

According to statements made by the U.S.S.R. concerning the release of long-lived radioactive materials from Chernobyl, the amounts were considerably less than those released by atmospheric nuclear-bomb testing. For example, Chernobyl emitted about 1 megacurie of cesium–137, whereas the United Nations Scientific Committee on the Effects of Atomic Radiation (UNSCEAR) has reported that atmospheric tests have produced 35 megacuries. Chernobyl emitted 700 curies of plutonium–239, while atmospheric tests have produced 200,000 curies.

"Following the Chernobyl disaster, Canadian nuclear advocates were quick to assure us that 'it can't happen here . . . .' The official record shows otherwise. Three organisations have undertaken independent examinations of the dangers of CANDU reactors: the Ontario Royal Commission on Electric Power Planning, the Select Committee on Ontario Hydro Affairs and the Atomic Energy Control Board. All concluded that meltdowns are possible in CANDU reactors and that the CANDU containment system can fail" (Gordon Edwards, CCNR).[42]

These statements are misleading.

As noted earlier, it is a truism that all accidents are possible. What Edwards does not quote are the conclusions of the three bodies mentioned with respect to the safety of CANDU reactors. The Royal Commission and the Select Committee both concluded that CANDU reactors were adequately safe and should be allowed to operate. The Atomic Energy Control Board obviously agrees with this view because it issues licences for the operation of CANDUs.

The key to the anti-nuclear game in Edwards's statements lies in the words "meltdowns are possible" and "the . . . containment system can fail." In neither case does Edwards mention the *probabilities* of these events. The probabilities *were* considered by the three organisations he mentions, and, as a result, all three gave CANDU reactors a safe bill of health. The probabilities of melt-downs and containment failures in CANDUs are so small that the *risks* from operating CANDUs are also very small. Hence the confidence in CANDU safety expressed by the three organisations.

"The Select Committee on Ontario Hydro Affairs said, 'It is not right to say that a catastrophic accident (in a CANDU reactor) is impossible. . . . The worst possible accident could involve the spread of radioactive poisons over large areas, killing thousands immediately' " (Gordon Edwards, CCNR).[43]

This statement is incomplete.

Edwards omitted to quote the immediately following statements from the Select Committee report which put the quotation above in context:

> There is always some chance that the worst can happen. In a situation where absolutes are misleading, the Committee is forced to make relative judgements. If there is some chance of a catastrophic accident, that chance must be suitably small. If it is not possible to say that Ontario's reactors are absolutely safe, then they must, if allowed to operate, be judged "acceptably safe" for continued operation. . . . The Committee concluded that on the basis of evidence examined so far that the nuclear reactors operated by Ontario Hydro are acceptably safe.

"According to figures published by the designers of the CANDU, the probability of a pipe break in the core of a CANDU reactor is greater than 25 per cent over its anticipated lifetime. Like the Soviet reactor which malfunctioned at Chernobyl, the Gentilly–2 reactor [a CANDU reactor in Quebec] is a pressure-tube design which automatically experiences a power surge in the event of such a pipe break. If this power surge is not terminated by automatic shut-down systems within one second, serious damage to the core of the reactor will result, and large quantities of radioactive gases and vapours will be released into the containment shell. A series of hydrogen gas explosions, such as those that occurred at Chalk River during the 1952 accident, could also result. (It is considered likely that this is how the Chernobyl reactor accident began; pipe break, power surge, explosions)" (Gordon Edwards, CCNR).[44]

These statements are inaccurate.

THE BARE-BUM PHOBIA

The bare-bum phobia can afflict anyone who wears trousers. It is characterised by the fear of showing a bare bum.

The earliest, and commonest, manifestation of the disease is a belief that the waist-band of the trousers will not provide adequate safety, so that a belt must be worn. The disease can then progress. Suspenders are added, followed by the introduction of a rope around the waist and more ropes over the shoulders to augment the belt and suspenders respectively. In the extreme manifestation of the disease a second pair of trousers, as sturdy as the first but of different material, is worn beneath the first pair, accompanied by suitable additions of belts, suspenders, and ropes.

Despite the unfortunate nature of this disease, it is welcome news that nuclear-reactor designers suffer from a nuclear equivalent of the bare-bum phobia, known as the bare-fuel phobia. Reactor designers have a phobia about their fuel being exposed naked instead of being covered decently by water. They go to extraordinary lengths to avoid being embarrassed in this way.

They insist that all shut-down systems in the reactor be duplicated, so that if one system does not work a second one is on standby. And if both systems fail simultaneously, the fuel is saved from exposure to public view by a concrete containment vessel almost two metres thick.

The existence of the bare-fuel phobia, as a disease, has not been recognised by the medical profession, and so there is no cure for it. This may seem unfortunate to some, but the knowledge that the disease in its extreme, but not terminal, state is endemic among reactor designers should be comforting to most of us.

A pipe break has already occurred in a CANDU reactor (the Pickering–2 reactor) without the consequences predicted by Edwards. The reactor control system automatically shut the reactor down—as it was designed to do in such an eventuality. No action was required on the part of the operator. The automatic shut-down systems (another line of defence-in-depth) were not brought into operation.

The attempt to equate a pipe break in a CANDU reactor with the accident at Chernobyl is misleading. Any power surge resulting from a pipe break in a CANDU reactor will be much less than the power surge which occurred at Chernobyl. The safety shut-down system in a CANDU reactor acts much faster than the one installed in the Chernobyl reactor.

The sequence of events at Chernobyl as described by Edwards is incorrect. The power surge occurred first (it was unconnected with a pipe break); a rapid steam expansion occurred next; and this expansion caused the pipes to break in an explosive manner. The information given by Edwards attempts to relate the CANDU reactor to the Chernobyl accident. But as an AECB report on Chernobyl stated, the two reactors are so different that no significant lessons could be derived from Chernobyl which would help to make CANDU reactors safer.

"It is sobering to realise that if such an accident were to occur at an eight-reactor CANDU complex (such as those nearing completion at Pickering and Bruce), all eight reactors might have to shut down for an extended period of time, since they are all connected to the same vacuum building" (Gordon Edwards, CCNR).[45]

This statement is partially inaccurate.

The eight reactors at the Bruce site are not all connected to the same vacuum building. One group of four reactors is about three kilometres from the other group of four, and each group has its own vacuum building.

"Since 1977, the Canadian Coalition for Nuclear Responsibility has been calling for a moratorium on further expansion of the nuclear industry in Canada. . . . The call for a moratorium has since been echoed by hundreds of other bodies throughout Canada, including the Ontario Royal Commission on Electric Power Planning, pending a solution to the problem of radioactive waste disposal" (Gordon Edwards, CCNR).[46]

This statement is misleading.

The passage to which Edwards alludes from the Interim Report of the Royal Commission is the following:

> An independent review committee should be established to report to the AECB on progress on waste disposal research and demonstration. If the committee is not satisfied with progress by 1985 a moratorium on additional nuclear power stations could be justified.[47] [The final report extended the date to 1990.]

This cautious statement is hardly a clarion call for a moratorium on nuclear power. On the same page of the Interim Report is the following statement: "On economic grounds, CANDU nuclear and coal generation are the major realistic options for new large scale base-load supply of electricity in Ontario in the late 1980s and 1990s." This endorsement of CANDU by the Royal Commission is not mentioned by Edwards.

"The Gentilly–2 reactor does not have a separate vacuum building [to contain radioactive steam and gases in the event of an accident] such as all operating reactors in Ontario have" (Gordon Edwards, CCNR).[48]

This statement is misleading.

In the event of a build-up of steam pressure in a reactor containment building during the course of an accident, two methods can be used to reduce this pressure. It can be vented into a separate vacuum building fitted with a water sprinkler system, as is done with Ontario's reactors, or a water sprinkler system can be deployed in the roof of the containment building which will condense the steam and thus reduce the pressure. Ontario's reactors, such as those at Bruce, are built in groups of four, and a single vacuum building connected to all four of them is an effective and economical solution to the problem of steam over-pressure. Where a single reactor is built, the sprinkler system inside the containment building is preferable. Both methods are effective.

"The only commercial reactor that AECL has ever owned—Douglas Point in Ontario—ran at a loss continuously for 17 years before it was finally shut down permanently" (Lawrence Solomon, Energy Probe).[49]

These statements are misleading.

The Douglas Point reactor was designed as a large-scale prototype for what eventually became the CANDU reactor system. It was not a commercial reactor. AECL, the owner, has never been in the business of supplying commercial electricity.

Like most prototypes, Douglas Point was not expected to make a profit, but the electrical power it generated during its experimental life was sold to Ontario Hydro at the same cost as coal-fired electricity. Although it suffered all the interruptions and shut-downs which are normal for a prototype system, Douglas Point actually made a profit on its electricity sales for two consecutive years in the mid-1970s.

"Iodine–131, one radioactive substance released [from nuclear reactors] both routinely and during accidents, and which presents a serious thyroid cancer risk, easily enters the food chain . . ." (David Poch, Energy Probe).[50]

These statements are misleading.

The amount of iodine–131 released during the routine operation of a nuclear power reactor is minuscule. Even during an accident such as Three Mile Island, the amount of iodine–131 released was only about 20 curies. Iodine–131 does not present a serious thyroid cancer risk. This radioisotope has been routinely prescribed for nearly forty years as a nuclear medicine diagnostic procedure and, in large quantities, for thyroid therapy. Some of the patients who have received treatment over this period have been the subject of several follow-up studies but have shown no evidence of significant excess cancers. The risk of thyroid cancer is not itself considered to be as serious as it once was. It is one of the more easily curable of cancers and today seldom poses a life-threatening risk.

"The Canadian public is being effectively left out of the decision-making process [on new nuclear power facilities]" (Gordon Edwards, CCNR).[51]

This statement is inaccurate.

Decisions on new nuclear power facilities are made by provincial governments, usually on the advice of their electrical utilities. Provincial governments are elected by the public.

It is believed that Edwards's problem with the decision-making process is one that he shares with others in the anti-nuclear establishment. They appear to believe that all decisions involving nuclear energy should be preceded by a public inquiry followed by a referendum. They do not seem to realise that in the Canadian democratic tradition referenda are only used for really important issues (such as deciding on the separation of Quebec from Canada), if at all.

"The gamma dose just outside the fence surrounding a nuclear plant is the dose which the operators of the plant like to quote when they assure the public of their safety. . . . But these same operators usually fail to mention the far more serious dose received by inhaling or swallowing the radioactive particles, gases and liquids which routinely leak into the environment from these plants" (David Poch, Energy Probe).[52]

". . . only the external gamma dose (i.e. where the source of radiation is external to the body) is included in the estimates [of radiation dose] for the reactor, thus omitting alpha or beta external doses and all internal doses . . ." (Rosalie Bertell, IICPH).[53]

These statements are inaccurate.

The licensed limit for the radiation dose due to the reactor to the most exposed person living at the boundary fence of a nuclear reactor is 5 millirems per year. This is much less than the natural radiation dose of 200 millirems per year received from environmental radiation.

The dose from a reactor is calculated assuming that the most exposed person lives at the boundary fence and is exposed to external radiation from the reactor for the whole year. It is also assumed that this person inhales only the air at the boundary fence, eats only food grown at the boundary fence, and drinks only water from the waste-water discharge outlet of the plant. Using these conditions, the plant is designed so that the maximum annual dose, including both internal and external components, is less than 5 millirems. In order to achieve the design limit, the plant is designed conservatively so that the average annual dose is less than 5 millirems.

RADIOACTIVE RELEASES

Lord Marshall was the chairman of the U.K.'s Central Electricity Generating Board (CEGB), which provides electricity to the U.K. grid, mainly from coal and nuclear generators. When giving evidence to a House of Lords select committee in 1986, Lord Marshall said:

> Earlier this year, British Nuclear Fuels [a fuel re-processing company in the U.K.] released into the Irish Sea some 400 kilograms of uranium, with the full knowledge of the regulators. This attracted considerable attention and, I believe, some 14 parliamentary questions.
>
> I have to inform you that yesterday the CEGB released about 300 kilograms of radioactive uranium, together with all its radioactive decay products, into the environment. Furthermore, we released some 300 kilograms of uranium the day before that. We shall be releasing the same amount of radioactive uranium today and we plan to do the same tomorrow. In fact we do it every day of the year as long as we burn coal in our power stations. And we do not call that "radioactive waste"; we call it coal ash.

"During operation, the Gentilly–2 reactor releases large quantities of radioactive tritium and carbon–14 into the environment, both of which have been implicated in causing genetic and development defects at low doses in animal studies" (Gordon Edwards, CCNR).[54]

This statement is misleading.

The maximum quantities of tritium and carbon–14 which may be released from the Gentilly–2 reactor (or any other reactor) are specified by the Atomic Energy Control Board (AECB) in the reactor operating licence. In setting the level of these quantities, the AECB is aware of the animal studies mentioned by Edwards, and the levels are set so that any effect on people will be negligibly small. The quantities of tritium and carbon–14 which are *actually* released from Gentilly–2 are well below the

Lord Marshall then pointed out that three recent releases of radio-active carbon dioxide from the U.K.'s gas-cooled nuclear reactors had caused considerable adverse comment in the U.K. press. But he went on to say:

> The total amount of gas released from all three incidents was less than 100 tons. . . . Again, I must inform you that yesterday the CEGB discharged some 600,000 tons of slightly radioactive carbon dioxide to the atmosphere. We do so every day—from our coal-fired power stations. . . . In both cases the risks to the public are insignificant.

Although the concentration of radioactive materials in coal is low, so much coal is burned to produce electricity that far more radio-active material is released into our environment from coal-fired power stations than from nuclear generating stations.

This fact should be borne in mind when listening to complaints from the anti-nuclear establishment that nuclear power is con-taminating our environment with radioactivity.

maximum licensed quantities, and thus the hazard to people is less than the already negligible hazard licensed by the AECB.

"Apart from moving away from the vicinity of a nuclear plant, there is very little that can be done by an individual to reduce his or her exposure due to routine or accidental emissions" (David Poch, Energy Probe).[55]

This statement is misleading.

If a person living at the boundary fence of a nuclear power plant moved away from the plant in order to be safer, the move should not take him more than half a kilometre farther from his work. Poch fails to mention that the risk of driving that extra distance to work and back every day is about the same as the risk from the additional radiation dose from living near a nuclear reactor operating under normal conditions.

"If there is a reactor melt-down in Canada people will die. Whole cities could die. The world could die. I see members laughing. They think it is a joke. It is no joke" (Ian Waddell, Member of Parliament, NDP).[56]

The first three statements are inaccurate. The next two are true. The last is inaccurate.

Ian Waddell is one of the more vociferous members of the anti-nuclear faction in the New Democratic Party (NDP). Although there can be no doubt about his sincerity, he does not seem to realise that honourable members were probably laughing at his apparent complete acceptance of misinformation provided by the anti-nuclear establishment.

NUCLEAR LIABILITY ACT

In 1986 Energy Probe started a public campaign against the Nuclear Liability Act. In April 1987 it challenged the legality of the Act in the Supreme Court of Ontario. Its application was heard in August and judgement was delivered the following month. The application was dismissed on the grounds that Energy Probe had no standing to bring such an action, but Energy Probe filed a motion of appeal in November 1987. The appeal was successful and it was then the turn of the government to appeal this decision in the Supreme Court of Canada. In October 1989 the Supreme Court supported the Ontario Appeal Court's decision that Energy Probe did have standing to pursue its case, and Energy Probe will now proceed with its challenge to the Nuclear Liability Act in the Supreme Court of Ontario.

In this section some of the claims made by Energy Probe representatives during their public campaign against the Nuclear Liability Act will be examined.

"It [the Nuclear Liability Act] removes all liability of companies that supply parts to nuclear reactors should the parts fail, leading to an accident" (Energy Probe, Press Release).[57]

"The federal government has passed legislation to guarantee that, in the event of a nuclear accident, the GEs and Westinghouses have absolute

WATCHDOG

The Nuclear Liability Act received royal assent in 1976. In 1986 Energy Probe started attacking it, finally deciding to launch a constitutional challenge against it.

In its promotional literature, Energy Probe is fond of referring to itself as an independent watchdog. Independent it may be, but in this instance it looks as if the watchdog had been asleep in its kennel for ten years.

100% protection and you have virtually none" (Norman Rubin, Energy Probe).[58]

"An inevitable side effect of the Act . . . is to remove important incentives to accident prevention. Not only do GE *and Westinghouse have less incentive to be careful, but the insurance industry is less likely to scrutinise nuclear companies or to suggest safety improvements, as it does to other sectors" (David Poch, Energy Probe).*[59]

"Members of this [nuclear] fraternity can lie, cheat, steal, fabricate safety documents and engineering specifications, and knowingly sell faulty products to unsuspecting utilities without facing any civil liability" (David Poch, Energy Probe).[60]

These statements are misleading.

The Nuclear Liability Act places all liability for *third-party* damages on the operator of a nuclear facility. He is responsible for damages to a third party if an accident takes place. He cannot, in turn, claim from the supplier of a defective part even if that part has contributed to the accident.

One reason why the government passed the Act was to ensure that in the event of an accident, claimants would be treated equitably and rapidly. Without the Act, claimants for damages would have to fight their way past lawyers for the dozens of companies who had supplied parts for the reactor and who would all be denying responsibility. If a small-sized supplier were eventually found responsible for the accident, it would likely go bankrupt before the claims were settled.

Out of this attempt by the government to serve the Canadian public,

Energy Probe has produced the misleading statements listed above. The statements are misleading because the Nuclear Liability Act applies only to third-party claims. There is nothing in the Act to prevent the operator of the nuclear facility which has had the accident from suing the component supplier for *the damage to his facility*.

As noted in the first part of this chapter, the most likely result of a very severe reactor accident is that the reactor will be destroyed but that there will not be any releases of radioactive material which could affect the public. Damage to the reactor could amount to a billion dollars yet there would be no reason for third-party damage claims from the public. If component suppliers are sued for damages by the operator of the reactor, the amount they could be liable for is very large compared with any realistic estimate of the claims which could be made by the public.

It is known that in some cases component suppliers have a clause written into their contracts excluding them from liability to the operator if their components are the cause of an accident. This type of contract is independent of the provisions of the Nuclear Liability Act. However, this clause would only be included in a supplier's contract if the purchaser were convinced of the reliability and probity of the supplier. No purchaser would conclude a contract with such a clause if the supplier were likely to "lie, cheat, steal, fabricate safety documents . . . and knowingly sell faulty products," as stated by David Poch.

"No insurance is obtainable to protect either home owners or businesses in the event of a nuclear accident" (Energy Probe, Press Release).[61]

". . . Canadian insurance companies protect their solvency by excluding coverage for nuclear accidents in every homeowner insurance policy" (David Poch, Energy Probe).[62]

"Citizens of Quebec are unable to purchase insurance to protect themselves or their property in case of a nuclear accident" (Gordon Edwards, CCNR).[63]

These statements are misleading.

Under the Nuclear Liability Act, the insurance industry is already insuring the public against a nuclear accident. The reason why further insurance is not available is the well-known reluctance by the insurance industry to pay out twice for the same accident.

"If the nuclear industry believes its own claims for the safety of CANDU it . . . should either be in a position to satisfy risk experts in the insurance industry that the risk is low or be content to self-insure. Quite obviously the nuclear industry has not been able to satisfy itself or the insurance industry" (Energy Probe, Press Release).[64]

"The biggest lobby against requiring insurance of any kind was that of the insurance industry itself, which puts nuclear power in the same class as wars, insurrections and acts of God—infrequent events that can wreak incalculable damage and so are too risky to insure" (David Poch, Energy Probe).[65]

These statements are misleading.

Energy Probe staff appear to believe that the only insurance that the nuclear industry carries is the compulsory $75 million third-party liability it is forced to carry because of the Nuclear Liability Act. This is an understandable mistake because Ontario Hydro, the nuclear utility with which Energy Probe is primarily concerned, is such a large corporation that it self-insures almost all of its activities. Indeed, Ontario Hydro has stated that it would prefer self-insurance of its nuclear reactors to compulsory insurance under the Nuclear Liability Act.

However, a smaller utility, New Brunswick Power Corporation, carries replacement insurance on its nuclear power reactor at Point Lepreau. The coverage is provided by the insurance industry. It amounts to nearly $800 million. The annual premium is nearly $4.5 million.

A consistent theme of Energy Probe's attack on the Nuclear Liability Act is the implication that the nuclear industry is so dangerous that it can only be insured if the government legislates that the liability be limited to $75 million. Energy Probe never mentions that the New Brunswick reactor is insured by the commercial insurance industry (an industry which well understands risk) for its replacement value, a sum which is ten times the amount of insurance legislated under the Nuclear Liability Act.

In the event of an accident, the damage inside the reactor would likely be much greater than the damage to the public outside, so that the ratio of insurance in both cases, given above, would seem to be reasonable.

"It will be a long court case. . . . It will be expensive. And pitted against us will be the combined resources of the federal government, the utilities

and the corporate giants that comprise the nuclear industry" (Norman Rubin, Energy Probe).[66]

These statements are misleading.

The anti-nuclear establishment likes to portray itself as a concerned little David fighting an uncaring nuclear Goliath. What the public may not yet fully realise is that in the nuclear energy context, the David and Goliath image has been turned on its ear. Today, it is often found that little David is the purveyor of misinformation, while Goliath is behaving as a model of corporate integrity.

CHAPTER 4

Nuclear Fuel Waste

The Facts

On THE SUBJECT OF THE DISPOSAL OF NUCLEAR FUEL WASTES, experts in the field hold one view, while most of the general public holds a view which is completely opposite. Experts in the field believe that safe disposal is possible, even simple, and that the hazards to man and the environment now and in the future are negligible. The public, on the other hand, views used fuel wastes as very dangerous and believes that they will provide a serious hazard to our descendants for many generations into the future.

To understand the experts' point of view, the layperson must have some knowledge of the nature and volume of the wastes to be disposed of, and of the methods used to isolate the wastes from the biosphere. Once these two aspects are put together, the reason for scientific confidence in the proposed methods of disposal should be apparent.

THE NATURE OF URANIUM FUEL

Uranium fuel is the material used in nuclear reactors to generate electricity. At the same time it produces radioactive wastes as a by-product. Uranium fuel consists of uranium oxide pellets which have been heat-treated to render them into a very hard, insoluble form best described as "ceramic" uranium oxide. The pellets are cylindrical in shape, about twelve millimetres in diameter and twelve millimetres thick. They are ground to very fine tolerances to fit snugly inside a metal sheath.[1]

The uranium oxide fuel for the CANDU reactor consists solely of oxides of the two different sorts of uranium (i.e., two different isotopes) found in nature. These are uranium–238, which is by far the most abundant (99.3 per cent), and uranium–235, which is much less abundant (only 0.7 per cent). It is the latter, the uranium–235, which is fissioned in the reactor to provide heat and radioactive fission products. The highly abundant uranium–238 is not very useful for the direct production of heat because it does not fission to any appreciable extent. However, it does absorb neutrons to produce radioactive activation products such as plutonium–239. This radioisotope is also fissionable and can be extracted from the used fuel and recycled.

Both the isotopes present in natural uranium (uranium–235 and uranium–238) are unstable. They decay by emitting high-energy radiation. Radioisotopes have one distinguishing feature which must be borne in mind. When they give off radiation (i.e., decay), fewer radioisotopes remain so that the amount of radioisotopes present in used fuel wastes is continually decreasing.

The rate of decay varies widely among different radioisotopes. Some decay with a half-life of less than a second. This means that they decay almost completely to produce other isotopes, which may be stable or unstable, in less than a minute. Others have half-lives of billions of years. These latter radioisotopes are decaying so slowly that they can almost be considered to be stable since they produce minuscule amounts of radioactivity over periods of tens or hundreds of years. Thus it is not necessary to worry about either the very short-lived or the very long-lived radioisotopes. The former disappear so quickly that shielding people for brief periods from their effects is no problem. The latter disappear so slowly that their rate of production of radiation is inconsequential. It is the radioisotopes with half-lives between the two extremes that can cause some problems.

The two uranium radioisotopes, uranium–238 and uranium–235, have half-lives of 4.5 billion years and 0.7 billion years respectively. They decay so slowly that uranium fuel is safe to handle before it is put into the reactor. No precautions against radioactivity are taken during the manufacture of uranium fuel rods except normal "good housekeeping" measures. Dust is kept to a minimum, and gloves are worn, as is protective clothing, which is changed at the end of each work day. Although uranium is almost non-radio-toxic, it can be chemically toxic. If it gets into the bloodstream, it is about as toxic as lead. The chemical toxicity, not the radio-toxicity, is the more significant problem to address when dealing with uranium.

As noted earlier, the uranium oxide pellets are fitted inside a fuel tube. The tubes are made of a zirconium alloy called "zircaloy."[2] This alloy has low neutron-absorption properties; it is also strong and very corrosion-resistant. The uranium pellets are packed into the tube, and the tube is sealed with a cap which is welded in place. The tubes are then assembled in a bundle of nineteen to thirty-seven tubes, and this fuel bundle is inserted into the reactor.

THE FUEL IN THE REACTOR

Inside the reactor the uranium–235 and the uranium–238 are bombarded with neutrons. Some of the uranium–235 atoms fission; they split into two fragments of unequal size (fission products) with the simultaneous emission of neutrons which keep the nuclear reaction going. The fission products are radioactive and provide a large number of different radioisotopes with varying half-lives. Uranium–238 absorbs neutrons and produces several heavier isotopes (actinides, also known as the trans-uranic radioisotopes). Most of the fission and actinide products stay where they are formed within the uranium pellet. Exceptions are the volatile fission products, such as iodine, which can migrate to the surface of the pellet. About 1–10 per cent of these volatile fission products will normally be found at the surface of the uranium pellet.

The average fuel bundle stays in the reactor for about 1.5 years. By this time much of the uranium–235 has been fissioned, and a small amount of uranium–238 has been converted to trans-uranic radioisotopes. When it is discharged from the reactor, the bulk of the material in the used fuel is still uranium. The used fuel bundles contain about 99 per cent of unchanged uranium and about 1 per cent of other radioactive materials.[3]

There are over one hundred different radioisotopes in the fuel when it is removed from the reactor. They can be divided into three groups with short, medium, and long half-lives. It is convenient to define a short half-life as one year or less, medium as a hundred years or less, and long as all the rest. Using this classification, most of the radioisotopes in the used fuel have short half-lives, with about a dozen classified as medium, and another dozen classified as long. These radioisotopes are all decaying and giving off energy. As a result, the fuel is generating both heat and radio-activity and must be managed with great care.

THE FUEL OUT OF THE REACTOR

When the used fuel is taken out of the reactor, it is immediately placed in a large water-filled pool. This storage procedure is used in Canada and in other countries with nuclear power reactors.[4] The water in the pool performs a number of functions: it is sufficiently deep to absorb almost all the radiation from the fuel, so that operators working near the pool require no additional protection; the water in the pool is circulated through cooling coils, so that the heat from the fuel is continually dissipated; and the water is also circulated through ion-exchange columns to purify it and to detect whether fuel bundles are leaking. The water itself does not become radioactive.

There has been enough Canadian and world-wide experience in the use of water pools to show that this procedure for storing used fuel is safe, reliable, and cheap and that it can be used for many decades. There need be no hurry to remove the fuel from the pool. It can stay there for fifty, or even a hundred, years if necessary.

During this time much of the radioactive material will decay. For example, if we consider radioisotopes with short half-lives of one year or less, all of them will have decayed to essentially nothing after a few years. A radioisotope with a half-life of one year will decay to one one-millionth of its original radioactivity after twenty years (i.e., $1/2 \times 1/2 \times 1/2 \ldots$ multiplied twenty times equals approximately 1/1,000,000).

Plans call for keeping used fuel in pools for at least twenty years. During this period 99.96 per cent of the radioactive material originally present will decay to stable elements. *By far the largest proportion of the radioactive material in used fuel will not be disposed of. It will decay while in storage, before disposal takes place.* Nonetheless, there will still be sufficient medium and long half-life radioisotopes requiring disposal, so that eventually a disposal facility must be prepared.

DESCRIPTION OF A DISPOSAL FACILITY

People usually dispose of waste either by burning it or burying it. Burning will not destroy radioactive waste—it is necessary to bury it. If the waste is buried, it is necessary to make sure that it does not return to the biosphere in harmful quantities. The principal route by which it can return is for it to dissolve in water which then finds its way back to the surface. Therefore one requirement for a burial place is that there should be a minimum of water movement through it.

There are several geological formations which fulfill this condition. Underground salt beds are one. If there were any significant flow of water through the salt, it would have long since been dissolved. A second possibility is granite-type rock, which is known to have little water movement through it. This is the type of rock which will probably be preferred as a potential waste disposal repository in Canada.[5]

Granite rock formations in the Canadian Shield have been stable for hundreds of millions of years and can be expected to be stable for hundreds of millions of years into the future. Plutons, which are nuggets of granite up to several kilometres in diameter, are of particular interest. Water flows through the cracks very slowly. They usually contain no minerals of value. They appear to be an ideal repository for wastes.

In the current repository design, a shaft would be driven 500–1,000 metres deep into the granite, and a number of tunnels would be excavated from the foot of the shaft. A series of rooms would be dug out from the side of each tunnel. The radioactive waste would be sealed in corrosion-resistant containers at the surface, and these containers would be placed in holes dug in the floor of each room. The space around the containers would be filled with a special clay which absorbs metallic elements and would therefore slow the movement of most radioactive materials through it. When the room was full, it would be backfilled with a mixture of clay and sand to further retard the movement of the waste elements. When all the rooms were filled with waste and the repository was ready for closure, the shaft would be sealed.[6]

From this brief description of a waste repository it is apparent that there are a number of barriers to prevent the escape of radioactive material from the used fuel and its appearance at the surface. These separate barriers and their expected effectiveness will now receive more detailed consideration.

THE FUEL CONTAINER

The radioactive used fuel bundles would be taken from their storage site in the water pools to the waste repository. About seventy-two bundles would be placed in each corrosion-resistant container. The container would then be sealed and emplaced underground.

A considerable amount of experimental work has been conducted to find the best container material. The prime candidates at present are titanium, copper, nickel-based alloys such as Inconel and Hastelloy, and ceramics. The container must last for five hundred years. By then, all the medium-life radioactive material will have decayed away. After five hundred years, 99.9995 per cent of the radioactive products originally present in the used fuel has disappeared.

It is important to realise two facts about the container. *(1) Until the container has been breached by corrosion, absolutely no radioactive material can even start on its passage back to the surface. (2) After five hundred years, there is very little radioactive waste material left in the uranium.* Currently the median lifetime of a titanium container, the preferred material in Canada, is expected to be well over ten thousand years.

THE FUEL

Once the container has been breached, groundwater will corrode the zirconium sheath and expose the uranium oxide fuel to the water. Some radioisotopes from the used fuel will be instantly accessible. These are the volatile radioisotopes which have been released by the fuel pellets while the fuel was in the reactor. As noted above, a small proportion of these radioisotopes, about 1–10 per cent, will have accumulated on the surfaces of the pellets. Most of these volatile radioisotopes will have decayed to nothing before the container is breached. A notable exception is iodine–129, which has a half-life of sixteen million years. The fraction of this radioisotope which has diffused outside the uranium pellets is available for instant dissolution in water.

The remainder of the isotopes, all of which have very long half-lives, are still enclosed in the uranium pellets and will only be released as the pellets dissolve in the water. The rate of dissolution will depend on such parameters as the flow of water past the pellets, the temperature of the water, and the type and concentration of materials dissolved in the water.

Under the conditions expected to be found in a typical repository vault, the release of radioisotopes due to the dissolution of the uranium pellets will be very, very slow. At the expected median rate of dissolution it will take ten million billion years for the used fuel to dissolve and the radioactive materials to be released. This is an unimaginable length of time. The earth is only six billion years old, and the time since the creation of the universe by the "big bang" has been estimated to be only fifteen billion years. *The rate of dissolution of the uranium oxide pellets is comparable to the rate of dissolution of the granite rock in which they are laid to rest.*

THE REPOSITORY

When the containers are placed in the repository, they are surrounded by an absorbing clay. The rooms in the repository vault are also backfilled with a similar clay mixed with sand. The clay performs two functions. As water seeps into the vault, the clay swells and closes up any small cavities in the vault, thus slowing down the movement of water. The clay also absorbs most of the radioactive materials in the water, a process which will further retard their movement through the vault. A notable exception to this latter effect is iodine–129, whose movement is retarded very little by the clay.

The clay is a naturally occurring material which has been in the earth for millions of years. It is sufficiently stable to retain its unique absorbent properties for millions of years into the future.

THE GEOSPHERE

The geosphere is the term used to describe the geological formation in which the radioisotopes are buried—in our case, probably granite. As noted above, the flow rate of water through granite is very low, but it is not zero. Granite contains fissures and cracks which provide long and tortuous paths from the repository vault to the surface.

The actual transit time from the vault to the surface will usually depend on the nature of the groundwater path, which in turn will depend on the properties of the granite. This transit time is expected to be in the order of millions of years, and thus only the very long half-life radioisotopes could be carried to the surface and still retain their radioactivity. None of these radioisotopes is particularly hazardous.

EXPERIMENTAL RESULTS

A research program designed to examine the nature of the variables described above is being carried out by Atomic Energy of Canada Limited at its Whiteshell Nuclear Research Establishment in Manitoba. Information on the longevity of the containers, the rate of dissolution of uranium oxide, the transit time through the vault, and the transit time through the geosphere is being collected.

Each step is expressed as a computerised model, and the models are joined to give, under varying conditions, the estimated rate of appearance of radioisotopes at the surface. Finally, the latter are transformed into the effective radiation dose which the most exposed person near the groundwater exit would receive. In some cases, the possible error levels in each step are wide, but ongoing work will narrow them and thus provide more accurate estimates of the final population dose. This latter is the bottom line of the whole research program. Already enough information has been assembled to give good estimates of the final dose to the population.

It is known that there will be zero dose to the population for tens or probably hundreds of thousands of years after the vault has been closed.[7] This estimate is based on the confidence that most of the containers will not be breached until all the medium half-life radioactive materials have decayed and that in the cases of the few containers which are breached the radioactive materials would take a long time to travel to the surface. Most of the radiation dose arising from the radioactive materials and reaching the surface during the first ten million years would be contributed by iodine–129 (half-life sixteen million years). Almost all of this dose is contributed by the "instantly released" iodine–129 outside the uranium oxide pellets.

As noted previously, when iodine enters the body it concentrates in the thyroid gland. Experience gained from using radioactive iodine for medical diagnosis and therapy shows that, in small quantities, it does not readily produce thyroid cancers. It is also known that thyroid cancers can usually be cured and are seldom life-threatening. In other words, iodine–129 is one of the more harmless of the radioisotopes which could escape from a waste disposal repository.

In summary, there are two controlling mechanisms affecting the appearance in the biosphere of radiation dose from radioactive wastes.

The dose from the instantly available fraction of the radioactive materials (1–10 per cent) found outside the uranium oxide pellets after water has penetrated the container is primarily controlled by their slow rate of movement from the vault to the surface. The production of radiation dose at the surface by the radioactive materials remaining inside the uranium oxide pellets is controlled by the even slower rate of dissolution of the uranium oxide.

CREDIBILITY OF THE RESULTS

The belief that used fuel wastes are a present and continuing hazard to life on this planet is so widespread that it may be difficult for some people to accept that this belief is wrong. It would be useful to have some external indicators that the scientific predictions of negligible harm into the distant future are likely to be correct. Fortunately three such indicators are available.

(1) About five hundred years after the used fuel has been emplaced, the radio-toxicity of the contents of the vault would be about the same as the radio-toxicity of a high-grade uranium ore deposit. Such deposits are spread across Canada from Newfoundland to British Columbia. Some high-grade deposits are located near the surface. We know that the release of radioactive materials from these deposits presents little hazard. It is often difficult to detect them by their radioactivity despite the fact that radioactivity can be detected at extremely low levels.[8] Because uranium ore deposits are so lacking in hazard, where the deposits are large enough to justify a mine, townships have been established nearby to house the mining community. Examples are Elliot Lake in northern Ontario and Uranium City in northwest Saskatchewan.

After closure, a nuclear fuel waste repository will be no more potentially hazardous to a community than a uranium ore deposit. The repository will probably be even less hazardous because of the multiple barriers around the used fuel wastes. They should ensure better containment of the radioactive materials than nature has provided for the radioactive materials in uranium ore deposits.

(2) After about ten thousand years the next ice-age is predicted to be upon us, and a repository in the Canadian Shield will then be covered by several hundred metres of ice. The area will be uninhabitable for about one hundred thousand years until the ice retreats. During this time there can be no realistic chance of hazard to human life due to the repository, and at the end of this period there will be no significant amounts of hazardous radioactivity left in the wastes.

(3) One of the radioactive materials in spent fuel which is wrongly

supposed to be particularly radio-toxic is plutonium–239. This radioisotope has a half-life of about twenty-four thousand years, which has led
to the belief that it will be impossible to isolate it from the environment
long enough to allow it to decay to harmless levels.

Several hundred million years ago in what is now Gabon in West Africa,
a rich uranium deposit became reactive when water started to flow through
it. The uranium in the deposit at that time had a higher abundance of
uranium–235 than is found today, and it began to fission, just as uranium
does in a water-moderated nuclear reactor. Plutonium–239 was formed
as a result of this natural nuclear reaction, and although it has long since
decayed away, its daughter products are still found close to the parent
material from which they were formed, despite the water flow. They have
only migrated a fraction of a centimetre in millions of years.[9]

This is not surprising considering the insolubility of the uranium ore
in which the plutonium was formed, but it does lend credibility to those
experimental results which show that even under the most adverse conditions plutonium–239 in a waste repository will move so slowly that it will
contribute only a negligible amount to the total radiation dose at the
surface.

WHY THE CONTROVERSY?

Opposition groups which sprang up with the spread of nuclear power in
the 1970s emphasised the dangers of public exposures to radiation. These
groups believed that potential nuclear power plant accidents were threaten-
ing present generations and that nuclear fuel wastes could threaten future
generations. The phrase "we don't know what to do with nuclear wastes"
was quickly accepted by opposition groups, and spread to the general
population as an accepted fact.

Why was the nuclear scientific community, which was aware of some
of the facts of waste disposal, muted during this period? It seemed obvious,
for example, that a corrosion-resistant container could be designed to ensure
complete isolation of the waste from the biosphere for a few hundred years
until all the short and medium half-life radioisotopes had decayed away.
After all, we possess today Bronze Age artifacts which were manufactured
five thousand years ago, and natural silver and gold have survived since
the earth's formation. Modern knowledge of corrosion-resistant materials
is immeasurably greater now than it was in the Bronze Age. But the scientific community could not prove how long modern containers would last
in the environment found within suitable geologic media such as granite.

Scientists also knew that ceramic uranium oxide was highly insoluble
in water. However, there was no certain knowledge of how this would

affect the rate of release of radioactive materials from the used fuel waste. Another major unknown at that time was the condition likely to be found inside granite geological formations. Would they be as solid as they appeared to be or would they be riddled with major fractures? What would be the flow rate of water through the granite and hence through the vault containing the fuel? What were the chemical conditions of the water which would control container-material corrosion rates and uranium oxide corrosion rates?

Much of the basic scientific evidence was missing, and as a result nuclear scientists were reluctant to engage in debate over nuclear fuel waste management. This left the field wide open to the spread of misinformation about used-fuel waste disposal. However, many countries set up research programs to fill in the gaps in scientific knowledge. In Canada, a joint agreement between the federal and Ontario governments led to research work being undertaken by Atomic Energy of Canada Limited (AECL) at its Whiteshell Nuclear Research Establishment in 1978. This major scientific program has been funded at over $30 million per year.

The program is monitored by a Technical Advisory Committee (TAC) consisting of independent experts nominated by professional societies whose interests are related to the research problems being studied. These societies are: the Biological Council of Canada, the Chemical Institute of Canada, the Engineering Institute of Canada, the Canadian Geoscience Council, the Canadian Federation of Biological Societies, and the Canadian Information Processing Society. The TAC is in agreement with the content and direction of the research program.

As a result of scientific research many of the reservations expressed about deep geological disposal in the mid-1970s are now known to be inapplicable. In 1985 AECL published an interim account of its results and expressed confidence that its method of disposal in granite rock would be adequately safe.[10] AECL is not alone in this opinion. Earlier in 1985, waste disposal experts from twenty industrialised countries published a collective opinion in which they asserted that nuclear fuel waste disposal could be safely accomplished using available technology.[11] It remains to transmit this scientific confidence to the general public.

The Game

The following statements are made routinely by the anti-nuclear establishment: "We don't know what to do with nuclear wastes"; "Nuclear wastes will be dangerous for thousands of years"; and "Staggering volumes of nuclear wastes are piling up." These slogans have been put across to the general public so successfully that a majority believes them to be true. They are in fact good examples of the ten-second inaccuracy.

At the time of writing (1989), AECL's research program into used-fuel waste disposal is almost complete, and its results are very promising. The government has stated that it will hold public hearings into AECL's assessment, and thus the good news that we *do* know how to manage nuclear wastes safely should then get wide publicity.

This prospect has caused the anti-nuclear establishment to back-pedal furiously. Whereas the storage of nuclear wastes was deemed unsafe to human life a few years ago, storage of these same wastes is now seen to be very desirable. The anti-nuclear establishment now uses arguments which purport to show the benefits of storage on the surface compared with disposal underground.

The statement "We don't know what to do with nuclear waste" is being replaced with other statements such as the truism "We can't predict the future." For example, according to the anti-nuclear establishment the future stability of rock formations which have been stable for hundreds of millions of years cannot be guaranteed because geology is not a predictive science. Or, computer models can be wrong; therefore they should not be used to predict the future.

Watching this intellectual gear-changing among members of the anti-nuclear establishment is amusing for the pro-nuclear advocate. But the fun will soon be over. A public hearing into AECL's research work will be held in the early 1990s, and hopefully the public will then realise that what it has been told by the anti-nuclear establishment was just another strategy in the anti-nuclear game.

Comments on other statements made by the anti-nuclear establishment on the subject of high-level nuclear waste disposal are given below.

❖ ❖ ❖

"We are talking about the most lethal, long-lived toxic substances on

the face of the earth" (Donovan Timmers, Concerned Citizens of Manitoba).[12]

". . . nuclear waste disposal is doing incredible harm to life on this planet" (Dan Heap, Member of Parliament, NDP).[13]

". . . we are creating thousands of tons of incredibly lethal wastes . . ." (Norman Rubin, Energy Probe).[14]

"High level radioactive wastes produced by reactors are capable, in principle, of causing millions to billions of fatal cancer deaths . . . an admittedly unlikely scenario" (Gordon Edwards, CCNR).[15]

All these statements are misleading.

They are typical of the tactics used repeatedly by the anti-nuclear establishment to frighten people. Nuclear fuel wastes, which decay with time, should be compared with other toxic materials which are produced in large quantities and which are with us permanently. For one illustrative example, it can be noted that the U.S.A. produces two thousand times more lethal doses of chlorine and twenty-five times more lethal doses of ammonia annually than it does of radioactive wastes. Both these materials are used as household items. People have not been frightened by the supposed dangers of chlorine or ammonia even though these hazardous substances are generally not managed as safely as nuclear wastes.

Despite the fact that nuclear fuel wastes from nuclear power reactors have been circulating in industrialised countries for thirty years, the record shows no accidents involving fatalities and very few with injuries during that period. There have not even been any significant "near-misses"— those nuclear non-events which are routinely described as "catastrophic accidents" by the anti-nuclear establishment.

Like many other materials in our society, radioactive wastes can be hazardous if they are not managed properly. The care with which radioactive wastes have been treated has ensured their safety. Most other industries could learn much from the nuclear industry in the proper management of wastes.

"The wastes remain at dangerously high levels of radioactivity for tens of thousands of years" (David Hallman, United Church of Canada).[16]

". . . large quantities of high-level reactor wastes, which will remain toxic for millennia . . ." (David Poch, Energy Probe).[17]

These statements are inaccurate.

After about five hundred years, a used-fuel waste deposit will be no more dangerous than a high-grade uranium ore deposit. There are many such deposits in Canada. Some of them are so close to the surface that they are mined using open-pit methods. Even these deposits are difficult to detect because the escape of radioactivity from them is so slow. A nuclear waste repository would produce no more radioactivity at the surface than a uranium ore-body because the man-made barriers are expected to be at least as effective as natural barriers in delaying the passage of radioactive materials from the disposal vault to the surface.

"The disposal of high-level radioactive waste (spent nuclear fuel) is financially onerous, environmentally uncertain, and potentially divisive" (Gordon Edwards, CCNR).[18]

The first two statements are inaccurate.

The cost of waste disposal *and* reactor decommissioning are estimated to be less than 5 per cent of the cost of nuclear electricity generation. These costs have been included in Ontario Hydro's base rate for several years, so that Ontario residents have been paying the future costs of eventual waste disposal and decommissioning as they pay their current electricity bills. This increased cost is hardly "onerous" at less than 5 per cent of their current electricity bills, which are among the lowest in the world.

There is nothing environmentally uncertain about spent fuel disposal. Almost all waste disposal experts agree that it can be accomplished without any significant effect on the environment. However, disposal could be divisive. According to public opinion polls, players of the anti-nuclear game have been so successful in transmitting their message about the nature of radioactive waste management that a large-scale educational program will be required to show the public that waste disposal is a problem with a relatively easy solution. The public hearings into AECL's assessment of its waste disposal concept will be a good place to begin this educational process.

"Prohibit permanent underground storage of radioactive wastes anywhere

in Canada. . . . Develop a full-scale research effort into a system for permanent, on-site, monitored, retrievable storage of nuclear wastes" (Walter Robbins, Concerned Citizens of Manitoba).[19]

This statement is a good example of back-pedalling.

The government chose eventual permanent underground disposal over permanent surface storage because it would not be fair to future generations to leave them with a legacy of problems that we have not solved. It was also necessary to refute the allegation that "we don't know what to do with nuclear wastes." Now that it is possible to demonstrate that underground geological disposal is adequately safe, there is no reason to think in terms of permanent surface storage. However, demonstration of a safe underground geological disposal concept will remove a major plank from the anti-nuclear platform. Hence the back-pedalling.

"The 'spent' fuel from a nuclear power plant is millions of times more hazardous than the uranium going in" (David Poch, Energy Probe).[20]

"Used in an atomic reactor, the products [of uranium] gain in destructive power, persistence and the ability to produce cancers" (Elinor D. U. Powell, M.D., F.R.C.P.C., Physicians for Social Responsibility).[21]

These statements are inaccurate.

To understand why they are inaccurate, consider the fate of an atom of uranium–235 which is fissioned, and the fate of one that is not. A fissioned atom produces *two* radioactive fragments, both of which have relatively short half-lives before decaying to, usually, stable states. A non-fissioned atom of uranium–235 will decay through *twelve* different radioisotopes before it achieves a stable state as an isotope of lead.

There is no doubt that the uranium going into a reactor is much more hazardous than the fissioned uranium coming out. Although it will take a long time for the hazard to express itself (the half-life of uranium–235 is 700 million years), over the very long term a non-fissioned uranium atom is potentially more hazardous than a fissioned uranium atom. A corollary of this statement is that putting uranium through a nuclear reactor is a method of slightly *reducing* the amount of radioactivity in our environment—over the very long term.

VALUABLE WASTE

When told by pro-nuclear advocates that we *do* know what to do with spent fuel waste, the public may justifiably ask, "Then why aren't you doing it?"

The best answer to this question is that *we do not have any spent fuel waste in Canada.* The reason for this surprising statement is quite simple.

Spent fuel contains plutonium–239, which is a fissionable radioactive isotope similar to uranium–235. Plutonium can be separated from spent fuel by chemical reprocessing and used to produce more fission energy. At present, reprocessing is not carried out in Canada because it is too expensive compared with the cost of using ordinary uranium. But at some time in the next century, when the current glut of uranium on the market disappears, it will become economic to extract plutonium from spent fuel. The residue from that process will be the true "spent fuel waste."

Meanwhile, storage is the best method of management during the period of rapid decay, and the spent fuel can be stored cheaply and safely in the water-filled pools at the reactor sites. Because of its future value, it will not be declared as "waste" ready for disposal.

Estimates show that by the end of this century the energy in the plutonium in spent fuel stored in Canada will be about the same as the energy stored in the Athabasca tar-sands.

❖ ❖❖❖

"When AECL comes forward with its 1,000 or so documents, where are we going to have the people to question the experts, the people with technical knowledge who have the budgets to do a serious job of reviewing this from an independent point of view?" (Gordon Edwards, CCNR).[22]

This statement is misleading.

But one can almost sympathise with Edwards's dilemma. The anti-nuclear establishment now realises that the scientific case which will be presented by AECL assessing an underground geological disposal repository will be overwhelmingly favourable to the concept.

What makes Edwards's statement misleading is his failure to acknowledge the existence of the Technical Advisory Committee (TAC). This committee consists of senior scientists nominated by the various professional societies in Canada whose disciplines are relevant to the research work being carried out by AECL. The TAC is exactly what Edwards wants, "the people with technological knowledge who have the budgets to do a serious job of reviewing this from an independent point of view." It has been monitoring AECL's work from the outset of the program. It has ensured that the science is good and that the direction being taken by the research program is the proper one.

No other scientific project in Canada has been as closely monitored by peer reviews as this one. This may be unfortunate for the anti-nuclear establishment, but it is good news for those in the population who wish to see a safe method of waste disposal developed.

"*The most misleading part of the advertisement, however, is the first paragraph which contrasts the electrical power generated for 750,000 people with high level radioactive waste amounting to 'only a four-foot cube'. . . . It also fails to mention that the reactor waste could not actually be stored in a four foot cube. The waste has an extremely high temperature. It is still capable of fissioning and must be surrounded by sufficient water to absorb the neutrons and prevent a chain reaction starting spontaneously. The space needed to store a four foot cube of fission waste is about 10,000 times the actual size of the cube. This is roughly the size of a football field with a depth of 10 feet*" (Rosalie Bertell, IICPH).[23]

These statements are inaccurate.

The advertisement to which Bertell refers was produced in the U.S.A. by America's electric energy companies. It is apparent from the advertisement that they are referring to the waste left after reprocessing spent nuclear fuel. This waste contains virtually no uranium or plutonium. It contains mainly fission products which are only about 1 per cent of the original fuel. This amount can easily be accommodated in a four-foot cube of glass. Since the uranium and plutonium have been removed, the waste will *not* be capable of fissioning. The extra volume around the cube to allow for cooling and shielding will be small, about three times the volume of the cube and not ten thousand times the volume as claimed by Bertell. Her figure is in error by a factor of about three thousand.

GETTING THE NUMBERS RIGHT

Scientists frequently deal with numbers, and if their arithmetic goes awry they tend to become embarrassed. Dr. Rosalie Bertell has been quoted as saying that some 150 megatons of fission-product wastes from atmospheric weapons testing in the stratosphere are gradually coming down all over the place.[24]

But Bertell has never considered how 150 million tonnes of fission products could have got into the stratosphere in the first place. A jumbo jet can carry about 50 tonnes of payload. It would take three million jumbo flights to transport the 150 million tonnes of fissionable material.

Her statement does not recognise the fact that the yield from fission explosions is expressed in terms of comparable conventional explosives. A one megaton nuclear explosion will have about the same effect as a megaton of dynamite, but it will be accomplished by a very much smaller mass of fissionable material.

A one megaton explosion is about equivalent to 1.45×10^{26} fissions. From this it can be calculated that 150 megatons of explosive power can be provided by the fissioning of about 8.5 tonnes of fissionable material. It is this 8.5 tonnes that is in the stratosphere waiting to come down, not 150 million tonnes. Bertell is wrong by a factor of nearly twenty million.

"... the rock in the Precambrian Shield is so incredibly fractured and so wet, there is a great deal of doubt as to whether this option would ever be viable" (Walter Robbins, Concerned Citizens of Manitoba).[25]

"Some experts think the repository will flood and casks will deteriorate, resulting in large-scale ecosystem radioactive pollution" (Donovan Timmers, Concerned Citizens of Manitoba).[26]

These statements are misleading.

It is known that granite rock in the Canadian Shield is fractured and also that it is permeated with water so that a waste repository would soon be flooded. However, it is also known that the movement of this water is very slow. Much of this water is referred to as "paleolithic," which means it has been down there for hundreds of thousands of years. This gives us a good idea of how slowly water moves inside some granite rock formations. The time this water will take to make its way to the surface is also measured in hundreds of thousands of years. The radioisotope causing the major radiation dose to people which the water would carry will be iodine–129 (half-life sixteen million years). Most other radioisotopes will have decayed long before the water reaches the surface.

"... to get the waste into the repository, one has to dig a hole through the rock. No matter what you do to that hole, you can never restore that shaft to the integrity it had when it was rock. So this is the Achilles heel of the entire geological disposal problem" (Gordon Edwards, CCNR).[27]

This statement is inaccurate.

It has been obvious to the world's scientists from the outset of their research programs that the shaft which was sunk into a geological medium could be the Achilles heel as far as movement of water back to the surface is concerned. As a result of research into this problem in Canada, AECL scientists are now convinced that they can plug a shaft so that it will be even less permeable to water than the surrounding granite rock. A probable method would be a series of impermeable concrete plugs placed across the shaft and grouted into the walls of the shaft.

"How does one propose to prove the disposal of radioactive waste is going to be safe? One uses geological science and mathematical science. . . . Geology as presently understood is not a predictive science. It is not a science capable of making precise predictions in the way physics or chemistry is" (Gordon Edwards, CCNR).[28]

These statements are misleading.

Edwards implies that the safety of a nuclear fuel waste repository is governed mainly by geology. It is not. It is governed primarily by physics and chemistry: by the rates of decay of radioactive isotopes and by the corrosion rates of corrosion-resistant materials. These are known with very good accuracy and they are very predictable.

It was noted in the first part of this chapter that after about five hundred years the toxicity of the contents of a waste repository would be about the same as the toxicity of a high-grade uranium ore deposit. Therefore, after five hundred years the waste can be considered adequately safe since we do not worry about the safety of uranium ore deposits. This level of safety depends solely on the radioactive decay rates of the radioisotopes.

The containment during this period will be provided by the corrosion-resistant vessel in which the spent fuel is sealed. Corrosion rates can be determined by physical and chemical measurements. Precise predictions can be made about corrosion rates under various conditions.

Geology is a factor in ensuring the safety of a waste repository which applies in the long term. It will only come into play after the containers have corroded (about ten thousand years), and then its major role will be to reduce the radiation dose to the most exposed person in the population from "negligibly small" to "even smaller"!

". . . the modellers and the technologists are never going to be able to guarantee the safety of a nuclear waste repository. It is simply beyond the scope of conceivable science to guarantee that such a thing will not have serious negative impacts" (Norman Rubin, Energy Probe).[29]

These statements are misleading.

Rubin is playing a semantic game, demanding certainty from the nuclear industry in an area where it is clearly not possible to give it—and then condemning the industry for being dangerous. The "modellers and the technologists" will be able to provide estimates over time of radiation dose rates from a nuclear waste repository for the most exposed person and the probability that those dose rates will be accurate within certain limits. Since those dose rates will be extremely small, the error margins can be wide and still the results will give no cause for concern.

As for giving *guarantees*, it is not the function of science to give guarantees, since there can be no guarantees for the future. However, the scientific "modellers and technologists" have usually done a much better job of forecasting the future than members of most other disciplines. It is this forecasting that has produced the technological richness of modern life.

"The real reason for the industry's sense of urgency [for waste disposal] has little to do with environmental or safety concerns. . . . The spent-fuel bays adjacent to the reactors are rapidly filling up. They want to empty the pools in order to make room for more" (Gordon Edwards, CCNR).[30]

These statements are inaccurate.

There is *no* urgency on the part of the nuclear industry to dispose of its spent fuel. This fuel contains a valuable energy resource, plutonium–239, and it would be foolish to dispose of the fuel until it was known whether it is possible to use this resource economically.

Spent fuel is stored at reactor sites in pools about the size of an Olympic swimming pool but about six times deeper. These pools are relatively cheap to construct. One of them can contain about seven thousand tonnes of spent fuel. Canada is currently producing about two thousand tonnes of spent fuel per year from all its reactors. There is obviously no danger of running out of this type of storage.

"AECL's long history of pre-judgement of the success of its research programs should in itself provide sufficient grounds to disqualify it from proceeding with further work on waste management" (Donovan Timmers, Concerned Citizens of Manitoba).[31]

This statement is misleading.

AECL's research programs have produced the world's first prototype, and the first full-scale heavy-water nuclear power reactor. They have produced on-load refuelling machines, safe low-power reactors, hundred-tonne quantities of heavy water, and cobalt–60 cancer-therapy machines. These are just a few of the results of "AECL's long history of pre-judgement of the success of its research programs."

Since the Second World War, AECL has conducted one of the most successful research programs ever launched in Canada. Much of its research has been mission-oriented; therefore there has been a pre-judgement of its success. It is not evident why an organisation which has so successfully completed most of its mission-oriented research programs should be disqualified from conducting more of the same.

QUANTITATIVE HAZARDS

Professor Bernard Cohen of the University of Pittsburgh has devoted a great deal of effort to studying the hazards of high-level radioactive wastes.

He has calculated that if the waste is buried about six hundred metres underground, then the eventual effect from the amount of wastes produced by one year of light-water reactor plant operation will be 0.018 cancer deaths. To my knowledge, this figure has never been challenged by the anti-nuclear establishment.

To put this figure into perspective, Cohen compares it with the consequences of operating a similar coal-fired plant for one year. According to a National Academy of Sciences study commissioned by a U.S. Senate committee, annual emissions from a coal-fired power plant result in twenty-five deaths and sixty thousand cases of respiratory disease.

Once again, quantitative safety figures show that nuclear power is much safer than the alternative.

However, the members of the anti-nuclear establishment never use comparative quantitative figures in their campaign against radiation. Rather, they speak in vague qualitative terms of "thousands of lethal cancer doses" even though these doses are contained safely in nuclear fuel wastes.

". . . transportation of spent fuel becomes a significant concern to millions of people living along the transportation routes in the Canadian Shield . . ." (Carol Duyf, Concerned Citizens of Manitoba).[32]

This statement is inaccurate.

Used-fuel waste has been transported throughout the world for several decades without any significant accidents. Nonetheless, the myth about the hazards of the transportation of radioactive material is one that is carefully cultivated by the anti-nuclear establishment. In Canada the mode of transportation (air, ship, rail, or road) is regulated by the Department of Transport. The transportation container is regulated by the Atomic Energy Control Board (AECB). All container types must undergo stringent tests before they are accepted for use. Hundreds of thousands of radioactive shipments, some of them used fuel, are made annually across North America and world-wide without incident. The anti-nuclear establishment obscures this excellent safety record while succeeding in frightening some people about the almost non-existent hazards of transporting radioactive wastes.

"Those titanium containers will then be filled with molten lead and sealed before burial in the underground repository" (Gordon Edwards, CCNR).[33]

This statement is out-of-date.

The concept of filling waste containers with molten lead, in order to reduce the external radiation field during handling, was considered by AECL. But it soon became apparent that when the containers corroded and the lead escaped into the environment, it would be a greater hazard to health than the radioactivity. This fact neatly illustrates the *relative* harmlessness of radioactive wastes after disposal compared with another well-known material used widely in our society.

"To most ecologists, nuclear power represents the ultimate extension of the throwaway society by producing mountains of radioactive garbage which cannot be safely recycled for any human use" (Gordon Edwards, CCNR).[34]

These statements about nuclear fuel waste are inaccurate.

The amount of waste produced in a nuclear reactor is small—not "mountainous." This is one of the advantages of nuclear power over alternatives such as coal. The amount of used-fuel waste produced in Canada up to 1988 was only enough to fill a hockey rink to the height of the boards. In addition, nuclear fuel waste can be recycled to produce plutonium–239, which could be a valuable energy resource for Canada in the next century.

CHAPTER 5

Uranium Mining

The Facts

URANIUM ORE HAS BEEN MINED IN CANADA SINCE 1932. IN THAT year Eldorado Gold Mines Limited opened a pitchblende mine at Port Radium on Great Bear Lake in the Northwest Territories for the purpose of extracting radium. The ore was shipped to Eldorado's refinery at Port Hope in Ontario, where the radium was extracted from the uranium and sold. The uranium was an unwanted by-product.[1]

At the beginning of the Second World War, radium markets were disrupted and the Eldorado mine was closed. However, it was opened again in 1942 to produce uranium for the Manhattan Project in the U.S.A. as part of the Allied war effort.

After the Second World War there was a uranium exploration boom in Canada fuelled by the U.S. nuclear weapons program, and a large number of new mines were opened, mainly in Ontario and northwest Saskatchewan. The uranium mining boom turned to a bust in 1959 when the U.S.A. announced that its stockpile of uranium for weapons production was sufficient and current contracts would not be extended. There was no other outlet for uranium at that time, and the Canadian uranium industry went into a precipitous decline. From a peak of twenty-six mines operating in 1959, only three mines were operating in 1965. This situation continued for ten years, and it was not until 1975 that a new mine was brought into production.[2]

Since 1975 the uranium industry has expanded again. In 1987 there were eight licensed mines in Canada, and they were all of considerable size. Canada is now the world's largest exporter of uranium with export sales valued at about $1 billion annually.

During its history the uranium mining industry has been the source of two major issues which have led to attacks on the industry by the antinuclear establishment. These issues are the effect of radon on the health of uranium miners and the environmental contamination from uranium tailings piles. Both will be discussed after a brief description of the industry.

URANIUM MINING

Uranium is a widespread constituent of the earth's crust with an average abundance of 3.4 parts per million. The ores suitable for mining contain in excess of 0.05 per cent uranium by weight (500 parts per million), with some rich deposits having greater than 10 per cent (100,000 parts per million). Mining in Canada is centred in Ontario in the Elliot Lake region, and in northern Saskatchewan, although ore bodies have been discovered in other provinces. Uranium also occurs in the oceans, but at a concentration too low to be worth recovering at today's prices.

Uranium ore is mined using the same techniques and much of the same equipment as for any other ore. Canadian uranium mining is carried out deep underground in Ontario, but in Saskatchewan the ore deposits are so close to the surface that open-pit mining is used. In both mining processes, ore is broken out by blasting, crushed to approximately fifteen centimetres in diameter, and then transported to the mill. In underground mines large quantities of air are circulated through the mine. The air flow ensures proper ventilation and carries away most of the radon gas and its decay products plus some of the dust released from the broken rock. In open-pit mines radon gas is not a major problem.

Significant quantities of water are also produced from the mine. The water comes from its use in drilling and dust control as well as from inleakage of groundwater and (in the case of open-pit mines) precipitation. In most cases this mine water is contaminated to some degree by minerals and chemicals. To avoid discharging it directly into the environment, it is generally pumped to the milling process, where it is used as process water.

In underground mining the amount of non–ore-grade rock removed is generally minimised, but cannot be completely eliminated. In open-pit mining the quantities of overburden which must be removed to obtain access to the ore are normally much greater. This solid waste, provided it is low in radioactivity, is often used in the construction of dams for the milling wastes or segregated in separate storage dumps for other construction or land rehabilitation purposes.

URANIUM MILLING

In the normal milling process, uranium ores are crushed and ground to approximately 0.15 millimetre particle size to expose the mineral surfaces to the chemicals employed to dissolve the metal values and for ease of bulk handling in slurry form. The uranium is then leached from the finely ground ore, usually by sulphuric acid. The final mill product is called "yellowcake." Most of the chemicals not incorporated in the yellowcake, and all the water not recycled, are piped to the waste management areas as a slurry with the solid residues which are called mill tailings.

The quantity of solid wastes transported in this slurry depends on the concentration of the ore. For ore containing 0.05 to 0.15 per cent uranium, approximately one tonne of tailings is produced per kilogram of product. Along with each tonne of solids, approximately two tonnes of liquid wastes are discharged.

To handle the large quantities of waste products, every uranium mill has a waste management area, which consists of two separate parts. The first and larger of these is the tailings basin into which the tailings slurry is pumped and in which the solid residues collect. This basin is usually a natural depression in the ground. The second is a settling pond used to retain the precipitates formed as a result of chemically treating the liquid overflow from the tailings basin.

URANIUM REFINING

Refining is the name given to the chemical purification and other steps needed to convert the milling product (yellowcake) into a product acceptable for the next stage in the process. Eldorado has been refining uranium at Port Hope, Ontario, since 1942 and also operates a newer refinery at Blind River, Ontario.

The refinery has two main products—ceramic-grade uranium oxide powder for CANDU reactor fuel and uranium hexafluoride for export to enrichment plants and eventual use in light-water reactors. In the past, the Port Hope refinery has also produced radium, uranium metal, aluminum-uranium alloy, and uranium carbide and retains the capability of doing so. Variations on the present processes and the dismantling of old equipment have also resulted in a variety of wastes different from those now produced.

Several sites in Port Hope have been used by Eldorado both for storage and for burial of different waste products. Some sites were on Port Hope municipal property; others, such as those at Welcome and Port Granby, were purchased by the company. Port Granby is the only waste management site which is still operational in the Port Hope area and, along with the Welcome site, is subject to supervision and control by the Atomic Energy Control Board.

URANIUM FUEL FABRICATION

The fuel fabrication process consists of uranium oxide powder preparation, pressing, sintering, and grinding. The resulting pellets are loaded into zirconium alloy tubes, which are then welded shut and assembled into bundles before packing and shipping.

Radioactive wastes arise mostly from the grinding of the uranium oxide pellets but also from items which are rejected at one of the many inspection points. Most of the grinding wastes and the pellet scrap are returned to Eldorado for recycling through their uranium refinery. The wastes from housekeeping have a very low level of contamination but are shipped to the Chalk River Nuclear Laboratories waste management site. The management of wastes from the Canadian companies operating fuel fabrication plants does not present any difficulty.

RADON AND ITS DAUGHTERS

When uranium decays, one of its decay products is the element radon, which under normal conditions is a gas. Radon is an inert gas, which means it is chemically inactive and does not form compounds with other elements.

The isotope of radon produced by the decay of uranium is radon–222. This isotope is radioactive with a half-life of 3.8 days, and it decays by alpha particle emission. Radon–222 is not particularly hazardous to health. It is chemically inert, and if inhaled it will be promptly exhaled again and not retained in the lungs. The small amount of decay which would take place while it is briefly in the lungs does not make it a significant hazard.

However, radon–222 decays through a series of daughter products before it arrives at its final form, a stable isotope of lead. These daughter products are solids and not gaseous; therefore they can attach themselves to dust particles or can serve as nuclei for the condensation of water vapour, so that when they are inhaled they are retained in the lungs. Some of the daughters are also alpha emitters, and if sufficient amounts of them are inhaled into the lungs the cumulative radiation dose can, if high enough, eventually cause lung cancer.[3]

The assessment of the degree of risk posed by radon daughters in a mine atmosphere is complicated by the complexity of the physical and biological processes involved, such as the amount of dust and humidity in the mine atmosphere, the breathing rate and type of breathing (through the mouth or nose) of the individual, the amount of mucus and its distribution in the bronchial passages, and the additive action of cigarette smoking on the severity of the effect.

The effect of radon and its daughters on the health of miners was recognised long before radon itself had been discovered. As noted earlier, in the sixteenth century it was reported that silver miners near the Erz Mountains in Europe were dying from lung diseases. While other noxious substances present in mine atmospheres were also contributing to these lung diseases, subsequent investigations have shown that radon daughters in these mines would almost certainly have been a major contributing factor.

Since uranium is widely dispersed in the earth's crust, most forms of mining can present a risk to mine workers from radon daughters released to ill-ventilated areas. A high incidence of lung cancer attributed to radon daughters has been reported among fluorspar miners in St. Lawrence, Newfoundland. It is not necessary for the mine to be specifically a uranium producer for the radon risk to be present.[4]

At the time of the uranium boom in the second half of the 1950s, both the health authorities and the uranium mining companies were aware that health risks to miners could be increased because of radon daughters in uranium mines, but the extent of the risk could not be fully assessed. A recommendation for a maximum concentration of radon in air had been made as early as 1940, but there was confusion over whether this concentration applied to radon, to its daughters, or to both.

It was also not possible in the early years of uranium mining to measure radon or its daughters in mines to any degree of accuracy. Accurate measurements could be made with delicate instruments under clean laboratory conditions, but it was not until the 1950s that the U.S. Public Health Service introduced a method of measuring radon and its daughters which could be used in the dirty, dusty, humid atmosphere normally found at the rock-face in a working mine.

Meanwhile, to reduce concentrations of radon and its daughters to acceptable levels, all uranium mines built during the boom of the 1950s were fitted with much higher volume ventilation systems than was normal in conventional hard-rock mines. The first of these mines, the Beaverlodge Mine of Eldorado Mining and Refining Limited opened in 1952, was subject to a joint government and industry study in 1954 and in the light of knowledge available at that time was found to be acceptably safe in all respects, including radiological safety.

The realisation that there could be a lung cancer problem among uranium miners came about gradually, mainly through the deliberations of the Advisory Committee on Occupational Health of the Ontario Mining Association. In the early 1960s this committee began setting up occupational records designed to assess the present and future risk of lung cancer in uranium miners. A Nominal Roll of uranium miners was developed by the medical statistics unit of the Workmen's Compensation Board, and figures of mortality by cause of death were compiled.

A report on the findings was published in July 1974.[5] It recorded forty-one lung cancer deaths observed in a population of eight thousand miners in Ontario during 1955–1972. The report estimated that this represented an excess of twenty-eight over the thirteen expected lung cancer deaths by reference to all contemporary deaths of Ontario males.

In September 1974 the Government of Ontario, responding to this and other questions concerning the effectiveness of mine safety programs, appointed James M. Ham as commissioner to investigate matters related to the health and safety of workers in mines. Part of that investigation was the health issue raised by the exposure of uranium miners to ionising radiation. Using updated data based on the Ontario Uranium Nominal Roll, the commissioner found that in the period from 1955 to 1974 a total of thirty-six excess deaths due to lung cancer were recorded for a population of just over fifteen thousand miners.[6] The commissioner's findings on lung cancer aroused considerable agitation in nuclear and anti-nuclear circles with demands that the regulatory authorities take prompt and vigorous action.[7]

In the early years of uranium mining the federal regulatory agency, the Atomic Energy Control Board (AECB), had delegated health and safety matters in uranium mines to provincial mines and health authorities. This was a reasonable thing to do. Under the Canadian constitution, all mining is a provincial responsibility except for uranium mining, which the federal government had reserved to itself under the 1946 Atomic Energy Control Act. The provincial governments had had extensive experience in regulating mining; the AECB had had none. Consequently all mine licences issued by the AECB specified that the mine operators must comply with any applicable provincial statutes and regulations dealing with mine safety and cognate matters.

After the Ham Commission report criticised the split in regulatory authority for uranium mines, the AECB took a stronger interest in uranium mining. Staff were hired to provide control and supervision of the mines, and in 1978 the AECB revised its radiation protection regulations to include for the first time a maximum exposure limit for radon daughters. The maximum hazard to uranium miners from radiation in their workplace is now limited, so that it is the same as for other radiation workers.

To put the radiological hazard to uranium miners into a proper perspective it should be noted that during the period covered by the Ham Commission report, the period when the hazard from radon and its daughters was at its highest, the risk to uranium miners from violent accidents was five times as great as the risk from lung cancer. The risk of lung cancer has since been considerably reduced. Mining is a relatively hazardous occupation, and it is to be hoped that all mining risks can be further reduced whether they are radiological or non-radiological.

URANIUM MILL TAILINGS

The major hazards from uranium mill tailings are the conventional hazards of instability of the tailings piles, acid generation, and heavy-metal dispersion. They have these hazards in common with the 3,500 million tonnes of hard-rock mill tailings which are scattered across Canada in hundreds of sites totalling 230 square kilometres. However, the main distinguishing feature of uranium tailings is the presence of radioactivity, and it is this feature to which most concern is addressed and most attention paid, even though it is not a major hazard.

Uranium tailings have accumulated in Canada since the milling of uranium ores started in 1952. To date more than 150 million tonnes of uranium tailings have accumulated in surface dumps, and tailings are being produced at the rate of approximately 7 million tonnes per year.

The human race has lived with the effects of the distribution and redistribution of natural radioisotopes throughout its existence. The concentration of radioactivity in the tailings is low enough that it poses no acute risk to human health. However, this radioactivity is, as a result of the mining operation, more accessible to the biosphere than when it was in the ore-body and therefore presents a small additional hazard to the local population.

In the past, uranium mining companies abandoned their tailings following the historical practice of most mining operations. Today, the uranium mining companies are required to obtain the approval of the AECB before decommissioning their mines and tailings facilities. Before giving such approval, the AECB requires evidence that the radioactive wastes have been treated in such a way that they present no significant hazard to people or to the environment.[8]

The radioactivity present in tailings can be transported through the atmosphere and by surface or underground waters. For example, the inert gas radon can diffuse into the atmosphere. As it has a short half-life and is very dense, it is not carried very far from its source. Within two kilometres downwind from the tailings pile, its atmospheric concentration is indistinguishable from the natural background.

The release of radioactive materials by dissolution and discharge in natural waters could also present some risk to man. Such radioisotopes could be ingested with water or as part of the food chain. The most hazardous radioactive material which could enter natural waters is radium. In recognition of this, overflow water and seepage from the tailings piles is collected in a settling pond where it is treated to remove the radium before the water is allowed to flow into a natural watercourse.

The permanent (i.e., non-radioactive) components of the tailings can also give rise to pollution problems. In addition to the heavy-metal content, some of the constituent elements of the ores and many of the chemicals used in mining and ore treatment have significant potential for environmental degradation. It should be noted that such degradation is associated with many other hard-rock mines and is not peculiar to uranium mining. For example, about 500 million tonnes of tailings from hard-rock mining in Ontario contain significant amounts of acid-generating sulphides.

The most prominent potential non-radioactive pollutant in uranium tailings is the iron sulphide present in the Elliot Lake ore-body. This material when exposed to air and water and assisted by bacterial action can produce sulphuric acid. For example, the deterioration of the Serpent River basin (downstream from Elliot Lake) as a fishing habitat was almost entirely due to this process. Continuing remedial action involving chemical treatment of all acidic effluents has now removed this source of environmental contamination.

Tailings are normally deposited in naturally occurring basins behind engineered dams. Detailed consideration of factors such as geology, hydrology, and seismicity have to be taken into account in the design of tailings dams. Guidelines have been issued by the AECB which require both dams and basin floors to have low permeability and long-term stability.

After the mixture of solid residues and liquid wastes is discharged into the tailings basin, separation of liquids and solids takes place. The solids settle into the basin, and the liquids decant into a settling pond, the second part of the waste management area. As this decanted liquid contains chemicals and radioisotopes in concentrations too high for release to public waters, further treatment is necessary. Most of the radium is removed from the sulphate-bearing liquors at operating sites by adding a solution of barium chloride to the overflow to co-precipitate a mixture of barium and radium sulphates. This settles as a sludge on the bottom of the settling pond. Settling is completed after a retention period of three to six days.

The precipitated material has a high radium content, and during the decommissioning process provision must be made for its collection and disposition prior to closeout of the operation. At many of the sites where the milling operations were discontinued in the 1960s, runoff and seepage are collected and treated for radium removal and, where necessary, also for acidity.

The present surveillance methods are designed to ensure that negligible quantities of radioactive materials and polluting chemicals are released to the biosphere in the water effluent and seepage. Removal of solid wastes by the public for any purpose is also prohibited. Airborne release of dust particles is now being minimised by planting vegetation. By such means, the risks from radiation damage to the health of the local population are practically eliminated. Enforcement of such preventive measures is required by the licensing procedures of the AECB and provincial authorities, and the measures are carried out by the mining companies.

Numerical estimates have been made of the radioactive hazards of tailings piles which serve to put their risks into perspective. By using the linear, no-threshold hypothesis, about twelve hundred out of every one million deaths in Canada from all causes may be attributed to the effect of naturally existing background radiation. Using the same basis for calculation, the radon and other radioactive materials released from the mill tailings projected to be deposited in Saskatchewan, for example, over the next thirty years have been estimated by Environment Canada to result in approximately one additional cancer death per century in the province. Compared with other industrial activities, including other forms of mining, uranium mining is a very safe occupation.

The Game

Uranium is mined in only two provinces in Canada, Saskatchewan and Ontario. The opposition to uranium mining is much stronger in Saskatchewan than in Ontario, but the reason for this is not completely understood. It may be because there are nuclear power reactors in Ontario but none in Saskatchewan. The presence of nuclear power reactors sometimes reduces much of the radiation paranoia associated with nuclear materials. Or it may be because the most vociferous opponent of uranium mining in Saskatchewan is a church ecumenical group known as the Inter-Church Uranium Committee. If the major churches are against something, then surely that thing must be evil and must be opposed by the public. Unless, of course, the churches and their leaders have been misled.

The arguments of the anti-nuclear establishment against uranium mining have all been put on display in a statement issued in June 1983 by church leaders in Saskatchewan entitled "Christian Leaders Call for a Halt to Uranium Mining for the Sake of Peace." This is a remarkable document signed by the following church leaders: Most Rev. Noel Delaquis, Roman Catholic Bishop of Gravelbourg; Mr. Edgar W. Epp, Executive Director, Mennonite Central Committee; Most Rev. Charles Halpin, Roman Catholic Archbishop of Regina; Dr. John W. Kleiner, Professor of Christian Ethics and Church History, Lutheran Theological Seminary; Bishop G. W. (Lee) Leutkehoelter, Central Canada Synod, Lutheran Church in America; Most Rev. James P. Mahoney, Roman Catholic Bishop of Saskatoon; Most Rev. Blaise Morand, Roman Catholic Bishop of Prince Albert; Dr. Paul W. Newman, Past President, Saskatchewan Conference, United Church of Canada; Most Rev. Michael G. Peers, Anglican Archbishop of Qu'Appelle; Rt. Rev. H.V.R. Short, Anglican Bishop of Saskatchewan; Rev. Wendell Stevens, President, Saskatchewan Conference, United Church of Canada; Most Rev. Jerome Weber, Roman Catholic Abbot Ordinary of Muenster; Rt. Rev. Roland A. Wood, Anglican Bishop of Saskatoon.

According to the signatories, making peace is the most pressing task of our time. Peacemakers strive to end all forms of violence against their neighbours, their environment, and themselves. In a series of thirteen pithy paragraphs, the church leaders explain why halting uranium mining will assist in the cause of peace. Each paragraph consists of one or more statements, and these statements comprise the core of the anti-nuclear establishment's arguments against uranium mining. Each paragraph will be examined below, and comments will be made on its accuracy.

The first group of paragraphs is under the subheading "Uranium Is . . . Fueling Weapons."

"Canadian uranium was initially developed to supply the nuclear weapons program of the United States."

This statement is misleading because it is made without context.

No mention is made of the fact that at that time there was a world-wide struggle going on against fascism, and that the free world was fighting for its life. That struggle was supported by the Canadian public and the Canadian churches.

"Canadian nuclear reactors sold for generating electricity have enabled other countries to develop nuclear weapons. Uranium mined in Saskatchewan is often used in these reactors. Saskatchewan uranium can thus be channelled to fuel weapons."

These statements are inaccurate.

India used a Canadian *research* reactor and indigenous uranium to produce a simple nuclear explosive device in 1974, which was claimed to be for "peaceful purposes." It is the only nuclear device exploded by India.

No Canadian nuclear reactors sold for generating electricity have been used to develop nuclear weapons. In addition, no country has used a reactor primarily designed for electricity production to produce weapons. The nuclear weapons states have all used small dedicated reactors which produce a better grade of weapons material than an operating power reactor.

Canadian uranium was used in the U.S. and U.K. weapons programs until 1965. Since that date no Canadian uranium has been sold for use in nuclear weapons manufactured by any country.

"Attempts at international nuclear safeguards are not working. More and more countries are joining the nuclear weapons 'club.'"

These statements are inaccurate.

Attempts at international nuclear safeguards *are* working as evidenced by the fact that fewer and fewer countries are joining the nuclear weapons "club." The facts are as follows. In the decade following the first nuclear explosion by the U.S.A., 1945–1955, three countries became members of the nuclear weapons "club," the U.S.A., the U.S.S.R., and the U.K. In the next decade, 1955–1965, France and China joined the club. In the decade from 1965 to 1975, there were no official additions to the club. During this decade India exploded its solitary nuclear device. Because India has exploded no further devices, it is not considered by the international community to be a "nuclear weapons state." Since 1975 there have been no additions to the "club," either official or unofficial. A few additional countries, such as Israel and South Africa, are suspected of possessing nuclear weapons. However, actual possession cannot be confirmed until a weapon is tested.

"World-wide proliferation of weapons continues."

This statement is misleading.

If it is read in conjunction with the above statements, it would imply that horizontal proliferation is continuing. Horizontal proliferation is the increase in the number of nuclear weapons states. As shown, this is not the case. However, vertical proliferation is continuing. This is the type of proliferation caused by the nuclear weapons states increasing the number of nuclear weapons in their stockpiles. It is to be hoped that the recent thaw in relations between the U.S.A. and the U.S.S.R. will reverse the trend of vertical proliferation.

A second group of paragraphs is under the subheading "Uranium Is . . . Risking Health."

"The nuclear industry, from uranium mining through reactors to bombs, produces both radiation and highly radioactive 'waste.'"

This statement is true.

However, it would have been fair to the nuclear industry to point out that the public has not been affected by the radiation or the radioactive "waste."

"Ionising radiation is a threat to human health. It has been shown to induce genetic disease and deformity, spontaneous abortions, leukemia and cancer."

These statements are misleading.

Placing these statements immediately after the previous statement implies that the nuclear industry has produced levels of radiation that are a threat to public health. This is far from the truth. The very low levels of radiation from the nuclear industry to which the public is exposed have never been shown to cause genetic disease, deformity, spontaneous abortions, leukemia, cancer, or any other disease.

"The problem of waste disposal has not been resolved. Wastes from the mining and milling of uranium produce a low level radiation that poses a constant threat to health and to the environment."

These statements are inaccurate.

There is no problem connected with the safe management of uranium mining and milling wastes. These wastes have been managed safely for many years to the satisfaction of the federal nuclear regulatory agency, the Atomic Energy Control Board, and the provincial environmental departments. One reason why they are so easy to manage is that their level of radioactivity is so low that they do not produce any significant threat to health or to the environment.

"Other steps in the nuclear fuel cycle produce high-level radioactive wastes that require secure isolation for thousands of years."

This statement is inaccurate.

As was seen in the chapter on nuclear fuel waste, high-level waste needs to be kept securely isolated for only about five hundred years. After that time the waste has decayed to a level which would permit it to be handled for short periods without undue hazard. The myth that fuel wastes are hazardous for thousands of years has been continually spread by the anti-nuclear establishment.

"It is not possible to give assurances of safety for this number of years into the future. Consequently, the burden of responsibility for assuring waste containment is placed on all future generations."

These statements are inaccurate.

After five hundred years, a high-level waste repository is no more dangerous than a high-level uranium ore deposit. There are many such deposits in Canada and they are not considered dangerous; in fact, we sometimes build towns near them to house the families of the miners who are working in the mines. We do not consider high-level uranium mines to be a burden on future generations.

Maintaining the safety of the waste for five hundred years is simple (see the chapter on nuclear fuel waste). The titanium containers in which the waste will be placed are expected to last at least ten thousand years, and until these containers are breached by corrosion no radioactive material can escape and start finding its way back to the surface. Even after the containers have been breached, the other barriers provided in the waste repository will probably keep the waste better contained than uranium in the ground.

The final group of paragraphs is under the subheading "Uranium Is . . . a Questionable Investment."

"The most active investors in Saskatchewan's uranium industry are a provincial and a federal crown corporation. Low risk factors in the industry's royalty structure, as well as government support services for the industry, have attracted large, private investors. Some of these investors are actively involved in weapons production."

These statements are misleading.

It is true that investors in Canada's uranium industry include federal and provincial crown corporations and private companies. However, even if one of the private companies were to be involved in weapons production, Canadian uranium could not be used for that purpose.

Canada has not sold uranium for weapons production since 1965. Since that time Canada has built up a safeguards regime to ensure that our nuclear materials, equipment, and supplies are not used for nuclear weapons purposes. Canada's safeguards regime is considered internationally to be one of the most stringent in the world.

"The industry depends on capital intensive technology which creates few jobs in comparison with alternative possibilities. Moreover, the uranium market is filled with uncertainty."

These statements are misleading.

Most modern heavy industry and all sectors of the mining industry are capital intensive and create few jobs. Is it being suggested that all these industries should close down? It is more likely that this silly criticism of the uranium industry arises from a lack of comparison with other industries—a common fault of the anti-nuclear establishment.

The second criticism is just as silly as the first. Is there any market which is not filled with uncertainty? In fact, as far as demand is concerned, the uranium market is more predictable than most. It takes about ten years to build a nuclear reactor; therefore the market for uranium for the next ten years is always known with some precision. However, Canada's share of this market is not known nearly as accurately.

"Uranium mining does not provide a viable future for communities. The people of Northern Saskatchewan are directly affected but have very little input into the development of this industry. Alternatives to a uranium-based economy in the North must be developed."

These statements are misleading.

The first statement ignores the fact that the new mines in northern Saskatchewan have not attracted residential communities. The miners are flown in to the mines to work long shifts for a period and are then flown out again. In this way, the social disruption which occurred when the mines near Uranium City closed down should be minimised and the potential number of mining "ghost towns" scattered across Canada is reduced.

The second statement ignores the fact that public inquiries were held before mines were opened in Saskatchewan. The leaders of these inquiries went out of their way to ensure that northern Saskatchewan residents had an input into their deliberations.

The third statement ignores the fact that the uranium industry has been beneficial to northern Saskatchewan. If alternative industries are developed, they must be in addition to uranium and not designed to replace it.

"A permanent, alternative economy in the North will benefit all Saskatchewan."

This statement is true.

The uranium deposits in northern Saskatchewan are enormous. But no matter how large they are it must be anticipated that they will be exhausted eventually. More permanent industries should be developed in the area in anticipation of that time.

This concludes the statements made by the Saskatchewan church leaders in their remarkable document. It includes two sets of statements which are true, five which are inaccurate, and six which are misleading.

Why did these thirteen well-meaning and intelligent gentlemen sign such an inaccurate manifesto? It is evident that they did not seek the facts from responsible officials in the federal or provincial governments or provincial crown corporations. They seem to have relied on the advice of junior clergy who themselves had been playing the anti-nuclear game.

A colleague of mine wrote to one of the bishops protesting the errors in the document. He received a cordial reply, but the detailed reply to his criticisms was appended by a junior cleric who, the bishop admitted, had strongly anti-nuclear views. This cleric did not admit any one of the mistakes in the manifesto. He simply either repeated them or went into detailed justifications which were sometimes more bizarre than the original inaccurate statements.

The anti-nuclear game can be played with all types of people. One can only hope that these church leaders have learned something from their experience. The thought of clergymen making inaccurate statements to their flocks, because they fail to inform themselves of the facts, is a disturbing one.

Saskatchewan clergymen are not the only critics of uranium mining in Canada. The regular sources of anti-nuclear information have also commented on this topic, and some of their statements are quoted below, with suitable responses.

"Saskatchewan Churches are disturbed by the failure on the part of the government to clean up tailings as mines are abandoned. Several such situations exist presently where the wastes are blown in the wind and are making their way into water systems" (David Hallman, United Church of Canada).[9]

". . . uranium tailings . . . are very voluminous. They are of a very fine consistency. They blow in the air when the wind comes by. They get washed into the river systems" (Gordon Edwards, CCNR).[10]

These statements are probably inaccurate.

However, without a knowledge of the tailings piles Hallman and Edwards are referring to, it is impossible to be more specific about these statements.

All tailings piles, whether from active or abandoned mines, are under the jurisdiction of the federal regulatory agency, the Atomic Energy Control Board, and are also under the surveillance of the relevant provincial environment authority. Neither agency would allow the conditions described by these authors. The myth of tailings "blowing in the wind" is often repeated by the anti-nuclear establishment, but it is not specified where these tailings piles are located.

"According to a computer model I prepared . . . to estimate the remote health effects of the radon gas and its daughters on Canadians . . . the existing tailings are now causing, remotely, one 'excess cancer death' about every twenty-one months in the Canadian population" (Norman Rubin, Energy Probe).[12]

This statement is misleading.

It is another case of Energy Probe apparently frightening people about something which is of no consequence. Firstly, the number of deaths should be quoted as "between zero and one excess cancer death, about every twenty-one months," and secondly, a calculated death rate that low once again illustrates that nuclear energy is so safe that its use should be mandatory.

Rubin does not explain that since uranium is a natural part of the soil, its decay product, radon, is also a natural part of the soil. As a result, radon gas is continually seeping out of the soil into the atmosphere. When, for example, farmers plough their land, radon is released at an even greater rate than when the soil is undisturbed.

The U.S.A. is a major uranium producer, and it has been estimated that tailings piles in that country release about 0.5 million curies of radon per year. Natural emissions from the soil in the U.S.A. amount to 120 million curies per year, which makes the emissions from tailings piles relatively small.[13]

But the main danger to people in the U.S.A., if Rubin is to be believed, is to farmers. Soil tillage produces about 3 million curies of radon per year, and much of it is probably inhaled by farmers sitting on top of their tractors. If radon were truly a hazard, we would expect to find lung cancer endemic among farmers. It is not.

"These radon emissions (from tailings piles) . . . will eventually cause about 62,000 excess cancer deaths . . . in the enormous number of people we expect to live in the Eastern half of Canada over the course of the next hundred thousand years or so" (Norman Rubin, Energy Probe).[14]

This statement is inaccurate.

Again, the multiplication of a small radiation dose by a very large population and extending this radiation exposure over a very long period of time enables Rubin to produce figures for cancer deaths which may very well frighten the public. No mention is made of the fact that the cancer deaths due to this very small radiation dose could be zero.

Also, Rubin appears unaware that people will be living in eastern Canada only for about 10 per cent of the next hundred thousand years. In about ten thousand years the next ice-age is predicted to arrive, and eastern Canada will then be buried under ice and therefore uninhabitable for the next one hundred thousand years or so.

KEY LAKE

Sir Walter Marshall, the former head of the U.K. Atomic Energy Authority, once said of the nuclear controversy: "Public perception [of the nuclear industry] is hindered by the symbiosis of the anti-nuclear lobby (who need the exposure to survive) and the public media (who need controversy to entertain)."[11]

This symbiosis was evident in the media treatment of a water spill at the Key Lake uranium mine in northern Saskatchewan.

The Key Lake mine is an open-pit mine, and in this type of mine water can accumulate in the pit. At Key Lake the water is pumped out and stored in reservoirs so that it can be used later as process water in the uranium milling circuit. One day in early 1985, a workman went home and left the pump running. As a result, the reservoir overflowed and tens of thousands of litres of water poured onto the ground, most of it eventually finding its way into a small lake nearby.

The anti-uranium groups in Saskatchewan, particularly the Inter-Church Uranium Committee, let out a howl that was soon picked up by the media. The spill at Key Lake was described as an

"Canada maintains that its system of 'safeguards' adequately keeps track of Canadian uranium to ensure that none of it contributes to the global nuclear arms race. Research conducted by Greenpeace and other organisations has repeatedly contradicted the Government's assurances about the uses to which Canadian uranium is put" (Greenpeace, leaflet on "Nuclear Exports and Government Secrecy").[16]

The latter statement is inaccurate.

Or, if accurate, Greenpeace has carefully kept the results of its research away from the Canadian public. Much of the research carried out by the anti-nuclear establishment is always about to be published but somehow never quite sees the light of day.

"environmental disaster." The CBC featured the "disaster" as the lead story in its broadcasts for two days. A national inquiry was demanded by the anti-nuclear establishment, together with immediate closure of all Saskatchewan uranium mines.

Canada's nuclear watch-dog, the Atomic Energy Control Board, sent officials to visit the site, as did the Saskatchewan Department of the Environment. Both agencies agreed there was no hazard from the spill, but their voices went almost unheard in the media clamour.

What was never mentioned by the media in communicating this "environmental disaster" to the public was the fact that the spilt material was groundwater. It was water containing minute quantities of naturally occurring radioactivity which had been pumped out of the ground and which had been inadvertently returned to the ground.

The anti-nuclear establishment in Saskatchewan got their public exposure from this incident, and the media got their sensational story. Unfortunately, there was no one to worry about whether the public got the facts.

"Does selling [Saskatchewan] uranium outweigh the creation of toxic northern waste lands where no one may hunt, fish, harvest or play?" (John Willis, Greenpeace).[17]

This question is misleading.

The radioactive material dispersed into the northern Saskatchewan environment by uranium mining is negligible. It is monitored and controlled by the federal agency, the Atomic Energy Control Board, and by the provincial Department of the Environment. Those lakes close to the mines that receive discharged waste water have shown no evidence of significantly increased radioactive contamination since the mines were opened. The areas around each mine where hunting, harvesting, or recreational activities have been halted temporarily are very small. These areas are comparable with the areas taken up by other (non-uranium) mining activities in other parts of Canada. The population of northern Saskatchewan is very sparse. The nearest Indian band to the Rabbit Lake mine, one of the largest mines in the area, is located about thirty kilometres away on the opposite side of Wollaston Lake.

POPULARITY

Greenpeace seems to have the knack of making itself unpopular wherever it goes—unpopular with both sides of an issue.

When Greenpeace director Patrick Moore arrived in Saskatchewan in 1981 to launch an anti-uranium mining campaign (under the slogan "Greenpeace has arrived"), the irate mayor of Uranium City, Rose Wasylenka, said he should be thrown to the whales. She also threatened to ask the police to escort him out of town if he did not leave voluntarily.

The anti-nuclear establishment in Saskatchewan was also upset with Greenpeace. In a letter to the Saskatoon *Star Phoenix*, two of them said that Patrick Moore's "arrogant statements" made him an "unacceptable saviour." Did he think "we . . . have been sitting around with straw in our hair and our minds in neutral?" They stated emphatically: ". . . we do not want or need Patrick Moore and his Greenpeace lot in this province."[15]

After this less than enthusiastic reception, Greenpeace seems to have departed the province and left Saskatchewan alone until its next foray into the province in 1987.

"The people who live in the vicinity of the Sequoyah Fuels uranium conversion plant in Oklahoma know that Canada's 'peaceful' atom is the source of the extremely high cancer rate which they have discovered in their neighbourhood" (Greenpeace, leaflet on "Nuclear Exports and Government Secrecy").[18]

This statement is inaccurate.

Some Saskatchewan uranium goes to the Sequoyah Fuels plant in the U.S.A. for refining. There is no evidence of increased cancer near the plant, and, if there were, it would be difficult to implicate uranium as the cause. As already noted, the half-life of uranium is so long that it is almost a stable element, and consequently its radio-toxicity is very low. This is a basic fact about uranium which Greenpeace's research appears to have left uncovered. In the leaflet from which the above quotation is taken, Greenpeace claims to be working with the International Institute of Concern for Public Health to study the effect of uranium on the population near Sequoyah. No results of this research have surfaced to date (mid-1989).

FROGS AND CATFISH

In 1987 Greenpeace launched a second campaign against uranium mining in Saskatchewan. The campaign resurrected most of the anti-uranium arguments used by other groups, but it added a new twist of its own.

Deformed frogs and catfish.

According to Greenpeace, deformed frogs and catfish had been found near a uranium-fuels plant in the U.S.A. where some of Canada's uranium was processed. In one of its pamphlets Greenpeace even provided a photograph of what could have been a nine-legged frog.

One might be tempted to suggest that the author of the pamphlet had been watching too many late-night B-movies of the genre "Monster from the Radioactive Swamp."

On the other hand, if the catfish were also deformed by having nine legs (the pamphlet did not say they were not), this would explain the origin of the well-known American expletive "Jumpin' catfish."

"Approximately 85 per cent of the uranium mined in Canada is exported. A great deal of it goes to enrichment plants . . . for enrichment to weapons grade material. The overwhelming majority of that is going into the 50,000 plus nuclear weapons which are constantly being upgraded around the world" (Jim Fulton, Member of Parliament, NDP).[19]

Most of these statements are inaccurate.

Exported Canadian uranium is not enriched to weapons-grade material (over 90 per cent uranium–235) but only to nuclear-power-reactor-grade material (about 3 per cent). Canadian uranium entering and leaving the enrichment plants is carefully measured to ensure that none of it is diverted for use in nuclear weapons. Canada has not sold nuclear material, equipment, or supplies for nuclear weapons purposes since 1965. Since that time Canada has developed a stringent safeguards regime to ensure that its nuclear exports are used only in accordance with Canada's policy of non–nuclear-weapons use. Canada's safeguards regime is acknowledged internationally to be one of the most stringent in the world.

"There are also questions which must be raised about the safety of the transportation of yellowcake, the final product from a uranium mill, to its destination" (David Hallman, United Church of Canada).[20]

This statement is misleading.

It gives the false impression that yellowcake is a hazardous material. Yellowcake is uranium oxide containing very small amounts of impurities. As noted earlier, uranium has such a long half-life that it is nearly stable. Consequently, its radio-toxic hazard due to radioactive decay is negligible. Of slightly more consequence, the chemical toxicity of uranium is about the same as the metal lead. We discharge large quantities of lead into our environment daily through automobile emissions. The major hazard of transporting uranium comes from the truck involved in the transportation, not from the contents of the truck.

"Much of Canada's uranium mining takes place in the traditional homelands of Canada's aboriginal peoples and severely compromises their ability to negotiate equitable land claims settlements or to maintain lifestyles based on renewable resources" (NDP, Public Inquiry Backgrounder).[21]

These statements are misleading.

Uranium mining in Canada makes no more demands on native peoples' homelands than any other form of mining. It is not likely that the NDP would demand an end to all mining in Canada for this reason. As noted earlier, the closest Indian band to the mines near Wollaston Lake in northern Saskatchewan is the La Hache band, which is thirty kilometres away on the other side of the lake. As for destroying native lifestyles, when the Rabbit Lake mine was being prepared for production, it was necessary to purchase only one trap-line from a local Indian trapper. He then lived in relative affluence near the mine.

"After being used for the production of energy in a nuclear reactor, some of the uranium, during the process of fission, is transformed into plutonium, a substance which has no purpose other than to be made into nuclear weapons" (Elinor D. U. Powell, M.D., F.R.C.P.C., Physicians for Social Responsibility).[22]

This statement is inaccurate.

Plutonium will have a very useful role to play in the future as a fuel for Canada's nuclear power program.

This quotation was part of a brief submitted to the government of British Columbia by the PSR asking for a continuation of a B.C. moratorium on uranium mining. It contained the unfounded allegations that Canadian uranium was fuelling the nuclear arms race and the unquantified statements that uranium daughters will inevitably cause cancers. However, the most remarkable feature of the brief was a complete neglect of the benefits to be derived from nuclear energy powered by uranium. For this organisation of physicians it would appear that radioisotopes are not used in medical diagnosis and medical therapy, and that nuclear medicine departments do not exist in their local hospitals.

CHAPTER 6

Nuclear Proliferation

The Facts

THERE ARE TWO TYPES OF NUCLEAR WEAPONS PROLIFERATION—
vertical and horizontal. Vertical proliferation means increasing the number
of weapons and weapon systems within the arsenals of the nuclear weapons
states. This is a subject which is receiving a great deal of public attention
at present. Fortunately, the two major nuclear weapons states currently
seem increasingly inclined to halt, and reverse, the process of vertical
proliferation.

For Canada, vertical proliferation is not a direct issue. Canada does
not possess nuclear weapons, and it has no intention of acquiring any. This
policy was stated by C. D. Howe in the House of Commons as long ago
as December 1945,[1] and it is a policy that has been maintained by
successive governments ever since. However, since the effects of nuclear
war are unlikely to be confined to the immediate combatants, the Canadian
public has a strong interest in the issue of vertical proliferation, and it is
this interest that is being expressed by several disarmament groups today.

The question of horizontal proliferation is the one which will be
addressed in this chapter. Horizontal proliferation means the acquisition
of a nuclear weapons capability by countries which do not presently possess
it. There are only six countries in the world with a known capability of
manufacturing nuclear explosives—the U.S.A., the U.S.S.R., the U.K.,
France, China, and India. The first five of these are recognised under the
1968 Treaty on the Non-Proliferation of Nuclear Weapons (NPT) as nuclear
weapons states (NWS). India is a special case and will be considered in more
detail later. A few other countries are suspected of possessing nuclear
weapons, but until they are tested these suspicions cannot be confirmed.

The central issue of horizontal non-proliferation is to prevent the
number of NWS from becoming larger. This is an issue in which Canada,
together with every other country in the world, has a direct interest.
Canada, indeed, has a more direct interest in horizontal proliferation than
most other states since this country is one of a handful of nations which
actively pursue the export of nuclear materials, equipment, and technology. In particular, Canada exports both uranium and the CANDU nuclear
power reactor. Most of the criticism of Canada's non-proliferation policy
has been directed at these exports and the potential for nuclear weapons
proliferation that they entail.

The purported connection between the CANDU reactor and weapons can be described quite simply.[2] Nuclear power reactors produce plutonium; plutonium can be used for making nuclear weapons; therefore more nuclear power reactors will result in more nuclear weapons. This chapter will show that the connection between nuclear power and nuclear weapons is not as simple as described by this concept. In fact, it will be shown that to deny nuclear power to other countries may provide a greater impetus towards nuclear weapons proliferation than its widespread use.

Only two nuclear weapons have been exploded in anger. These were the two bombs dropped on Japan in August 1945 which brought the Second World War to an end. The world was horrified by the explosive force of these new weapons and there was a general desire to ensure that such weapons would never be used again. The fledgling United Nations, in the first resolution it passed, set up an Atomic Energy Commission in 1946 directed to prepare proposals for "extending between all nations an exchange of basic scientific information on peaceful ends"; "the control of atomic energy to ensure its use only for peaceful purposes"; "the elimination of atomic weapons"; and "effective safeguards by way of inspection and other means against the hazards of violations and evasions."[3] The commission laboured for two years but, due to fundamental differences of approach between the U.S.A. and the U.S.S.R., it finally had to admit failure. The Cold War, which was developing between the U.S.A. and the U.S.S.R., had claimed one of its early victims.

It was apparent from the first of the directives issued to the UN Atomic Energy Commission that the nations of the world believed that the benefits that could flow from the utilisation of nuclear energy should not be confined to the few but should be extended to all countries. It was equally apparent from the last directive that the nations of the world believed that some form of safeguards should be established to ensure that the spread of nuclear energy benefits should not result in the spread of nuclear weapons.

For a while, the U.S.A., the only nuclear weapons state, attempted to keep secret not only its nuclear weapons technology but also much of its nuclear technology peripheral to the manufacture of nuclear weapons. However, the U.S.S.R. exploded its first fission device in 1949, followed by a fusion device in 1952, and the U.K. also exploded a fission device in 1952. It was obvious that the spread of nuclear weapons could not be confined simply by keeping nuclear technology secret.

As a result, President Eisenhower made his "Atoms for Peace" speech to the UN in late 1953, proposing the establishment of an international agency which would be devoted to promoting the peaceful uses of nuclear energy. The UN unanimously adopted a resolution calling for the establishment of such an agency in December 1954, and the Statute of the International Atomic Energy Agency (IAEA) came into force in 1957.[4] It stated that one of the functions of the IAEA, in addition to promoting peaceful uses, would be to establish and administer safeguards which would ensure that nuclear materials were not used "in such a way as to further any military purpose."[5]

In 1955 the UN organised the first of a series of conferences on the peaceful uses of atomic energy, and many states, led by the U.S.A. and the U.S.S.R., contributed large amounts of information relating to raw-material production, reactor design and construction, health precautions, and medical and biological research which had been held secret until then. As an example of how rapidly nuclear technology was spreading at that time, the design of the NRX reactor at Chalk River was designated secret when it first came into operation in 1947. When a similar reactor was sold to India in 1956 (later called the CIRUS reactor), the design had already been declassified.

It no longer made sense to attempt to restrict the horizontal proliferation of nuclear weapons by denying non-weapon nuclear technology to non–nuclear weapons states. It was universally agreed that a more effective method would be to allow all nations to share the benefits of peaceful nuclear technology based on the condition that they accept international safeguards, including inspections of their facilities to ensure there were no "violations or evasions." The IAEA was given powers for detection but not for enforcement. If any illegal activities were detected by the IAEA or its members in any country, it would then be the responsibility of the UN to decide what further actions should be taken against that country.

Both before and after the creation of the IAEA, the nuclear powers had exported nuclear technology, equipment, and materials to other countries. In each case, bilateral agreements were signed between the exporting and importing countries that the supplies should be used only for peaceful purposes. When the IAEA was established, an increasing number of agreements were made between the importing countries and the IAEA which allowed agency inspectors, rather than inspectors from the exporting countries, to inspect nuclear programs for violations and evasions.

In addition, many of the older bilateral agreements were also renegotiated as agreements with the IAEA. For example, the 1963 and 1966 agreements between Canada and India concerning Canadian-supplied power reactors were replaced in 1971 by a Canada-India-IAEA agreement under which the IAEA assumed the responsibility for applying safeguards at the reactors. A similar agreement concerning another Canadian power reactor was negotiated with Pakistan in 1969.[6]

By the early 1960s there were signs that a few additional states were considering the acquisition of nuclear weapons. Then, in 1964, China exploded its first nuclear device. To many countries this event caused considerable shock. China was a country isolated from both the East and West power blocs and was largely agricultural, with a small industrial base and a correspondingly small scientific establishment. Yet despite these handicaps China had acquired the technology, equipment, and materials to produce a nuclear weapon.

This event prompted the two major powers, the U.S.A. and the U.S.S.R., to put aside part of their Cold War hostility and collaborate in producing identical drafts of a nuclear Non-Proliferation Treaty (NPT), which they presented to the Eighteen Nation Committee on Disarmament in January 1968. These drafts were discussed in the UN, and the General Assembly adopted the NPT in July 1968. The treaty was ratified by 40 nations and put into force in March 1970. As of 1988, a total of 136 nations were party to the NPT.

Under the NPT, nuclear weapons states (NWS) party to the treaty undertake not to transfer nuclear explosive devices to any nation and not to assist or encourage non–nuclear weapons states (NNWS) to manufacture nuclear weapons. For their part, NNWS party to the treaty agree not to receive nuclear explosive devices and not to seek or receive assistance in manufacturing them. In addition, each of the NNWS agrees to accept safeguards on all nuclear material used in peaceful nuclear activities carried out within its state. In return for these restrictions, an obligation exists between member states to facilitate the exchange of nuclear materials, technology, and equipment for the peaceful uses of nuclear energy.

During the UN debate on the NPT, a major objection to the treaty was the discriminatory provision that only NNWS would be required to submit their nuclear facilities to IAEA inspection while NWS would not. To meet this objection, the U.S.A. and the U.K. promised to put their peaceful nuclear facilities under IAEA safeguards when the treaty came into force. France and the U.S.S.R. have also agreed to accept IAEA safeguards on some of their facilities, and China is currently negotiating a safeguards agreement with the IAEA. In addition, the NWS party to the treaty (the U.K., U.S.S.R., and U.S.A.) promised to pursue negotiations in good faith to reduce the vertical proliferation of nuclear weapons.

During the late 1960s and early 1970s, many countries adopted nuclear power programs to provide an alternative energy source to oil and coal, and some countries without indigenous uranium reserves developed an interest in reprocessing uranium to recover fissionable plutonium. The U.S.A. had declassified its reprocessing technology in 1955, and by the early 1970s many people were uneasy about the large amounts of plutonium which could become available in many countries. This unease was reinforced by India's "peaceful nuclear explosion" of May 1974, which had used plutonium produced in the CIRUS research reactor from uranium indigenous to India.

In this atmosphere, the major nuclear suppliers formed the Nuclear Suppliers Group (NSG) to prepare guidelines for nuclear transfers. Canada and the U.S.A. were largely responsible for this initiative. The guidelines augment the IAEA statute and the NPT and feature a "trigger list" of nuclear items that would be transferred only upon assurances that they would not be used in any activity that would result in a nuclear explosive device. Special controls and considerations apply to the export of "sensitive technologies," such as enrichment and reprocessing technologies and their associated equipment and materials.

Canada had been closely involved in the development of the IAEA, the NPT, and the NSG and has always strongly supported their activities. Each has been the product of an international consensus designed to deter the horizontal proliferation of nuclear weapons. Yet Canada and other states supplying nuclear equipment and materials have come under strong criticism from the anti-nuclear establishment which claims that they could be promoting rather than deterring horizontal proliferation. The alternative proposed or implied by these groups would be the denial of nuclear technology to non–nuclear weapons states, which is contrary to the spirit of the NPT. It is necessary to examine this alternative solution to see whether it would be a more effective deterrent to horizontal proliferation than the current regime of conducting exports under safeguards.

Both sides would agree that neither method offers any iron-clad guarantees that it will prevent horizontal proliferation. Such guarantees are not possible. This was recognised as long ago as December 1945, just four months after the first explosion of nuclear weapons on Japan, by Canadian Prime Minister Mackenzie King. Speaking in the House of Commons he declared that ". . . the truth is that no system of safeguards that can be devised will, of itself, provide an effective guarantee against the production of nuclear weapons by a nation bent on aggression."[7] This statement is a recognition of the fact that once knowledge has been acquired, it is with us forever. With respect to knowledge of how to make nuclear explosives, this is an unpalatable fact but one which must be faced.

In the years since Mackenzie King made his statement, events have confirmed he was right. Not only has knowledge of nuclear technology spread, but we have discovered what he did not know at that time, that the raw material necessary to make bombs is also widely spread. Most countries of any significant size are now known to contain within their borders enough uranium to make nuclear weapons should they wish to do so. There are now probably several dozen countries in the world that are able to make nuclear weapons from their own indigenous human and material resources without recourse to any outside assistance. Under these circumstances, a safeguards program which would rely solely on denial of technology and materials would appear to have scant chance of success.

However, the anti-nuclear establishment suggests several reasons why the possession of a nuclear power reactor will actively aid any country wishing to acquire a weapons capability. It is claimed that a nuclear power program increases the technological strength of a country and provides it with a core of nuclear personnel who could be employed on weapons production. These personnel, assembled for a peaceful nuclear program, would be available to turn their skills to weapons production should this be required.

While this argument is true, it ignores the fact that a nuclear power program is not necessary for a country to acquire the skills necessary to manufacture nuclear weapons. A weapons capability can be achieved using a small research reactor (such as the CIRUS reactor used by India) and a small reprocessing plant to extract plutonium from uranium. Both the number and the degree of skills required to launch a nuclear weapons program are much less than those required for a nuclear power program. Nuclear weapons are much simpler to design and construct than nuclear power reactors. As evidence of this it should be noted that all NWS, except France, produced nuclear weapons long before they produced nuclear power reactors.

In addition, the existence of a small research reactor and reprocessing plant built with indigenous skills and resources could be kept secret for a period of time. This is an important consideration for a country wishing to acquire weapons. However, if a country were to attempt to divert irradiated uranium from a nuclear power plant, this would be quickly apparent to IAEA inspectors, and internal and external pressures against the weapons decision would be quickly mobilised.

It has also been argued on economic grounds that a nuclear power program will assist a country to acquire weapons. It is claimed that the marginal cost of producing weapons from a power program is less than starting from scratch since most of the cost would be recovered from the electricity produced by the power program. An argument based on the marginal costs of production would not appear to be very realistic. Once a country had decided to produce weapons, marginal economic factors would cease to be a prime consideration. A more significant economic factor which would have to be addressed would be the withdrawal of nuclear aid, which could lead to closing down or, at least, severely disrupting the operations of the power program, as happened in India. An overwhelming economic factor might be the imposition of economic sanctions on the country by the rest of the world once that country had made apparent its intentions to become a nuclear weapons state. In the context of these major economic risks, marginal economic costs would not be very important.

Another argument used against exporting nuclear power reactors is that a power program provides a legitimate cover for nuclear activities which would otherwise be exposed as unambiguously weapons-oriented. Without such a cover a country embarking on a weapons program is apt to be discovered. This argument ignores the fact noted above that a research reactor program is sufficient to provide the technology for making weapons; a country does not have to progress to a power program to provide it with a cover. Even more significant is the fact that a power program comes with a built-in safeguards regime administered by the IAEA. It would be more difficult to hide from IAEA inspectors a weapons program associated with a power reactor than to hide a similar program involving a clandestine research reactor.

The major argument against the "denial" approach for preventing horizontal proliferation does not involve showing that the arguments in favour of it have little validity. It is a consideration of what would happen if the "denial" approach were to be actually put in place. Proponents of the "denial" approach usually buttress their arguments by pointing out that most power reactor exports are made to developing countries whose governing regimes are "dictatorial," "repressive," "undemocratic," "militaristic," or any combination of these. Since liberal democracies are a minority of the world's governments, a policy of excluding all other countries from using nuclear power would inevitably exclude most of the developing countries in Asia, Africa, and South America.

The effect of excluding these countries from obtaining nuclear power reactors must be considered as part of the effect of applying the "denial" approach. It can first be stated that denying a nuclear power reactor to these countries on the grounds that they could not be trusted to use it for peaceful purposes only would constitute an unacceptable act of paternalism. Any such proposal would be rejected immediately by an overwhelming majority of the states in the United Nations, and the resulting effect on the IAEA and its safeguarding responsibilities would be devastating. It was difficult enough during the passage of the NPT to persuade states to accept the de facto division of the world into nuclear weapons states and non-nuclear weapons states. To persuade the majority of UN members to accept a further division of non-nuclear weapons states into "trustworthy" and "untrustworthy" would be impossible; particularly when the nuclear critics would want many of the more advanced developing countries placed in the latter category.

This does not mean that under the present non-proliferation regime, all nations have to be treated absolutely equally. There are a few nations in the world which are generally regarded by most other countries as being untrustworthy from a proliferation standpoint. Even though some of these nations may have signed the NPT there is a tacit consent by the rest of the world that they should be prevented, as far as possible, from obtaining any materials, equipment, or technology which would assist them in approaching a nuclear weapons capability. Although isolating a few countries in this way is considered acceptable by the many, isolating the many by a widespread adoption of a "denial" approach would be unacceptable to all.

In addition, adopting a policy of "denial" may have a completely opposite effect to that intended. If a country with a significant nuclear research program wished to obtain a nuclear power reactor and were told, in effect, that it was untrustworthy, the effect might be to persuade that country to seek nuclear autonomy at all costs. Treating a country as a nuclear pariah could create paranoia among its leaders and nationalistic fervour among its population. Under such conditions, a decision by that country to develop nuclear weapons would almost certainly be supported by its population.

It is interesting to examine the historical records of the two methods of deterring nuclear proliferation, the "denial" method and the "provision of technology with safeguards" method, to see whether one might be preferable to the other. Because there are only five recognised nuclear weapons states, that is four instances of horizontal proliferation, the evidence is necessarily sparse.

When the U.S.A., the first country to develop nuclear weapons, practised denial of this technology to other countries soon after the end of the Second World War, three countries—the U.S.S.R., the U.K., and France—attempted to produce nuclear weapons without U.S. assistance. Their efforts were successful. An argument can be made that these first steps in horizontal proliferation were promoted by the early application of the denial approach, but it is equally true that all three countries considered themselves to be world powers so that the acquisition of nuclear weapons to defend their legitimate interests was probably inevitable.

China acquired its nuclear weapons under somewhat similar circumstances. Until 1960 China was the recipient of various types of technological and scientific aid from the U.S.S.R., including some peaceful nuclear technology. Then a series of ideological differences caused the U.S.S.R. to withdraw all aid from China. Isolated from both East and West, China now found itself in the condition proposed above as being conducive to unilateral weapons development. Again, it is not known how much the "denial" of aid contributed to the decision to develop nuclear weapons, but only four years passed before China joined the "nuclear weapons club."

India's accession to the threshold of nuclear weapons capability provides a different type of insight into deterring proliferation. The nuclear explosion by India in 1974 was carried out underground. India has claimed consistently that the device was intended for "peaceful purposes." Indeed, it followed a series of underground explosions for peaceful purposes in the U.S.A., where Project Plowshares was intended to demonstrate the use of nuclear explosives for earth-moving purposes such as canal construction, mining, etc. However, most of the world did not accept India's "peaceful" explanation and, as a result, that country had to endure a considerable amount of international obloquy as well as being denied further international nuclear co-operation.

It is interesting to note that India has not exploded another nuclear device since that first test in 1974. Indian scientists have undoubtedly prepared a series of experiments designed to improve what must have been a crude first explosive device, but they have not been allowed by their government to actually proceed with testing. The international non-proliferation regime relies on world opinion to help reinforce a national will not to acquire nuclear weapons. It could be claimed that the absence of a second nuclear explosion in India represents a successful demonstration of the force of world opinion in deterring a country from pursuing a nuclear adventure.

Despite the doomsday scenarios regularly produced by the anti-nuclear establishment, it remains a fact that the rate of horizontal nuclear proliferation has decreased during the last forty years. Between 1945 and 1955, three countries (the U.S.A., U.S.S.R., and U.K.) acquired nuclear weapons. In the next decade, 1955–1965, two countries (France and China) did so. Between 1965 and 1975, only one country (India) even threatened to join the "nuclear weapons club" by exploding a "peaceful" nuclear device. There has been no addition to the "club" since 1975.

A number of countries are regularly cited by the anti-nuclear establishment as being on the verge of nuclear weapons acquisition, among them Pakistan, South Africa, and Israel. These "proliferation sensitive" states are all non-NPT members with whom Canada has had no nuclear co-operation since 1976. Whether any of these countries have a weapons potential will not be known until they carry out weapons testing, an event which cannot be conducted clandestinely.

The current small number of nuclear weapons states should be surprising. In the early 1960s it was widely believed the number would grow significantly. President Kennedy, for example, once predicted a world with between fifteen and twenty nuclear weapons states. It is interesting to consider the current small number in the light of the fact that since the 1950s the number of countries operating nuclear power reactors has increased from zero to twenty-six.

Meanwhile, the most effective means of deterrence remains bolstering the will of non–nuclear weapons states not to acquire weapons. In the opinion of most of the countries of the world, this can best be done through the current international non-proliferation regime. Several ways can be proposed for making this regime more rigorous, but any improvements must have the broad agreement of the international community of nations if they are to be effective. A non-proliferation regime based on the denial of nuclear assistance to other countries is not likely to be acceptable, and the actual effect of such a regime, if it were implemented, is likely to be the opposite to that intended.

One final point of speculation. Imagine that the physics of nuclear fission were not what it is, and that controlled nuclear fission reactions were not possible. In this case there would still be nuclear explosives, but there could be no nuclear reactors. Under these hypothetical conditions, the NPT would not be possible. Without peaceful uses of nuclear energy as a bargaining chip there could be no NPT, and hence there would be fewer constraints on countries which might wish to develop nuclear weapons. Consideration of this hypothetical world helps us realise that nuclear power, far from promoting nuclear weapons proliferation, may be credited with providing us with a means of reducing it.

The Game

The first two public demonstrations of the power within the atom occurred as nuclear explosions at Hiroshima and Nagasaki. It is therefore not surprising that the public associates the peaceful uses of nuclear energy with the use of nuclear energy for destructive explosive purposes.

Technically, the connection between the use of a controlled release of fission energy and its uncontrolled use as an explosive device is remote. Politically, the decision-making process in the two cases springs from completely different ideological motivations. Economically, one is a contributor to national wealth, while the other can be seen as a fiscal sink. Nonetheless, it must be agreed that there is a connection between the two uses of fission energy, albeit a very tenuous one.

Using this tenuous link the anti-nuclear establishment has tried to lead the public to believe that there is not only a very strong link between the two uses of fission energy, but that there is an inevitable connection. It wishes to convince the public that those countries using nuclear energy for peaceful purposes are almost certainly going to use it for weapons purposes as well. As noted in the first part of this chapter, the facts are against the anti-nuclear establishment in its contention that the connection is either strong or inevitable.

A secondary argument arising from the alleged dangers of nuclear proliferation is that they can only be controlled by enforcing such strict controls on all forms of nuclear energy that the inevitable result would be the creation of a police state.

It is in dealing with issues of nuclear proliferation that the anti-nuclear establishment merges itself with the nuclear disarmament groups. As a result, there is no shortage of quotations to illustrate how the nuclear proliferation game is being played. Some of them are considered below.

❖ ❖ ❖

"I therefore believe that the only real security lies in abolishing the uranium trade altogether. This, of course, means forgoing nuclear power as an energy source. . . . it seems a small price to pay to keep alive the dream of a nuclear disarmed world . . ." (Gordon Edwards, CCNR).[8]

These statements are misleading.

The myth that abolishing the trade in uranium, and thereby the use of nuclear power, will produce a world with no nuclear weapons is unfounded. Uranium is a fairly abundant and very widely dispersed mineral in the earth's crust. Most of the major countries of the world have a sufficiently large land mass that within their borders there will be enough uranium to allow them to build nuclear weapons if they wish to. Those countries with a coast line which cannot find uranium on land can extract it from sea water. It has been estimated that there is a thousand times as much uranium in the sea as on land.

The two major producers of nuclear weapons, the U.S.A. and the U.S.S.R., have very large uranium deposits, which they use for producing nuclear weapons materials. Edwards does not explain how abolishing the uranium trade will alter this situation. It must be suspected that, when using this argument, the anti-nuclear establishment is more interested in providing arguments for closing down the nuclear power industry than for providing realistic ways of reducing nuclear weapons proliferation.

"A single one-megaton bomb dropped on a nuclear reactor would have consequences far more devastating than the one-megaton bomb itself, because the entire core of the reactor would be vaporised, spreading lethal contamination over an enormous land mass. Responsible decision makers cannot afford to overlook the realities of modern life. One of these realities is the possibility of a major nuclear exchange between East and West in the next few decades" (Gordon Edwards, CCNR).[9]

These statements are misleading.

In the event of a major nuclear exchange between East and West, the effect of nuclear weapons falling on a few nuclear power plants will be small compared with the effects of the many bombs themselves. A larger number of immediate casualties would occur if hydro dams or chemical works were hit by the nuclear weapons.

"Nor can we afford to completely overlook the possibility of sabotage. It is not difficult to induce a catastrophic nuclear accident in a CANDU

reactor once access to the plant has been gained. . . . In fact, since spent fuel bays are often located outside containment buildings at CANDU power stations, nuclear sabotage is possible even without forced entry into the plant itself" (Gordon Edwards, CCNR).[10]

These statements are misleading.

It would be difficult to induce a catastrophic accident in a CANDU nuclear plant, even if the saboteur knew what he was doing. Accident sequences in nuclear power plants usually take a long time to develop, and many mitigating measures could be taken if they were necessary.

It would have been interesting if Edwards had tried to explain what a saboteur could do to a spent-fuel bay in order to put the local population at risk. Spent fuel consists of ceramic-grade uranium oxide encased in zirconium alloy sheaths. It is not soluble in water; it will not burn; and it cannot be easily dispersed into the environment.

Saboteurs and terrorists have many ways to make a statement against society. One of the more absurd methods would be to attempt to destroy a nuclear reactor or a spent-fuel bay. Immediate casualties would be very difficult to achieve, and the impact of possible cancers several decades into the future would surely miss the dramatic effect required by the terrorists to make their point. So far there have been no serious attempts to use operating nuclear reactors for terrorist demonstration purposes.

". . . as long as reactors deal with materials which are nuclear-weapons useable . . . and/or as long as nuclear reactors are attractive targets for sabotage . . . they will place a burden on individual freedoms and civil liberties . . ." (Norman Rubin, Energy Probe).[11]

". . . nuclear power cannot replace oil to any significant extent unless plutonium replaces uranium as the principal nuclear fuel. . . . The associated political cost of such a development may be unprecedented and irreversible, leading us toward a paramilitary police state" (Gordon Edwards, CCNR).[12]

These statements are misleading.

As a result of the campaign by the anti-nuclear establishment in the late 1970s to persuade the public that nuclear reactors were attractive

JAMES BOND LIVES

In the second half of the 1970s, the world experienced outbreaks of terrorism from organisations such as the Baader-Meinhof gang, Black September, and the Red Brigades. The anti-nuclear establishment immediately saw how to generate another argument against nuclear power.

Nuclear reactors, it proclaimed, are prime targets for terrorist activities, and if one were to be blown up the results would be devastating.

To supplement this argument, articles began to appear in the popular science magazines explaining in detail how nuclear reactors could be sabotaged.

Small units whose members were skilled in the arts of nuclear physics and the use of explosives could blacken their faces, blast their way through chain-link fences, storm the reactor control room with Uzi machine guns and impact grenades, and hold reactor operators hostage while they performed their nefarious tasks.

Alternatively, scuba divers, with blackened faces, could slip overboard from fast boats anchored off the reactor at night and insert plastic bags full of explosives in the water-intake pipe of the reactor.

Another scheme had a small-aircraft pilot, with a blackened face, dive the explosive-laden plane into the reactor in a suicide mission.

These stories were great fun to read, particularly when it was realised the authors were respectable middle-class members of the anti-nuclear establishment whose closest brush with illegality might be filing their annual income tax returns.

The authors had one thing in common. They were all saying to Ian Fleming, "Eat your heart out."

targets for saboteurs, the Atomic Energy Control Board reassessed its regulations for the security of all Canadian nuclear facilities including nuclear power stations. The board then published new regulations, which included requirements for the size of security fences, exclusion zones inside fences, number of guards on duty, etc. The regulations were promulgated by the Government of Canada in 1982. This is a far cry from denying anyone his "individual freedoms and civil liberties" or turning Canada into a "paramilitary police state." Rubin and Edwards may not have been aware that new security regulations were in force.

> "By nature, nuclear technology tends to encourage a repressive kind of secrecy, tends to justify a para-military preoccupation with security and tends to rationalise the gradual erosion of democracy" (Gordon Edwards, CCNR).[13]

These statements are inaccurate.

Since 1945 most of the wartime secrecy surrounding nuclear technology has been removed. There are only two areas where secrecy is still maintained. One is the manufacture of nuclear weapons, although even on this topic enough has been published for a country to manufacture a bomb if skilled scientists are provided with the required equipment and materials. The other is the routine commercial secrecy with which any manufacturer tries to preserve the exclusivity of his product. In this case there may be public secrecy, but nothing is hidden from the regulatory authorities who license the product. In neither of these instances is there a "repressive kind of secrecy." Neither is used to "justify a para-military preoccupation with security." Neither has had any effect on democracy.

> "While the U.S., like Canada, refrains from making warheads out of the spent fuel from its civilian reactors, it is becoming both increasingly true and increasingly clear that it does so only as a courtesy to the public-relations needs of its nuclear industry. As President Reagan's feelings of bomb-shortage intensify, he is making stronger overtures towards the spent fuel in the 'swimming pools' at the nuclear stations, both in the U.S. and (perhaps to lower his political costs) in the U.K." (Norman Rubin, Energy Probe).[14]

These statements are misleading.

THE PLUTONIUM ECONOMY

One of the by-products of the nuclear processes occurring in a nuclear reactor is the radioisotope plutonium–239, which is produced from uranium–238. It is a valuable by-product because plutonium–239, like uranium–235, can fission to produce energy. It can be extracted from spent fuel and then mixed with natural uranium and manufactured into fuel rods. These can go back into the reactor to produce more energy and also more plutonium from that otherwise useless isotope of uranium, uranium–238. In this way it is possible to increase manyfold the amount of energy which can be extracted from uranium.

The anti-nuclear establishment objects to this procedure. It claims that such a cycle will involve us in a "plutonium economy" in which we will come to rely on plutonium for our nuclear energy. This will lead us to a police state because plutonium must be protected with the utmost stringency.

In fact their dire warnings against relying on plutonium to produce our energy are largely beside the point.

The formation of plutonium–239 from fresh fuel begins almost as soon as the fuel goes into the reactor. As it is formed, it is exposed to neutrons and some of it fissions to produce energy while still in the reactor. By the time CANDU fuel is ready for discharge, over 40 per cent of the energy which it has produced has come from the fissioning of plutonium–239.

So we already have a 40 per cent plutonium nuclear economy.

Although the plutonium in spent fuel from nuclear power reactors can be made into nuclear explosives, this can only be accomplished with difficulty. When plutonium–239 is formed in the reactor, part of it is fissioned to produce energy and part of it reacts with neutrons to produce plutonium–240. This is an undesirable contaminant which is not readily fissionable. The longer the fuel is left in the reactor, the larger is the proportion of plutonium–240 which is built up.

In all normally running nuclear power reactors, the fuel is left in the reactor for a long time, typically about eighteen months. The plutonium in the fuel then contains a large proportion of plutonium–240, which is not a desirable material for weapons fabrication. Thus there is no incentive for any country to look to its nuclear power reactors for weapons-grade plutonium.

All countries with nuclear weapons programs have small dedicated reactors which make only nuclear weapons material. The fuel is shuffled through these reactors relatively quickly to prevent the build-up of plutonium–240. The resulting plutonium is a good grade of weapons-usable material.

Weapons-grade plutonium is made this way out of practical necessity, not because of the "public-relations needs" of the nuclear industry.

"... I am convinced ... that only by simultaneously eliminating the continuance, spread and perception of legitimacy of the nuclear energy industry, can we hope to combat both the 'horizontal' spread of nuclear weapons to non-weapons countries, and the superpowers' continuing 'vertical' nuclear arms race" (Norman Rubin, Energy Probe).[15]

These statements are unjustified by the facts.

The facts are that all the nuclear weapons states, except France, produced their first nuclear weapons *before* they produced nuclear power reactors. Indeed, China still has not produced nuclear electricity although it exploded its first nuclear device over twenty years ago. The spread of nuclear power to other countries has been accompanied by a *reduction* in the rate at which additional states have acquired a nuclear weapons capability. The legitimacy of the nuclear power industry is the cement which holds the nuclear Non-Proliferation Treaty (NPT) together.

Without the NPT some countries may decide not to deny themselves nuclear weapons. It is probably *because* there is a peaceful component to the atom that horizontal proliferation has proceeded as slowly as it has. The knowledge and capability of manufacturing nuclear weapons is widespread in today's world. This fact must be accepted and policies developed accordingly. The fact will not disappear by means of wishful thinking.

". . . the spread of nuclear energy, with its fissionable materials, its skills and its useful 'peaceful cover' for military activities, is virtually certain to lead to the spread of nuclear weapons" (Norman Rubin, Energy Probe).[16]

This statement is misleading.

As already noted, since the Second World War the rate at which countries have obtained nuclear weapons has declined sharply, while the rate at which nuclear power reactors have spread throughout the world has increased. If it were argued, as the anti-nuclear establishment sometimes does, that correlation equals causation, then it could be stated that the increased deployment of nuclear power *decreases* the rate at which countries acquire nuclear weapons capability. In fact, it would be more accurate to state that there seems to be only a tenuous relationship between the two.

". . . while the use of nuclear weapons continues (as in deployment), there is no way to separate 'peaceful' nuclear power from nuclear weaponry" (Dan Heap, Member of Parliament, NDP).[17]

"I want to deal as well with the whole question of nuclear proliferation. This is tied very clearly to the nuclear industry" (Simon de Jong, Member of Parliament, NDP).[18]

"Another area of concern is nuclear proliferation and how the use of nuclear energy leads to the use of nuclear material for weaponry" (Simon de Jong, Member of Parliament, NDP).[19]

These statements are inaccurate.

As noted previously, during a period when the number of countries employing nuclear power for peaceful purposes has increased from zero to twenty-six, the number of additional countries acquiring nuclear weapons capability has decreased to zero. Most members of the anti-nuclear establishment seem unaware of this basic fact of nuclear proliferation. Members of Parliament representing the New Democratic Party (NDP) seem to have been particularly taken in by the misinformation that the use of nuclear power inevitably leads to the acquisition of nuclear weapons.

INDIA'S BOMB

One article of faith in the anti-nuclear creed is that the spread of nuclear power reactors inevitably leads to the spread of nuclear weapons. The only evidence for this which is ever given by the anti-nuclear establishment is the explosion of a single "peaceful nuclear device" by India in 1974. Unfortunately their information is once again inaccurate.

The reactor which India used in order to produce the plutonium for its explosive device was a research reactor, not a power reactor. Pro-nuclear advocates have been saying for years that research reactors are much better facilities for making bomb material than power reactors: research reactors can be constructed at about one-tenth the cost of power reactors; they produce a much better grade of plutonium for weapons; and they are easier to operate clandestinely. Given these facts, nobody with a research reactor would want to produce plutonium from a power reactor.

Research reactors are always acquired before power reactors by nations with nuclear aspirations. Their technology is simpler and they make excellent training tools. The level of nuclear technology required to construct a research reactor and that required to make a bomb are roughly equivalent. Both are far easier to acquire than the more sophisticated technology required to produce a nuclear power reactor.

India is an exception. It had a nuclear power reactor operating before it produced its peaceful explosive device. Nonetheless, it used its research reactor and not a power reactor to produce the plutonium for the device.

"Large scale centralised technologies like today's CANDU *stations emerged in a society ruled by the military-industrial complex. . . . If a 'participatory society' is to be democratic, it must first take control of* CANDU *away from the military-industrial complex" (Dan Heap, Member of Parliament,* NDP).[20]

These statements are inaccurate.

The term "military-industrial complex" was coined about thirty years ago to describe a situation perceived in the U.S.A. It was not applicable to Canada then, and it is even less applicable now—particularly when discussing nuclear energy. The managers and workers in the provincial electrical utilities which own Canada's CANDU reactors—Ontario Hydro, the New Brunswick Electric Power Commission, and Hydro Quebec—would not recognise themselves when described as being part of a "military-industrial complex."

"The non-proliferation treaty seems ineffective except as a rationale for hindering third-world countries from attaining parity with NATO *and Warsaw blocs" (Dan Heap, Member of Parliament,* NDP).[21]

This statement is inaccurate.

Mr. Heap seems confused about the nature of the non-proliferation treaty (NPT). It is specifically designed to help Third World countries acquire peaceful nuclear technology. It only "hinders" them by insisting that they do not obtain nuclear weapons technology.

"The government has concealed from the public much of the relevant truth about our nuclear arms build up" (Dan Heap, Member of Parliament, NDP).[22]

This statement is inaccurate.

Canada has never developed any nuclear arms. The Canadian position on nuclear weapons was made clear by C. D. Howe in December 1945, when he stated in the House of Commons, ". . . we have not manufactured atomic bombs, we have no intention of manufacturing atomic bombs . . . ." This policy has been maintained by successive Canadian governments ever since.

CHAPTER 7

Alternative Energy Sources

The Facts

WHEN THE OPEC-INDUCED OIL CRISIS STRUCK THE WESTERN world in 1973, all countries scrambled to find alternative sources of energy which would make them less dependent on OPEC oil. A large number of energy alternatives were examined, ranging from the mundane peat-bog to the high-tech fusion reactor. In the last fifteen years our knowledge of many of these energy sources has increased considerably.

In the mid-1970s, many of the more exciting energy alternatives were solar powered. Large sums of money were invested in research on these alternatives, much of it by some of the major oil companies who had decided their field was really energy, not just oil. However, by the mid-1980s, when oil prices had sunk to less inflated levels, much of the enthusiasm for solar energy alternatives had evaporated. It had been found that the three major drawbacks to solar energy sources could only be overcome by uneconomic technical fixes. These three drawbacks are the *diffuse* nature of solar energy, the fact that it is *periodic*, and the fact that it is *intermittent*.

Because solar energy is a very *diffuse* form of energy, large collection structures covering large areas of land are required in order to utilise it. For example, the collection area required to provide sufficient solar energy to power a modern city is about twice the area of the city itself. In addition to the cost of the land, the structures are expensive to build, operate, and maintain. Solar energy does not provide a free lunch.

Solar energy is a *periodic* source of energy in a manner which makes it basically inefficient in our Canadian climate. For example, on a daily basis most solar energy is available during the day when it is needed least. It is not available at night when it is needed most. On an annual basis solar energy is most abundant in the summer, when it is required the least, and is the least available in the winter, when it is required the most.

In other words, solar energy is inefficient because solar energy *supply* is out of phase with human energy *demand*. It is not possible to conceive a technical fix which will alter this basic limitation. It can be ameliorated by providing storage for solar energy, but providing sufficient storage to carry over from summer to winter will be expensive. If solar energy is stored at the low density at which it is available, the size of the storage capacity will be prohibitive. If the energy is concentrated before storage, the additional cost of concentration (with its associated energy losses) must be added to the cost of storage. Again, solar energy provides no free lunch.

The *intermittent* nature of solar energy due to varying cloud cover of the earth adds to the problems due to its periodicity. Cloud cover can last for minutes or months and can reduce incident solar energy by less than 10 per cent or more than 90 per cent. A solution to the problem of intermittent supply is also storage, except that more storage will be required than to solve the problem of periodic supply alone.

One form of solar energy to which these strictures do not apply is hydro energy. The heat from the sun evaporates water from the surface of the earth and it returns as rain. The rain is eventually collected by large rivers which can be dammed. The two processes which make other forms of solar energy expensive, energy collection/concentration and energy storage, are provided by nature—mostly free. They make the generation of hydro power possible and economic.

When selecting among available large-scale electrical generating facilities, hydro located near sources of demand is almost always the first choice because it is most economic. However, when large-scale hydro is used up, the next most desirable alternative is not necessarily small-scale hydro. For example, Ontario Hydro in the 1960s had run out of large-scale hydro sites and turned to coal and nuclear as alternatives. Both of these sources were more economical than building small-scale hydro sites, and eventually Ontario Hydro found that nuclear was more economic than coal.

It should also be noted that large-scale hydro which is remote from demand centres is not always an economical choice. Building Quebec's James Bay hydro project about one thousand kilometres into the bush was very expensive. So was running power transmission lines from the hydro site to consumers in southern Quebec. It has been argued that Quebec could have got its power more cheaply by building nuclear power reactors on the St. Lawrence River, close to electricity demand centres.

Although large-scale hydro is a solar energy source, it is not considered to be an alternative energy source. This latter term is reserved for sources such as direct solar energy, wind energy, and biomass energy. These three could be joined by a few others such as energy from tides, waves, oceans, and geothermal sources, but none of these latter is expected to be a major economical source. One additional alternative energy source which may become very large, but which may be up to fifty years away from commercial exploitation, is fusion energy.

SOLAR ENERGY

Direct solar energy can be used in three ways.[1] (1) Solar panels are sometimes seen on houses or small industrial buildings. These active solar panels contain a liquid which is heated by the sun and which circulates into the building, where it is used either for direct heating or supplying hot water. The system is simple, consisting of pipes and pumps, a reservoir and a control system. Because the concept is simple and the parts are commonplace items, major reductions in the costs of the units are not foreseeable in the future. These units are often cost effective in those parts of the world with a lot of sunshine. They are seldom cost effective in more northern latitudes such as Canada.

(2) Photovoltaic systems consist of solar cells fabricated from a semi-conductor material which absorbs light and produces electricity. A number of semi-conductor materials can be used, the theoretically most efficient being gallium arsenide. A large area of solar cells is required to capture significant amounts of sunlight. The electricity produced by the cells can be used to power electrical devices. The cost of electricity from this source is falling, but it is still high compared with the cost of electricity from conventional sources.

(3) Passive solar energy systems are provided by design features in buildings which capture and retain solar heat. Such features include large south-facing windows and suitably placed masses of concrete (as room dividers) or stone fireplaces which heat up during the day and release their heat in the evening. Passive solar heating is not very expensive, but it is not very efficient either. Its practical use often collides with the aesthetics of housing design.

The prospects for major utilisation of direct solar systems in Canada are not very promising. Government subsidies for direct solar programs have been cut in recent years. Without them, direct solar energy cannot stand on its own economically. The peak years for direct solar systems in Canada were probably the mid-1980s, when these systems produced about 0.007 per cent of Canada's energy needs.

WIND ENERGY

Windmills have been around for the last thirteen hundred years. It has been estimated that in the seventeenth century there were twenty thousand windmills operating in the Netherlands alone. Most windmills were displaced by steam engines followed by diesel and electrical motors. Wind energy is an old technology making a new comeback, which makes it popular with those opposed to modern technology.

Today's windmills are quite unlike their predecessors. Horizontal axis machines carrying slim propellor-like blades up to one hundred metres in diameter are capable of generating several hundreds of kilowatts of energy. Vertical axis machines, which look like upright egg-beaters, have been a speciality of the Canadian wind energy program.

Internationally, the largest concentration of wind energy machines is in California. By 1985 more than seventeen thousand wind turbines generating more than 1,400 megawatts of energy had been erected, mainly in the Altamont, San Gorgonio, and Tehachapi passes in California.[2] Federal and state tax incentives stimulated the growth of wind energy farms in California to the extent that *Time* magazine has referred to them as "tax farms" rather than "wind farms." Some of these incentives have since been removed, and the rate of construction of new units has dropped considerably.

In Canada the world's largest vertical axis machine is near Cap Chat in Quebec's Gaspé region. The prototype machine is 96 metres tall, and the output is 4 megawatts. This unit will be used to verify design codes for factors such as vibrational characteristics and stress levels.

The intermittent nature of wind energy due to the variability of wind velocity means that a windmill cannot stand alone as a reliable energy source. As a result, Canada is also developing a hybrid wind/diesel generator. The wind energy will be used when available, and when it is not the diesel generator will cut in. It is hoped that half the normal amount of diesel fuel will be conserved by this arrangement. Such systems may be useful in remote areas where electricity is not normally available. They would be uneconomic in areas with access to normal electrical transmission lines.

BIOMASS ENERGY

Biomass energy is obtained by exploiting the energy of wood, animal manure, and crops such as straw and corn. The direct burning of wood was our oldest and our largest energy source until it was displaced by coal. Today, wood combustion is making a comeback as an energy source particularly in the forest industry, which burns its wood residues for energy. Wood also has a nostalgic value, and open fireplaces are still a feature in house design. These could perhaps be justified as a source of exercise if the house owner cut and split his own wood, but unfortunately the wood is usually delivered to the house in logs the right size for the fireplace.

There is no shortage of wood in Canada. It has been estimated that the total weight of trees in Canada is 26 billion tonnes, of which two-thirds can be accessed by existing transportation systems.[3] However, little of this timber need be harvested for energy purposes. Today, hybrid poplars have been developed which are very fast growing. In five years they can reach a height of ten metres with an average stump diameter of thirteen centimetres. These trees can be grown and harvested as if they were an agricultural crop. If wood becomes a significant source of energy, it will likely be grown on wood plantations adjacent to processing facilities rather than gathered from existing forests.

Apart from being used for combustion, wood is also a raw material used to produce value-added products such as ethanol and methanol which can be used as transportation fuels.[4] It is too expensive to be used now, but in the next century as oil becomes scarcer and more expensive it is possible that methanol will assume importance as an alternative to oil for many applications.

As with other alternative energy sources, biomass energy is being used only in special situations. It is not economically competitive with conventional energy sources.

ENERGY CONSERVATION

Of all the "sources" of energy promoted by the alternative energy advocates, the one which can most easily make a significant contribution to our energy economy is energy conservation. Conservation means reductions in demand rather than increases in supply such as we have considered hitherto. Unlike supply increases, reductions in demand, once achieved, are often permanent. In addition, the capital cost of conservation measures, where they are successful, can sometimes be paid back in a few years.

Even though conservation is an attractive energy "source," it will not provide us with a free lunch. It is an energy "source" which is in limited supply because the number of conservation measures which can be adopted is limited. For the foreseeable future, decreases in energy demand due to conservation will be overtaken by an increasing use of energy to maintain an improving standard of living and to supply the energy demands of a growing population.

In most of the world, including Canada, energy conservation was given a big boost by the increase in oil prices following the OPEC crisis in 1973. Various conservation measures were put in place, often with government encouragement and financial support. In Canada, the total primary energy required to produce one unit of gross domestic product (GDP) fell by 15.5 per cent over the decade 1974–1984 thanks to energy conservation.

The investments in conservation during this period were often applied to measures showing the most promise of a quick pay-back. The measures which remain to be taken will not be as easy or as inexpensive to apply. The majority of the existing equipment, vehicles, processes, buildings, etc., which are less energy-efficient will be left to the end of their useful lives before they are replaced by more energy-efficient substitutes.

It has been estimated by Canada's Department of Energy, Mines and Resources that further potential savings from the application of energy-efficiency measures could be about 10–20 per cent depending on the sector (industrial, commercial, transportation, residential). Because many of the easily acquired energy savings have been achieved already, realistic expectations of energy reduction due to conservation could be less than indicated by this estimate.

Following the OPEC oil crisis there was a large-scale switch from oil and gas to electricity for heating purposes. This switch, combined with an overall increase in electricity use for many purposes in our economy, has resulted in a rise in electricity consumption over the last decade while the consumption of most other energy sources has been declining. The average increase for electricity has been about 2–3 per cent per year, and increases of this magnitude are expected to continue.

It is obviously in the interests of all Canadians that conservation measures be pursued wherever they are practicable from technical, economic, or aesthetic considerations. However, conservation cannot be the answer to all our energy problems, particularly in the area of electricity generation. Conservation measures will not remove the demand for increased electrical generating capacity in the future.

The Game

The Canadian anti-nuclear establishment routinely proposes the use of alternative energy sources as a substitute for nuclear power. However, it has already been noted that it promotes alternative energy sources with much less fervour than it denounces nuclear power sources.

For example, it was mentioned in the Introduction to this book that even Energy Probe, whose proclaimed primary purpose is "to promote policies for Canada based on conservation and renewable energy" and whose complete statement of purpose does not include the word *nuclear*, seems to devote most of its efforts and resources to anti-nuclear activities, not pro–alternative energy activities. The same orientation has been adopted by the Canadian Coalition for Nuclear Responsibility (CCNR). The International Institute of Concern for Public Health (IICPH) mentions alternative energy sources hardly at all.

In order to obtain the full flavour of the anti-nuclear game as applied to alternative energy sources, it will be necessary to go outside the "Big Three" sources of information used hitherto and look at two new sources. One is Amory Lovins, who since 1976 has been the guru of the alternative energy movement world-wide, and the other is David Brooks, a Canadian who has taken some of Lovins's concepts and attempted to give them a more rational slant.

THE LOVINS LOVE-IN

For the anti-nuclear establishment to make a satisfactory case against the use of nuclear power, it is necessary for it to try to provide a convincing alternative in the form of some other source, or sources, of energy to replace nuclear. This alternative has been provided by Amory Lovins, who has developed a theory of alternative energy supply and has described it in its most convincing and persuasive form.

Amory Lovins was born in Washington, D.C. He studied at Harvard and then moved to Oxford University in England. The Friends of the Earth Limited published his first book, on mountain rambling, and his connection with this organisation led him to explore the technology and economics of energy production. It was this work which subsequently led to his increasing distaste for nuclear energy.

ECONOMIC ALTERNATIVES

An often expressed belief of the anti-nuclear establishment is that too much money is being spent on nuclear research and that if alternative energy sources were funded at the same level, they would soon be economically competitive with nuclear sources.

Unfortunately, this belief cannot be justified by the facts. One of the reasons why most of the multi-national companies have now backed out of research and development of alternative energy sources is that they could not find areas where they could usefully spend money on research. Breakthroughs in windmill efficiency or solar collector efficiency are always theoretically possible, but it is not known in a practical sense how they can be achieved.

As an illustration of this type of difficulty, Professor Bernard Cohen has estimated that if photovoltaic solar collectors are to be competitive with other forms of electrical generation, they must be manufactured at about the same cost per unit area as concrete paving slabs. One is a low-tech item, and the other is a high-tech item. The difficulty of achieving economic manufacturing parity between the two is obvious.

About every six months there is another optimistic story in the press about a "breakthrough" in photovoltaic research. However, none of these "breakthroughs" ever seems to amount to anything. This is not surprising when it is realised how difficult it must be to manufacture a hectare of semi-conductor material for the same cost as a hectare of concrete slabs.

The language in which Lovins's stance was originally expressed was not aggressively anti-nuclear but was rather in terms of the advantages of other types of energy supply. As the pro- versus anti-nuclear argument gathered momentum in the late 1970s, Lovins increasingly became a publicist for anti-nuclear sentiments. He now seems less inclined to argue that alternative energy supplies are so good that we do not need nuclear, and more to argue that nuclear is so bad that we must adopt a policy of exploiting alternatives in its place.

Lovins's ideas first attracted wide attention when he presented them in an article in the *Journal of International Affairs* in 1976 under the title "Energy Strategy: The Road Not Taken."[5] In the article, Lovins accepts the imminence of an energy shortage due to the depletion of fossil fuels, particularly oil and natural gas, and describes two scenarios for the production of energy in the U.S.A. up to the year 2025. One, which he calls the "hard technology path," is represented by a continuation of present policies, relying on centralised hard technologies such as coal, oil, and nuclear. The other, termed the "soft technology path," calls for more efficient use of energy and the development of renewable energy resources such as solar, wind, and biomass.

Lovins recognised that the hard technologies were in place, whereas the soft technologies needed development and implementation. To bridge the period between now and the emplacement of a soft technology supply, he suggested the use of coal in specially developed fluidised-bed reactors which can be used for small- or large-scale applications.

Existing conservation techniques such as improved thermal insulation in buildings, use of heat pumps, more efficient furnaces and car engines, etc., are approved by Lovins but are considered not enough in themselves since the basic energy supply still depends on hard technology. The ultimate move must be made away from hard technology towards soft technology. Examples of soft energy technologies are domestic and local solar heating (but not large solar stations), conversion of forestry and urban wastes to methanol and other liquid gases and fuels, and wind/hydraulic systems.

According to Lovins, a choice must be made now whether to pursue the hard or the soft path. No compromise is possible because the two paths are mutually exclusive.

The soft path, he believes, must be chosen since it could be the catalyst for social change. "The most important, difficult and neglected questions of energy strategy are not mainly technical or economic but rather social and ethical."[6] We could live "lifestyles of elegant frugality" surrounded by such recycled values as thrift, simplicity, diversity, neighbourliness, and craftsmanship. "In the new age of scarcity, our ingenious strivings to substitute abstract (therefore limitless) wants for concrete (therefore reasonably bounded) needs no longer seem virtuous."

As Lovins's ideas developed, the advantages of his soft energy path mushroomed until, in giving evidence to the inquiry which preceded the opening of the Cluff Lake uranium mine in Canada, they achieved full flower:

> . . . a soft energy path, properly done, can have advantages for every constituency. It offers:

— jobs for the unemployed,
— capital for business people,
— environmental protection for conservationists,
— better national security for the military,
— savings for consumers,
— opportunities for small business to innovate and for big business to recycle itself,
— existing technologies for the secular,
— rebirth of spiritual values for the religious,
— radical reforms for the young,
— traditional virtues for the old,
— world order and equity for the globalists,
— energy independence for isolationists,
— local autonomy for political conservatives,
— civil rights for political liberals.[7]

This is an incredible list. About the only advantage not offered by Lovins's soft energy path is a cure for dental plaque.

The extravagant claims made by Lovins in this list illustrate why his views are not taken seriously except by a small number of adherents such as the anti-nuclear establishment. If he were to restrain himself to a plea for more conservation and the development of better alternative energy technology, he might be taken more seriously. But his claim that soft and hard energy paths are mutually exclusive and his claims of imaginary improvements leading to a new utopia effectively put his views beyond the realm of serious consideration.

In addition, the five characteristics which Lovins has used to define the soft energy path have been accepted so uncritically that they have become dogma to many of Lovins's fans.[8] These five characteristics of soft technologies are listed below, together with some comments.

(1) "They rely on renewable energy flows that are always there whether we need them or not . . . such as sun and wind and vegetation . . . ."

A dictionary definition of "flow" is to "move steadily and smoothly along." Under this definition, sun and wind do not qualify as renewable energy sources since neither of them "flows." Both of them are highly variable and irregularly intermittent. In particular, the sun never seems to be there when we need it since, in northern climes, human energy demand and solar energy supply are 180 degrees out of phase.

(2) "They are diverse . . . an aggregate of very many individually modest contributions . . . ."

This characteristic must refer to the *size* of energy sources rather than the number of different sources available for use. Since this characteristic also appears in (4) below, it is discussed there.

> (3) "They are . . . relatively low technology . . . easy to understand and use . . . ."

The experience of industrialised countries since the industrial revolution began is that most technologies are becoming more complex and difficult to understand. Lovins does not explain why this progression in technology of the last two hundred years should be reversed for energy sources.

> (4) "They are matched in scale and in geographic distribution to end-use needs . . . ."

Taken in conjunction with (2) above this means that all energy sources must be of small scale (consistent with the well-known phrase "small is beautiful"). However, a return to small scale would also run counter to industrial experience of the last two hundred years. Many production units, whether for manufacturing, agriculture, or energy, have tended to increase in size, usually for the pragmatic reason of economies of scale. An insistence on a return to smaller units without any discussion of their merits and disadvantages appears to be dogmatic rather than reasonable.

> (5) "They are matched in energy quality to end-use needs . . . ."

This means using low-temperature energy sources (e.g., solar) for low-temperature applications (e.g., space and water heating) and reserving high-temperature sources for high-temperature applications. This is the "thermodynamic efficiency" argument of Lovins. However, no reason is given why thermodynamic efficiency should be the sole or even the major determinant in the selection of an energy source. There is also no reason given why economic efficiency, utilisation efficiency, or reliability efficiency should be ignored.

Lovins has had an influence on the nuclear controversy not because of his accuracy or his insights but simply because his extremism is found attractive by a number of different constituencies. Conservationists can see wholesale energy savings by phasing out the existing energy supply systems and putting substantially less in their place. Environmentalists can be convinced that less environmental damage will be caused by adopting alternative energy sources. Anti-technologists love his descriptions of simple

EXPERT OPINION

Every three years the World Energy Conference is convened so that energy experts from all countries can meet to discuss the world's energy situation. At the 1989 meeting of the fourteenth conference in Montreal, about 3,400 delegates from 91 countries listened to 160 technical papers and attended dozens of panel discussions.

The theme of the conference was "Energy for Tomorrow," and at the end of the conference the Honourable W. Kenneth Davis, chairman of the Program Committee, presented his conclusions drawn from the views expressed during the conference. He covered all aspects of energy use, and his comments on alternative and renewable energy sources are quoted below.[9]

"One important message from the Conference is that there was general agreement that solar energy was unlikely to be a major source of economic and environmentally benign energy for several decades."

"It must be recognised from a realistic point of view that alternative and renewable energy sources are not likely to provide a major part of the world's future energy requirements in the foreseeable future except for hydroelectric power which is likely to play a major role in some areas although the potential has been largely exploited in others."

"It must be recognised that not all alternative and renewable energy sources are environmentally benign either in the short or long term."

The views of these energy experts could all be wrong. But that is not likely.

technology futures, and communalists respond to his picture of an idyllic small-scale neighbourhood energy-supply system. In particular the anti-nuclear establishment cherishes his suggestion that nuclear power can be dispensed with. Lovins has a little of something for everyone.

However, it must be realised that the Amory Lovins style of thinking

OLD SOL

Ask any anti-nuclear activist what he would put in the place of
nuclear energy if it were abolished, and the answer will come
promptly, even fervently: solar energy. Old sol is likely to be his
god, but like many other gods, old sol is not quite what he seems.

For example, the commonest form of capturing solar power in
Canada is through solar heating panels, but if we look at this form
of solar energy carefully we find that it is anti-social.

First, one never sees solar panels on working-class houses—or on
average middle-class houses for that matter. They are only used
on expensive houses because of their high capital cost and long
periods of pay-back (if any). They are a rich man's toy, out of reach
of the pocket of the average workingman.

And not only are solar panels destined solely for the rich, but the
poor have to help pay for them.

The reason for this is quite simple. Solar panels in our Canadian
climate cannot provide enough heat and hot water all year round.

takes us back to another era—back to the nineteenth century in fact. In
those days it was fashionable to produce philosophic theories proposing
a Grand Design which would describe the precarious condition of the world
and point the way to a solution. The solutions proposed by these theories
could have a political basis, an economic basis, or a religious basis, but
whatever their starting point they would, if followed, promise a road to
a new millennium. In the twentieth century most of us have learned that
the world is a more complicated place than was thought a hundred years
earlier and that problems are now better approached in a more piecemeal
and pragmatic manner.

But not Lovins. His solution for all the world's ills is a prescription
derived from an energy basis. It is surely no coincidence that the road forward to his millennium is paved with that typical nineteenth-century energy
resource—coal. It is impossible to say whether the resource gave birth to
the philosophy or is a necessary result of it, but both point us back to the
past and give little guidance for the future.

The message conveyed by Lovins in all his writings is basically political and completely uncompromising. He has stated, "For all these rea-

At some time in the dead of winter supplementary heating will be required. This is when the rich man flicks a switch and turns on his electric heater.

But who is paying for his electrical generator when it is not in use? Those of us using electricity all year round are paying for the capital cost of our generator all year round. The rich man who relies on solar power for most of the year has his generating source sitting idle for that time, waiting to be used. The rest of us are subsidising that capital investment for a large part of the year.

The obvious way to avoid this inequity would be to charge the man with solar panels a higher price for his electricity to reflect the cost of his share of the capital investment. But it can be imagined the squeals of outrage from solar advocates if this were done. Any electrical utility doing this would be accused of trying to murder old sol.

The odd thing about all this is that solar advocates often profess a strong social consciousness. Even old sol himself seems to be a bit of a gamester.

sons, if nuclear power were clean, safe, economic, assured of ample fuel, and socially benign *per se*, it would still be unattractive because of the political implications of the kind of energy economy it would lock us into."[10] The committed anti-nuclear activist agrees with Lovins. He has no doubts about the righteousness of his cause, and he usually has no interest in considering other energy scenarios.[11]

DAVID BROOKS

To get a better idea of what is in store for us if the soft energy path is chosen rather than a hard energy path (or a combination of the two), the writings of a Canadian conservationist, David Brooks, will be examined. This author follows the Lovins soft energy path, but he is a more sensible proponent of it than Lovins and he is not as strongly anti-nuclear. We will look first at a paper prepared for the 1978 Couchiching Conference[12] and then at a book entitled *Life after Oil*.[13]

In his paper, Brooks proposes that there are five possible future energy scenarios for Canada based on growth rates. These range from the hard to the very soft energy options. The two options at either end of the scale he quickly dismisses. The hard path, which he labels "historic," consists of going ahead as we have been doing for the last thirty years with our energy consumption growing at a high rate of 4.5–6.0 per cent per year due to the active promotion of growth in energy production and consumption. Given the world's dwindling energy resources, Brooks believes this scenario is clearly not appropriate for the future.

The alternative at the extreme soft end of the energy consumption spectrum he labels the "buddhist" option. This would involve active discouragement of the use of energy, so that the annual rate of growth of energy consumption would be negative to a considerable degree. This option too is clearly untenable in the real world.

The other three scenarios, labelled "laissez-faire," "economic fix," and "zero energy growth," have annual growth rates respectively of 3.5–4.5 per cent, 1.0–2.0 per cent, and 0–1.0 per cent. Brooks considers all of them to be feasible, although he claims the first does not make too much sense and he expresses a strong preference for the last.

Towards the end of his paper, Brooks contrasts the disadvantages of following the relatively hard path of the "economic fix" with the advantages to be gained from pursuing the relatively soft path of "zero energy growth." It is here that he slips into the conventional energy conservationists' view of society and provides the reader with their standardised list of assumptions and assertions which have been adopted by the anti-nuclear establishment.

Brooks first cites the disadvantages of the harder energy path and claims that the "economic fix" scenario will lead to a "continuation of current trends towards the bureaucratisation of our institutions." Bureaucratisation is a buzz-word and it is assumed to be a bad thing in itself, even though no evidence is presented to show that it is. Should we consider bureaucratised welfare payments, unemployment benefits, and medical services to be bad? Bureaucratic growth is certainly not the answer to our contemporary problems, but it is not evident why bureaucratisation has become an anathema to the conservationists.

A by-product of the bureaucratisation of our institutions is "the management of our economic and our energy systems by a technological elite." The term "technological elite" is another buzz-word which serves as a red flag to the conservationists. In their lexicon, all technological elites should be avoided, but how this can be done is never explained. Even soft energy systems have a high-technological content and must be run by technological experts. These experts then become a "technological elite."

A contradiction in the conservationists' position becomes apparent when their dislike of a technological elite is compared with their claims that governments should spend more money on soft path research. Since research produces a higher level of technology and since a higher level of elite will be necessary to manage this higher technology, they are arguing for two incompatible courses of action. They are also, incidentally, arguing in favour of more bureaucratisation—this time of research into soft path energy systems.

A further disadvantage of our present centralised energy systems, according to Brooks, is that they are so highly integrated, "that a breakdown could not be tolerated." This argument contradicts the facts of Canadian life. It is *because* we have centralised systems that breakdowns are hardly ever noticed. The storm that brings down electricity lines leaves the user without electricity for a few hours at most. Our integrated, centralised system has work crews out making repairs before the storm is over. In addition, the average homeowner is seldom without gas or heating oil supplied by highly integrated industries despite the severity of the Canadian winter.

Yet to prevent the breakdown which supposedly cannot be tolerated, Brooks proposes another canard of the conservationists. It will be necessary to impose "the most rigorous measures, even to the extent of limiting civil rights." The "loss of civil rights" theme is one that is often played by the anti-nuclear establishment. Lovins has talked lovingly of the chaos that could be caused to our centralised energy supplies by a single rifleman. He has even written a book on the subject called *Brittle Power*.[14]

Unfortunately for the conservationists, this is not a realistic view of the world. Large centralised energy-supply systems have existed in many countries for several decades. The loss of civil rights due to the operation of these systems has been virtually zero. In the early 1980s, the Atomic Energy Control Board, Canada's nuclear regulatory agency, issued new and more stringent regulations for the protection of nuclear facilities. One wonders whether Brooks realised at the time that they had come into effect.

In his final argument against following the hard energy path, Brooks points out that it would entail "continued modification, if not absolute deterioration of the environment, and consequently no gain in the struggle to limit the incidence of cancer or other environment-related diseases." Of all the hard path energy sources, nuclear power is one of the more environmentally benign as far as environmental pollution is concerned. This argument also ignores the fact that the fight against disease, whether environmentally related or not, can only be conducted out of the surplus of wealth generated by our society, and that this surplus is vitally dependent on a wholesome supply of energy. Brooks also repeats the canard that cancer is increasing in our society because of an increasing amount of environmental pollution. The statistics for cancer fatalities for all forms of cancer, except lung cancer, have been showing a stable or declining trend for years. The major reason why lung cancer is bucking the trend is cigarette smoking.

Having cited the alleged disadvantages of the hard energy path, Brooks turns his attention to the merits of the soft energy path. The phraseology he uses to describe its benefits is typical of that used by soft energy advocates. The soft energy path would "move towards a diverse and flexible collection of energy technologies that are regionally, municipally or locally controlled." Our present hard energy path is already diverse (hydro, nuclear, oil, gas, coal), and, as noted above, it is flexible enough to cope with most Canadian climatic conditions. How alternative sources would be an improvement in this respect is not explained. Some of our energy sources are already regionally controlled; for example, electrical generation utilities are provincially owned and electrical distribution is locally controlled. The advantages of increasing local control are not expanded upon.

Brooks also claims that alternative technologies could "be built closer to human scale" and could be "readily understood by the citizenry." This latter statement harks back to the anti–"technological elite" attitude among conservationists mentioned earlier. However, Brooks does not explain how "the citizenry" will be able to understand the thermal hydraulics of a solar collector or the aerodynamics of a windmill. He does admit, however, that ". . . monetary incomes may be somewhat lower than they would have been under the hard path." This is a refreshing admission that we are all likely to be worse off if the conservationists have their way. Brooks's admission is certainly more candid than the Stanford Research Institute's mention of "voluntary simplicity" or Amory Lovins's euphemism, "elegant frugality."

However, the nub of Brooks's article, and the core of all the arguments of the proponents of the soft energy path, lies in his statement that "the choice of energy policy in Canada is ultimately less a choice between technologies than one between values. . . . the hard path and soft path imply radically different societies." Conservationists want not merely to change our energy options but to change our whole lives and the type of society within which we live them. They want a society with diverse, small-scale energy sources which are locally controlled and readily understood. This society would also be somewhat impoverished. Nuclear power, on the other hand, is centrally controlled, difficult to understand, and operated by a technological elite. Nuclear power produces large amounts of energy which can be exploited by the citizenry for its own benefit without a thought of "elegant frugality." It is not surprising that conservationists dislike it.

The characterisation of pro- and anti-nuclear activities in terms of hard and soft energy paths and the subsequent description of those activities in terms of opposing views of the ideal society have succeeded, for many people, in polarising the nuclear energy controversy. The fervour engendered by these views goes some way towards explaining the vehemence of the anti-nuclear assault.

This description of the ends desired by the alternative energy proponents also explains some of the indirectness of the anti-nuclear arguments, since they cannot openly explain their aims to the mass of the population. It can well be imagined that Lovins's offer to change our present style of living to a state of "elegant frugality" would be greeted by the man in the street with a reply which would be short, sharp, and unprintable.

CONSERVATION

As the large-scale deployment of alternative energy sources has receded further into impracticability, the anti-nuclear establishment has increasingly promoted the conservation of energy as a "replacement source" for nuclear energy.

Common sense dictates that conservation should be employed wherever practicable and economic, but it should not be promoted as a cure-all for the problems of energy shortage. For one thing, conservation is our most limited energy "source," and many of the simple conservation measures have already been taken. Those that remain will be more difficult and less economic to implement.

In addition, it is uncertain whether energy conservation measures will result in comparable energy savings. For example, consider the case of the houseowner who thoroughly insulates his house and finds at the end of a year that his fuel heating bill has decreased by, say, $400. What will he do with the money he has saved? He may decide that he can afford to run a second car. What now would be the net energy savings due to his conservation efforts?

Energy conservation probably leads to reductions in energy consumption, but nobody has yet demonstrated a quantitative relationship between the two.

"LIFE AFTER OIL"

So far, little has been said about the practicality of applying soft-energy-path principles to a mature industrialised society. However, an attempt has been made to apply these principles to Canada by David Brooks and two collaborators. Their efforts were funded by the Canadian government, for whom they produced a report: *2025: Soft Energy Paths*.[15] It was from this report that a more popular book was published entitled *Life after Oil*.

The book, and the report, are an examination of the soft energy alternatives for Canada and purport to show that by the year 2025 Canadian energy needs can largely be derived from soft energy sources. The soft energy path is seen in the conventional way as being decentralised (i.e., small-scale), renewable, and environmentally benign, as against the hard path, which is centralised, large-scale, technologically complex, non-renewable, and damaging to the environment.

Given these arbitrary definitions, energy sources can be declared as either acceptable or unacceptable to soft path advocates. Nuclear power, for example, is declared unacceptable. A number of standard anti-nuclear arguments for this decision are listed in the book: catastrophic accidents, weapons proliferation, terrorism, wastes, technological priesthood, health and safety of uranium miners, and economics. However, at a seminar at the Department of Energy, Mines and Resources when introducing the report, David Brooks, who is more thoughtful about nuclear power than some soft path advocates and realises that some of these arguments are invalid, stated that the major reason for rejecting nuclear energy was the size of the plants. If small is desirable, then it follows that large must be undesirable. Thus rejection of nuclear is based mainly on dogma.

The same dogmatic argument about size is made against large-scale hydro projects which, although based on renewable energy, are also viewed as undesirable. However, mini–hydro projects are acceptable. A second major argument against large-scale hydro plants is that they are environmentally destructive because of flooding and other hydrological effects.

Some criticisms have been levelled against the methodology used in *Life after Oil*. Here we will confine ourselves to comments on the rejection of nuclear power because of its size. The book proposes that the main substitute for oil by 2025 should be methanol derived from wood. To meet demand, it proposes that Canada build 315 methanol plants, each with a daily output capacity of 1,000 tonnes. The annual energy output in the form of methanol from such a plant would be about 7.3×10^6 gigajoules (a gigajoule is a unit of energy). The annual energy output in the form of electricity from a 300-megawatt CANDU reactor operating at 80 per cent capacity would be approximately 7.5×10^6 gigajoules, about the same as a methanol plant.

Although both plants have similar size energy *outputs*, the material *inputs* differ greatly. The daily raw-material input to a 300-megawatt CANDU reactor would be less than 0.1 tonnes of uranium, while the daily raw-material input to a 1,000-tonnes-per-day methanol plant would be about 2,600 tonnes of wood. As far as size is concerned, a 300-megawatt CANDU reactor should be more acceptable than a 1,000-tonnes-per-day methanol plant.

A similar argument is made against large-scale hydro projects. Apart from size, a major disadvantage cited by the book of large-scale hydro is the environmental damage caused by the reservoirs built up behind the hydro dam. This can be compared with the environmental damage caused by "farming" trees on a five-year cycle as proposed in the book.

It is recognised that the degree of environmental damage in each case is arguable. Although a hydro reservoir completely destroys the original natural ecology of the area under its surface, it provides some compensations in the form of fishing, recreation, and acceptable aesthetics. Cutting wood on a five-year rotation may not completely destroy the local ecology, but it is likely to remove land from recreational use completely, and the aesthetic impact would be very unattractive. For the calculations below, it will be assumed that the environmental damage in each case is complete, and equal to the area covered by the energy source.

In one possible scenario quoted in the book, it is proposed that the energy derived annually from biomass liquids (from wood) in 2025 will need to be 2,878 petajoules. The book states that "farming" wood will produce 10–13 tonnes per hectare per year on a five- to eight-year rotation. This will fall to about 2.5 tonnes in the northern parts of the prairie provinces. It will be assumed that under average Canadian conditions an average of 8 tonnes per hectare can be harvested every year.

Since 50 kilograms of methanol (from 130 kilograms of oven-dried wood) produce 1 gigajoule of energy, it will require about 4.4×10^7 hectares to produce 2,878 petajoules; that is, about 440,000 square kilometres. Thus biomass liquids are produced at an annual rate of 0.0065 petajoules per square kilometre of land. The reservoirs of the La Grande complex at James Bay cover about 12,200 square kilometres, and the complex produces about 13.5 gigawatts. At 80 per cent capacity factor, the complex will produce 340 petajoules per year. The annual production rate of energy is 0.028 petajoules per square kilometre of reservoir. Thus the production of biomass liquids from a tree farm will be nearly five times as destructive to the environment as the La Grande hydro complex.

Similarly the Peace River hydro project covers an area of about 1,800 square kilometres and produces 2.5 gigawatts of energy; that is, 63 petajoules per year. The annual energy production is thus about

0.035 petajoules per square kilometre, so that biomass liquids are nearly six times as environmentally damaging as the Peace River hydro project.

SPLIT WOOD—NOT ATOMS

Some proponents of alternative energy resources have the quaint idea that burning wood could replace uranium as a heat source for generating electricity. The slogan "Split Wood—Not Atoms" has been elevated to the status of bumper-sticker art.

Unfortunately alternative energy proponents have not put pen to paper to calculate whether it is possible to replace uranium with wood as a source of energy.

A standard face cord of wood, familiar to most domestic users, measures eight by four feet and is sixteen inches deep. When burned it will produce about 1.2×10^{10} joules of heat.

The new Darlington nuclear power station in Ontario has a gross thermal output of about 11,000 megawatts and will produce about 3.5×10^{17} joules per year.

To replace Darlington with a wood-burning power station would require every year a "face cord" of wood about 72,000 kilometres long. This "face cord" would stretch nearly twice around the world.

The logistics of cutting and transporting this amount of wood are staggering. Transportation alone would require two trucks arriving at the plant every minute of every day of the year. By contrast, Darlington can be fuelled by about one truckload of uranium per month.

The atmospheric pollution from burning wood and the potential for accidents while cutting and transporting it are considerable. Yet wood is touted by the alternative energy folks as a safe, non-polluting energy source.

In a rational world where people value safety and a clean environment, bumper stickers would proclaim, "Split Atoms—Not Wood." But we do not yet live in a rational world.

These examples reveal a major weakness in some of the proposals made by alternative energy advocates. Untested dogma is sometimes treated as revealed truth. As a result, simple mathematical calculations are not made to test whether the dogma is true. The ideas put forward by alternative energy advocates and by conservationists should always be tested before acceptance. At minimum, they should be tested against common sense. Preferably, they should be tested using some form of scientific discipline.

The last word on the subject of alternative energy and its proponents can be left to David Fishlock, science editor of the *Financial Times* of London:

> Nuclear energy is controversial because a sector of Western society, with political ambitions to revert from an industrialised to an agrarian and craft-based society, sees nuclear technology as the most potent force for stability in our present way of life. The "nuclear threat" is nothing more than its ability to deliver low-cost, dependable power. . . . [This] is an intolerable obstacle to [the Green Movement's] efforts to overturn industrialised society.[16]

CHAPTER 8

Risks of Nuclear Energy

The Facts

ALL HUMAN ACTIVITIES INVOLVE A RISK TO LIFE OR TO HEALTH. Achieving a state of safety or zero risk is not possible. The adjective *safe*, in its normal usage as an absolute term, cannot be applied to any activities that people engage in.

If no activity is safe, how can an activity be judged safe enough to indulge in? There can be no definitive answer to this question. It depends on considerations such as the size of the risk, who bears the risk, how much it will cost to reduce the risk, and what alternative risk will be put in its place. These are considerations which cannot always be decided on scientific grounds. Some must be decided on societal or economic grounds.

Nonetheless, if human society is to continue functioning, decisions on risk must be made continually. When confronting risks, sometimes it is more dangerous to do nothing than to do something. A decision to do nothing about a risk is just as much a decision on risk as a decision to reduce or alter or accept a risk.

In this chapter, the risks of nuclear electricity production will be looked at from two different perspectives. In the first, they will be compared with other methods of energy production. In the second, they will be compared with other risks of everyday living with which we are familiar. The reader will then be able to make a personal judgement, based on comparison, whether the risks of nuclear energy are worth the benefits obtained.

A COMPARISON OF THE RISKS OF ENERGY PRODUCTION

There have been two major comparisons of the risks of energy production conducted in North America. The first, carried out by Herbert Inhaber, was published in 1982 in his book *Energy Risk Assessment*.[1] Inhaber's approach to comparing risks from energy sources was new at the time. He was aware that no energy source was without risk, and he set out to tally all the risks associated with the construction and operation of various energy sources. Each energy source was tracked from start to finish. The materials which were used to construct each energy source had themselves an element of risk in their production, and this risk was tallied, together with the transportation risks of the component parts, the construction and operation risks, and the risks of accidents during operation.

Computing every last risk in this way made for very complicated calculations. In drafts, prepared and published before his book was completed, Inhaber made a number of errors which were pounced upon by his critics. Where the criticisms were justified, Inhaber corrected his results in the final manuscript, but it was found that although the magnitude of the risks had changed somewhat as a result of these recalculations, the ordering of the energy sources in terms of risk had not.

Inhaber expressed the total risk arising from each energy source as the total deaths (public and occupational) per megawatt year of energy generated as a function of the energy system. He found that natural gas was the safest energy system, followed by nuclear, hydroelectricity, wind, solar (thermal), photovoltaics, and solar space heating in that order. The most hazardous source was coal, followed by oil and methanol as the next most hazardous.

The publication of these results, which showed solar energy sources to be more dangerous than nuclear, caused an immense furore in energy circles. The anti-nuclear establishment believed that claiming nuclear energy was safer than solar energy was worse than demeaning motherhood or apple pie.

One of the most vociferous of Inhaber's critics was John Holdren of the University of California. In 1983, a year after Inhaber's book had been published, Holdren and five collaborators wrote a long paper which appeared in a book entitled *Health Risks of Energy Technologies*.[2] They attempted, the same as Inhaber, to calculate the risks of energy production from various sources by adding up all the incremental risks involved in producing and operating each different source. Holdren et al. subdivided the energy sources more narrowly than Inhaber and only calculated occupational risks. They did not include risks to members of the public.

Despite the differences of methodology, Holdren's ordering of the risks of energy sources was remarkably similar to Inhaber's. Holdren found that oil refining was the safest, followed by nuclear and hydroelectric. He also found that coal was the most hazardous, followed by methanol, solar (thermal) mass heating, and solar space heating. The other sources, including other solar sources, were in between.

Again, nuclear had been found safer than solar energy sources, but this time there was not a whisper from the anti-nuclear establishment. This was probably partly due to Holdren's standing as a member of the anti-nuclear establishment. It was also not in the interests of the anti-nuclear establishment to advertise the fact that one of their own had calculated nuclear energy to be safer than solar energy.

The results of these two studies have not prevented the anti-nuclear establishment from continuing to proclaim the dangers of nuclear energy—

but without ever comparing these dangers with other energy sources such as solar. A final point which should be made in this section is that *the degree of risk from all of these energy sources, whether nuclear, solar, or coal, is sufficiently low that none of them should be excluded from utilisation on the grounds of risk.*

A COMPARISON OF NUCLEAR ENERGY RISKS WITH OTHER RISKS

As noted at the beginning of this chapter, all human activities involve risk. In order to appreciate the risks of energy production they can be compared with other risks which we endure during our normal everyday lives. The measure which will be used when comparing risks is the ultimate effect of risk—death. It must be remembered that over a lifetime the total risk of death for all of us is unity—we all die.

Health statistics provide us with information on the causes of death as recorded in death certificates. The major causes are listed in Table 4 below.[3]

TABLE 4
Immediate Causes of Death in Canada, 1983

CAUSE	ANNUAL DEATH RATE PER 100,000	PER CENT OF TOTAL
Cardiovascular diseases	502	42.1
Cancer	296	24.7
Pneumonia, influenza, and tuberculosis	41	3.5
Motor vehicle accidents	33	2.8
Suicide	27	2.3
Occupational accidents	6	0.5
Other accidents	37	3.1
All other causes	251	21.0

The category "All other causes" contains several hundred causes of death, each of which accounts for a fraction of 1 per cent of the total death rate.

If it were desirable to improve our human lot by expending effort on death-preventing measures, it is obvious from the above Table where our money could be most profitably spent. A reduction in cardiovascular disease or cancer by a few per cent would be much more beneficial to the Canadian population than any other measures we could take. Logic dictates that we should give most attention (and money) to reducing these two death rates. Unfortunately, as we shall see later, we are not that logical.

The actual risk which a member of the public faces from the use of nuclear energy is very, very small. To put it into a perspective with other risks with which we are familiar, the following Table lists some types of activities which will increase the risk of death by one in a million.[4] This is a very small level of risk indeed and one which we would tend to ignore in everyday life.

TABLE 5
Activities Which Increase Risk of Death by One in a Million

ACTIVITY	CAUSE OF DEATH
Smoking 1.4 cigarettes	Cancer, heart disease
Spending three hours in a coal mine	Accident
Travelling 480 kilometres by car	Accident
Flying 1,600 kilometres by jet	Accident
Flying 0,600 kilometres by jet	Cancer caused by cosmic radiation
Living 2 months in a stone or brick building	Cancer caused by natural radioactivity
Living 2 days in a large city	Air pollution
Eating 500 grams of peanut butter	Liver cancer caused by aflatoxin B
Eating 100 charcoal-broiled steaks	Cancer from benzopyrene
Living 5 years at the boundary of a nuclear power plant	Cancer caused by radiation
Risk of accident due to living within 8 kilometres of a nuclear power plant for 50 years	Cancer caused by radiation

These risk comparisons illustrate how trivial are the risks from nuclear energy when they are compared with risks from other activities. For example, the annual risk of death to a member of the public living near a nuclear power plant due to an accident at that plant is the same as the annual risk of death due to eating two charcoal broiled steaks each year. In both cases the cause of death would be cancer. In each case the risk of death is negligible.

One of the difficulties in conveying an appreciation of low levels of risk to the public is selecting an adequate measure to define risk in absolute terms. Discussing risk in terms of a "one in a million chance of death" as presented above is useful for comparing risks, but it is difficult to comprehend a "one in a million" or a "one in a billion" chance of something happening because these chances are so very small.

A more graphic expression of risk of death has been used by Professor Bernard Cohen. It is called a "Loss of Life Expectancy" (LLE). It is calculated by assuming that the LLE of a person who dies as a result of an activity is spread over the entire group engaging in that activity. For example, if the risk of death from an activity is one in a million per year and one million people engage in that activity for one year, then one person in that group would be expected to die. For the sake of simplicity, it is assumed that the one person who dies loses half his life; that is, he dies at age 35 years rather than at age 70. Since his death could have occurred to any one person in the one million sample, his loss of life expectancy can be spread across the whole group, and the average LLE for the group indulging in that activity for a year will be 35 years divided by one million, which is 0.013 days. If the activity is indulged in for a lifetime of 70 years, the total LLE will be 0.91 days.

Table 6 lists some of the causes of LLE and the number of days each is expected to reduce normal life expectancy.[5]

TABLE 6
Loss of Life Expectancy Due to Various Causes

CAUSE	LLE (DAYS)
Being unmarried—male	3,500
Cigarette smoking—male	2,250
Heart disease	2,100
Being unmarried—female	1,600
Being 30% overweight	1,300
Being a coal miner	1,100
Cancer	980
Being 20% overweight	900
Cigarette smoking—female	800
Stroke	500
Dangerous job—accidents	300
Motor vehicle accidents	207
Accidents in the home	95
Suicide	95
Being murdered—homicide	90
Average job—accidents	74
Drowning	41
Falls	39
Accidents to pedestrians	37
Safest job—accidents	30
Fire—burns	27
Poison (solid, liquid)	17
Firearms accidents	11
Natural radiation	8
Coffee	6
Oral contraceptives	5
Accidents to bicyclists	5
Reactor accidents—UCS	2*
Reactor accidents—Rasmussen	0.02*
Radiation from nuclear industry	0.02*
PAP test	−4
Smoke alarm in home	−10
Air bags in car	−50
Mobile coronary care units	−125

N.B. Data are from U.S. sources. UCS is Union of Concerned Scientists, the most prominent anti-nuclear critics in the U.S.A. Items marked with an asterisk are deliberately worst-case figures. They assume that all U.S. electrical power is nuclear.

Some of the hazards to life revealed by this list are startling. Being unmarried and accidents in the home are two major hazards to life which are not usually considered when risks are being discussed.

The hazard represented by nuclear energy is vanishingly small when compared to most of the other everyday risks. Even when the risk of reactor accidents is assumed to be as high as claimed by the U.S. anti-nuclear organisation, the Union of Concerned Scientists, it is still negligible when compared with other risks.

It is interesting to note that the list also includes a few life-saving activities such as PAP tests and smoke detectors. In order to improve our longevity, it is necessary that life-extending measures be encouraged and life-shortening measures discouraged in our society. Governments should maximise the number of coronary mobile units in operation and try to discourage people from being single, overweight, and smokers.

Unfortunately, the only leadership displayed by governments is in encouraging exercise and discouraging smoking. One reason may be that governments and the general population seem unaware of the relative hazards of various activities. Tests have been carried out in which people have been asked to rank various activities or technologies in terms of their hazards. Some items such as smoking and motor vehicles are usually ranked quite closely to their ranking on an objective scale. Others are way off. The one activity which is usually ranked most differently from its position on an objective scale is nuclear energy. However, when scientists participate in this test, it is found that they have a much better appreciation of the true level of safety of nuclear energy than non-scientists.

Although included in the Table above as a possible contributor to LLE, it has been argued by some risk analysts that nuclear energy could be included as a GLE—a "Gain in Life Expectancy."[6] The reasoning behind this argument is quite simple. There is a known correlation between energy consumption and life expectancy. As one increases, so does the other. In most developed countries there is a well-established historical relationship between per capita energy consumption and the average age of death. Similarly those underdeveloped countries with low average ages of death are those with low per capita energy consumptions. High energy consumption in a society enables it to produce high levels of wealth. Some of this wealth is used to provide hospitals, sewers, social benefits, etc. All of these modern social support systems contribute not only to the quality of life but also to the quantity of life; that is, to life expectancy.

Ernest Siddall, a Canadian risk analyst, has quantified the relationship between energy production and its effect on increasing life expectancy. He concludes that a nuclear generating station the size of Pickering A, with 2,000 megawatts capacity and operating for 70 per cent of the time (producing 1,400 megawatts), can be credited with saving 136 lives per year.[7] A coal-fired station of the same size could be credited with saving the same number of lives except that pollution from coal burning causes 26 deaths per year for each 1,000 megawatts of electricity produced. Thus 1,400 megawatts of coal-fired generation will cause 36 deaths, so that the net saving in lives each year from coal-fired generation would be 104.

Thus even coal-fired generation, which as noted above is the most "dangerous" energy source, saves lives simply because the energy produced is used to create wealth, a proportion of which can be used to save lives. There is no doubt that as our individual wealth increases, the quantity and quality of our lives increase. Rich people live longer than poor people. Yet it is the comfortably-off stratum of our society, the stratum exposed to the lowest level of personal risk, which worries most about that risk. In doing so, it has to some extent managed to persuade society to spend vast sums of money in attempts to reduce risks which are already negligible. Meanwhile other risks, which are considerable, are being ignored.

Ernest Siddall and Bernard Cohen have both compiled lists of activities on which money is being spent to save lives and have estimated what has been spent in each case for each life saved. Their results show there is a very wide variation in the cost of saving one life.[8] For example, the World Health Organisation (WHO) estimates that over five million childhood deaths could be averted each year in Third World countries at a cost ranging from $50 per life saved through immunisation against measles in Gambia and Cameroon, to $210 per life saved by a combination of immunisations in Indonesia. WHO also estimates that three million childhood deaths could be averted annually by oral rehydration therapy for diarrhea. The cost per life saved would range from $150 in Honduras to $550 in Egypt.

In the Western world, all the inexpensive ways of saving lives are already in place, and the cost of saving an extra life is much higher than in the Third World countries. However, some measures are still in a reasonable range of costs. For instance, a program to persuade sexually active women to have regular PAP tests for cervical cancer costs an estimated $50,000 per life saved. A multiple cancer screening test costs about $52,000 per life saved.

Making road transportation safer is a fertile field for saving lives. Measures range from improved traffic signs and improved lighting, at $31,000 and $80,000 respectively per life saved, to permanent grooving in roads to minimise skidding, which would cost $320,000 per life saved. Installing air-bags in cars would also cost $320,000 per life saved.

But the really high costs of saving an extra life come from activities in the nuclear industry. After the Three Mile Island accident, hydrogen recombiners were made mandatory in U.S. nuclear power reactors, at a cost of $3 billion per potential life saved. Regulatory rachetting in the U.S.A., the process by which regulatory authorities keep adding one safety requirement after another—just because they are there—has cost the U.S.A. an estimated $2.5 billion per potential life saved. In Canada, where our regulatory authorities have been more reasonable, the cost of regulatory rachetting has been $250 million per potential life saved. The cost of the U.S. waste disposal program has been estimated at $220 million per potential life saved.

The costs of risk reduction in the nuclear industry are far greater than in any other industry. The reason for their imposition has been the stimulus provided by public fear. Fortunately the Canadian nuclear industry has been able to compete economically despite this burden. The U.S. nuclear industry is finding it more difficult.

The major difficulty in accepting the costs of saving a life described above is the obscene difference between the cost of saving a child's life in the Third World and the cost of pandering to an artificially stimulated fear of radiation in the economically developed world. How much better off the world would be if some of the money wasted on unnecessary safety improvements to nuclear power stations in developed countries could be spent on saving children's lives in Third World countries.

The Game

The populations now living in Western industrialised societies such as Canada are exposed to fewer risks than any other peoples in the history of the world. Yet paradoxically parts of these same populations seem to be more worried about risks than any previous generations.[9] It would appear that without the real dangers of disease, starvation, or violence faced by our ancestors some people need to magnify the relatively small risks which exist in industrialised countries just to bring an apprehension of danger into their lives.

The anti-nuclear establishment is aware of this modern fearfulness and pitches its message to take advantage of it. By refusing to either quantify or compare dangers, it has succeeded in confusing the issue of risk for many people.

> *"There is no such thing as a 'safe dose' of radiation. Any dose, ever so small, entails an increase in the incidence of cancers, congenital malformations and anomalies in the growing process"* (Gordon Edwards, CCNR).[10]

> *". . . the AECB itself agrees that every little bit [of radiation] hurts (i.e. there is no safe amount)"* (David Poch, Energy Probe).[11]

These statements are misleading.

As was seen in chapter 2, we do not know the risks from low levels of radiation dose. Consequently it is *assumed*, for purposes of radiation protection, that the effects of radiation can be extrapolated from high levels, where effects are known, down to low levels, and that the extrapolation is linear and without a threshold dose. This is known to be a safe extrapolation in that it will exaggerate the effects of low levels of radiation rather than minimise them.

It is known that high levels of radiation dose can produce cancers. However, there is no reliable evidence that congenital malformations or anomalies in the growing process are produced in people at either high or low levels of radiation. It is easy to frighten people by exaggerating the risks of radiation, particularly when those risks are improperly described both quantitatively and qualitatively.

FIRE

We are fortunate that an anti-fire establishment did not spring up when fire was first discovered many thousands of years ago. Otherwise fire would have been treated then in the same way as radiation is treated now by the anti-nuclear establishment. Imagine the reactions of an anti-fire establishment.

It would have demanded an immediate ban on the use of fire on the grounds that it posed an unacceptable hazard to people and the environment. After all, an uncontrolled fire might kill thousands and destroy vast areas of forests.

The anti-fire establishment would have argued that although small quantities of fire could warm cold bodies and cook raw food, even very small quantities could be lethal. Because a bonfire's heat could kill a person standing too close to it, the heat could also produce a measurable chance of death for people standing some distance from the fire. We would have been told, "There is no safe level of fire."

Fortunately, an anti-fire establishment did not appear with the discovery of fire. Perhaps pre-historic man had a better appreciation of risks and benefits than today's anti-nuclear establishment.

"Absorption or ingestion of radioactive substances, including tritium, creates a cancer risk for the person exposed, a risk of mutation for descendants of the person exposed and a risk to unborn children in utero" (David Poch, Energy Probe).[12]

This statement is misleading.

Unless some indication is given of the level of risk from a particular amount of tritium, the statement above will likely have the effect of frightening people. The facts are that (1) the amount of tritium released by the nuclear industry is carefully monitored by the Atomic Energy Control Board (AECB); (2) the amount routinely released is always well below the level established as safe by the AECB; and (3) the quantity of tritium already in the environment from natural sources is much greater than the amount released by the nuclear industry.

"Children eating irradiated food have developed chromosomal abnormalities according to one of a few studies conducted on humans, while animal studies have found kidney disease, abnormal blood cells, testicular damage, reduced fertility and premature death" (Patricia Adams, Energy Probe).[13]

These statements are misleading.

The anti-nuclear establishment has campaigned for a long time to prevent the use of food irradiation. This process increases the shelf-life of many foods, and although it may have only marginal uses in countries with good transportation systems and good refrigeration facilities, it could be useful in reducing food spoilage in many developing countries. Despite the potential importance of this process, the anti-nuclear establishment has opposed any use of food irradiation anywhere in the world—even in developing countries where it could save lives.

Typical of the misinformation they broadcast is the one study from India which showed chromosomal abnormalities in children fed with irradiated wheat. This study has been repeated elsewhere without repeating the effect. It would appear that the Indian study was flawed.

It is considered by the vast majority of scientists, who have examined *all* the evidence about food irradiation, that it is a safe procedure. This opinion is held by the World Health Organisation and the Food and Agricultural Organisation of the United Nations as well as by Canadian government scientists in the Departments of Health and Welfare, and Agriculture.

The list of ailments found in animals who have been fed massive quantities of irradiated food is common to many experiments involving animal feeding. These experiments would simply seem to show that animals cannot be fed massive quantities of anything without harmful effects to their health.

RAILWAYS

Some of the objections made to the first railway construction are curiously reminiscent of the objections made today by the anti-nuclear establishment to the use of nuclear energy.

For example, from a safety standpoint it was claimed that there was a risk that railways would

— suffocate passengers at speeds greater than 30 km/h,
— cause blood vessels to burst at that speed, and
— have accidents in which hundreds would die.

From an environmental standpoint there was a risk that railways would

— cause smoke pollution to cover the countryside,
— produce devastating fires from sparks from the engines, and
— cause cows to drop dead at the sight of a train.

From a social standpoint there was a risk that railways would

— be uneconomic, and
— allow the lower classes to move about needlessly.

The anti-railway establishment of the time advocated the use of alternative technology such as wind- and water-powered engines or the use of atmospheric pressure as a propellant.

The current anti-nuclear establishment seems to have simply adapted the arguments used by its anti-railway predecessors.

"[nuclear reactor decommissioning] is a difficult, dangerous and very expensive job [requiring] the transportation and disposal of countless truck-loads of radioactive rubble" (Gordon Edwards, CCNR).[14]

This statement is inaccurate.

Reactor decommissioning is neither difficult, dangerous, nor expensive.[15] Several reactors in various parts of the world have already been decommissioned, and current techniques can perform this type of operation safely and cheaply. In 1952 the NRX reactor at Chalk River suffered a partial melt-down. The reactor core was taken apart and removed, and another was assembled in about a year. Decommissioning techniques have improved considerably since 1952.

The major part (over 80 per cent) of a nuclear power plant never becomes radioactive and can be demolished or reused without restrictions. It has been estimated that the quantities of waste from a large (1,000 megawatt) reactor would amount to a few hundred cubic metres of waste requiring deep underground disposal, a few thousand cubic metres which can be disposed of as normal operating waste, and about fifty thousand cubic metres of non-radioactive waste which can be taken away as land-fill.

"Replace the International Commission on Radiological Protection with an independent scientific agency dealing only with the health risks of exposure to ionising radiation, not *with trade-offs of health for presumed benefits" (Rosalie Bertell, IICPH).*[16]

This is a typical wish of the anti-nuclear establishment.

They would like to convince the public that the *only* risks they face come from the use of nuclear energy; that risks to public health from nuclear energy are considerable; that all other energy sources are risk-free; and that knowledge of the vast benefits of nuclear energy (described in the next chapter) should be inaccessible to the general public. It would be difficult to find a better reason why a book such as this is required than this statement by Rosalie Bertell.

"Clearly, any safety standard that allows anything more than absolutely no exposure [to radiation] is putting worker and public lives at risk" (David Poch, Energy Probe).[17]

This statement is misleading.

This statement illustrates clearly how the risk game is played by the anti-nuclear establishment. First, it is implied that there could be a risk-free state. Then it is implied that since a particular activity of the nuclear industry is not risk-free, we should abandon it in favour of a risk-free alternative. There is always an attempt to convince the public that only nuclear energy involves any risk component. There is never an attempt to *compare* risks of alternatives.

COURAGE

The members of the anti-nuclear establishment often fly hither and yon to "warn" the public about the risks of low levels of radiation produced by the nuclear industry.

As noted in chapter 2, a person receives a radiation dose of about 4 millirems during a return flight in a jet aircraft from Halifax to Vancouver. This is more than the radiation dose received from the nuclear industry by the average person in a lifetime. Thus, if we believe that the reactor industry poses a significant risk to our health, we must also believe that the radiation dose we receive while flying even short distances poses an even greater risk.

What, then, are we to make of the members of the anti-nuclear establishment who fly hither and yon to "warn" us of the risks of nuclear energy?

Are they incredibly courageous people to take such risks on our behalf?

Or do they believe that low levels of radiation are not really as dangerous as they proclaim?

CHAPTER 9

Benefits of Nuclear Energy

The Facts

THE BENEFITS OF NUCLEAR ENERGY ARE SELDOM MENTIONED BY the anti-nuclear establishment, and they are seldom perceived by the general public. Nonetheless, these benefits are real and manifold. There is hardly any aspect of modern life untouched by nuclear energy.

The best-known benefit is the production of nuclear generated electricity, but there is also a myriad of uses for artificially produced radioactive isotopes. The benefits of nuclear electricity can be stated in economic terms. The benefits of radioisotopes in improving our quality of life usually cannot be quantified. However, when compared with the risks of nuclear energy, the benefits show an overwhelming advantage.

NUCLEAR GENERATED ELECTRICITY

About twenty-six countries now have nuclear power programs. Those with the largest programs are listed in Table 7.[1]

TABLE 7
Total and Nuclear Electricity Generation (1988)

	ELECTRICITY GENERATION (TWH)		
COUNTRY	TOTAL	NUCLEAR	PER CENT
France	372	260	70
Belgium	62	41	66
Sweden	141	66	47
Switzerland	58	22	37
Finland	51	18	36
Spain	133	48	36
Germany F.R.	403	138	34
Japan	642	175	27
United States	2,701	527	20
United Kingdom	283	53	19
Canada	487	78	16

In many industrialised countries, nuclear generated electricity now accounts for a significant proportion of the total electrical generation. One reason for this is the economic advantage of using nuclear energy over the only reasonable alternative—coal. Another reason is that in most industrialised countries the potentially cheapest electrical source, large-scale hydroelectric generation, has been exploited to the maximum extent possible. Oil and gas are depleting energy sources which are unlikely to be economically viable in the long term for electricity generation. Solar-derived energy sources are also considered to be uneconomic except in special circumstances, such as in remote communities. This leaves coal and nuclear as the only credible alternatives for large-scale electrical generation.[2]

In Canada the relative economics of the two sources varies across the country. For example, Ontario has few indigenous coal reserves and must import coal from Pennsylvania. This is one reason why the total cost of a kilowatt-hour of electricity generated by coal is more than a kilowatt-hour produced by nuclear energy. Alberta, on the other hand, has large reserves of low-sulphur coal requiring a minimum of acid-rain reduction equipment, and in Alberta coal is found to be cheaper than nuclear. In New Brunswick, which has access to sulphur-bearing coal requiring acid-rain emission reduction measures, nuclear costs about the same as coal.

In Ontario, which has the largest nuclear power program in Canada, the savings from the use of nuclear rather than coal generation amount to about $1 billion per year. In addition, Canada has already saved about $14.5 billion (1988 dollars) in foreign exchange, since without nuclear energy in Ontario it would be necessary to import coal from the U.S.A.[3]

Direct savings are not the only economic advantage of nuclear power. The nuclear industry, Canada-wide, provides about thirty thousand direct jobs, many of them high-tech, and about one hundred thousand jobs over-all, including indirect employment.[4] The industry contributes about $4 billion per year to the Canadian economy, about the same as the contributions made by the chemical and automobile industries. These returns are the result of a federal government research and development investment in the nuclear industry of about $5 billion since 1945.

The safety record of Canada's nuclear power industry is exemplary. In nearly two hundred reactor-years of operation there has not been a radiation-related death either to the public or to the operators of the nuclear power stations. Ontario Hydro statistics show that their nuclear power workers are safer on the job than when they are away from work. Although worker safety at Ontario Hydro's hydraulic stations and coal-fired thermal stations has been very good, worker safety at its nuclear stations has been superior.

The environmental benefits of using nuclear power are considerable. If Ontario Hydro had used coal-fired instead of nuclear generated electricity since its nuclear program started in the early 1970s, an additional 7.8 million tonnes of acid gas would have been released into the atmosphere.

In addition, about 20 million tonnes of ashes would have been produced. These ashes would take up about twenty-five thousand times the amount of space required for used nuclear fuel wastes and would release more radio-active material into the environment than nuclear fuel wastes.

The quantity of radioactive material released to the environment from Canada's nuclear power stations has been negligible compared with the radioactivity already there. Only our ability to detect radioactivity at very low levels allows us to measure the excess.

Given the considerable benefits and the low level of risks in the production of nuclear generated electricity, it is not surprising that so many countries have adopted the nuclear power option. In addition to electricity generation, there are many other areas where nuclear energy is conferring considerable benefits on the world community.

MEDICINE

Radioisotopes have been widely used in medicine for both *therapy* and *diagnosis* for many years. The radioisotope cobalt–60 has been used for cancer therapy since the early 1950s. Cobalt–60 emits a high-energy gamma ray. A thin beam of these rays is directed towards the tumour, and enough energy is absorbed by the cancerous cells to kill them. Cancerous cells are more susceptible to destruction by radiation than normal cells, but care must be taken during radiation to minimise the amount of damage to healthy cells.

Canada has played a major role in the supply of cancer therapy units world-wide and has installed over fifteen hundred units representing 75 per cent of the international market. By the end of 1986, treatment by Canadian units had extended the lives of cancer patients by an estimated 17 million person years.

The use of radioisotopes in medical diagnosis has been widespread for many years both for in vivo and for in vitro diagnosis. When employed in vivo, the radioisotope is introduced into the body by injection, ingestion, or inhalation. The chemical form of the radioisotope is custom-designed so that most of it will locate in a specific body organ. The radioisotope is taken up by the organ, and its distribution shows whether all, or part, of the organ has a cancerous disfunction. The radioisotopic distribution can be "photographed" by using the radiation it emits. If necessary, the functioning of an organ can be followed by taking a sequence of "photographs."[5]

The most widely used radioisotope for in vivo medical diagnosis is technetium–99m.[6] The element technetium is not found in nature. It is one of the fission products of uranium–235. It can be separated from the other fission products and then incorporated into a variety of compounds which are designed to be taken up by specific organs of the body.

This ability to be incorporated into organ-specific compounds is one of the great attractions of technetium–99m as an in vivo diagnostic tool. Another attraction is its short half-life of six hours, long enough to allow the diagnostic test to be completed but short enough to ensure a minimum radiation dose to the patient. The radiation emitted by technetium–99m is principally a 140-kilovolt gamma ray. This energy is low enough to be readily shielded, but high enough so that little is absorbed by body tissue on its way to produce the "photograph" outside the body. All the atoms of technetium–99m are radioactive, so that only a very small quantity is required to provide enough radiation for use in a diagnostic test. With all these advantageous properties, it is easy to understand why technetium–99m is the almost perfect diagnostic radioisotope.[7]

The in vitro use of radioisotopes in medical diagnosis is also widespread. This method of diagnosis is carried out outside the body on samples of body fluids. A variety of hormones and other chemicals found in body fluids can be measured by in vitro analysis.[8] A solution of a radioisotope is added to the body fluids, and a separation of the required material is carried out. By knowing how much radioactivity was added, and by measuring the amount in the sample after separation, it is possible to estimate accurately very small concentrations of vital constituents in the fluids. The radioisotope most widely used for this technique is iodine–125. The name of the technique is radio-immunoassay. A Nobel Prize was awarded to Rosalyn Yalow of New York for its discovery.

Canada is the world's largest supplier of radioisotopes for in vivo and in vitro medical diagnosis. Using these radioisotopes, about 10–12 million diagnostic procedures are carried out annually in Canada, and world-wide the number likely exceeds 300 million. It is estimated that one-third of all medical diagnostic procedures done in North America utilise radioisotopes. The value of these procedures, in providing accurate diagnoses, and in the reduction of human trauma due to using radioisotopes rather than exploratory surgery as a diagnostic tool, is incalculable.

In medical research, radioisotope tracers are powerful tools for unravelling natural biologic systems. They have been used to provide much information about the complex structures of living cells and their genetic systems, and to investigate biological processes.

More than one-half of the world's disposable medical products are sterilised with cobalt–60 gamma radiation. Articles such as syringes, needles, sutures, gloves, gowns, sponges, and catheters are packaged by the manufacturer in clean but not sterile conditions. The packages are then passed through a powerful cobalt–60 gamma radiation field. The gamma rays penetrate the packaging and kill all organisms inside. The contents of the package remain sterile until the package is opened in the hospital operating theatre.[9]

INDUSTRY

Industry also uses radioisotopes for a variety of beneficial purposes.[10] Radiographers use gamma radiation to detect structural faults, impurities, and porosities in metal components such as aircraft castings and welds in oil and gas pipelines. Sophisticated electronic gauges, such as level and density gauges, use radiation in industrial processes to measure and control the thickness of sheet material, including plastic films, metal foils, and metal or plastic coatings on a wide variety of materials. Radioisotopes are also used by industry as tracers to find leaks, follow flow patterns, and monitor chemical reactions.

Ionisation smoke detectors containing small radioactive emitters are widely used industrially and domestically to protect people and property against the hazards of fire.

AGRICULTURE

In agriculture, radioisotopes are used to measure the uptake of nutrients by plants and animals, and to study topics such as trace element deficiencies and the effects of fertilisers.

Fertilisers labelled with a radioactive isotope of phosphorus or with a stable isotope of nitrogen show how much of the fertiliser is taken up from the soil by plants and how much is lost to the environment. The efficient use of fertilisers is important not only because they are expensive but also because the wrong use of fertilisers or over-fertilisation may cause environmental damage. These experiments have led to improved fertiliser techniques and improved crop production in all parts of the world.

Radiation-induced mutations of plant genes have produced many properties in plants which are of value to the agricultural community. Mutations giving earlier or later maturing times in crops such as wheat, rice, and barley allow crops to escape frost, drought, or pests. Increased disease resistance and increased yields obtained by radiation-induced mutations can both help produce bigger crops. Improved agronomic characteristics can be induced in plants such as better winter hardiness, greater heat tolerance, and better adaptability to poor soil conditions. There are now about three hundred useful radiation-induced mutants covering a whole range of agricultural products from fruit crops to cut flowers.

Insect control through the sterile insect technique has been achieved, or is in progress, for the Mediterranean fruit fly, the tsetse fly, melon fly, and screw-worm fly among others.[11] In this technique, laboratory-reared male insects are irradiated with sufficient radiation dose to sterilise them. These sterilised males are then released in very large numbers in infested areas. They mate with the females, but they do not produce offspring. It is possible to reduce the insect population drastically by repeated applications of this technique. An early successful application was the eradication of the screw-worm fly on the Caribbean island of Curacao. Since then other populations of insects have been eradicated, and programs are currently under way in many countries.

The measurement of the radioisotopes tritium and carbon–14 and the stable isotope oxygen–18 in ground and surface waters has provided information in many parts of the world on water supplies. During the examination of surface waters, the dynamics of water movement into and out of lakes and reservoirs have been established, as have rates of charge and discharge of rivers. Measurements have been made of leakage through dams and the transport of sediments either suspended in water or in river beds. Ground waters have been examined to determine their origin, availability, and renewability. These studies are important in water resource management, particularly in arid parts of the globe.

Radiation-attenuated vaccines are routinely used to protect farm animals from diseases. Radiation is used to reduce the pathogenicity of the particular parasite stage used in the production of the vaccine without decreasing its immunising capability. For example, radio-vaccines have been developed against lungworm diseases in cattle and sheep, and against canine hookworm.

Radiation can also be a valuable tool in food preservation.[12] Up to half the food harvest in some countries is lost by spoilage. Part of this loss can be avoided by irradiating the food with gamma rays from cobalt–60. In 1983 the Codex Alimentarius Commission proposed allowing food irradiation under certain conditions and incorporated these conditions in its International Standards for Irradiated Foods. Currently there are about ten irradiators world-wide dedicated solely to food irradiation and about twenty-five multi-purpose irradiators which irradiate some food products. About twenty-eight countries have approved some applications of food irradiation, and it is estimated that over 500,000 tonnes of food were irradiated in 1986. Food preservation by irradiation can often provide considerable benefits, and its use is expected to grow considerably, particularly in developing countries.

The benefits of nuclear energy are so numerous, diverse, and widespread that all countries in the world have gained from its use. Any one of the benefits listed above justifies the small, controlled risks of nuclear energy. Taken together, they present an overwhelming justification.

The Game

The anti-nuclear establishment often denigrates some of the benefits that nuclear energy brings to society. Primarily, its choler is directed against nuclear generated electricity. To this end Energy Probe has conducted what amounts to a crusade against Ontario Hydro.

Any objective evaluation of Ontario Hydro would show it to be a company which is not without faults. But it would also show that it is one of the most competent and best run organisations in Canada. However, listening to Energy Probe one wonders if the same can be said of its competence and efficiency.

The quotations below demonstrate how the anti-nuclear establishment spreads its message that there are no benefits arising from the use of nuclear energy.

". . . uranium has only two alternative destinations. It invariably ends up either in nuclear weapons or in nuclear wastes" (Gordon Edwards, CCNR).[13]

This statement is misleading.

It ignores all the benefits which flow from the peaceful uses of nuclear energy derived from uranium. These benefits, to areas such as medicine, industry, research, and agriculture, are spelled out in the first half of this chapter.

"In economic terms, nuclear power has been a multi-billion-dollar boondoggle which could not survive without massive governmental bail-outs" (Gordon Edwards, CCNR).[14]

"But CANDU has become an economic black hole; the federal Government has poured hundreds of millions of dollars into this technology with no hope of ever recovering the money" (David Suzuki, Energy Probe).[15]

These statements are inaccurate.

Since 1945 the federal government has spent about $5 billion in research and development (R & D) into nuclear science and engineering. Currently, expenditures are between $0.1 and $0.2 billion per year. Much of this money, but by no means all of it, has gone into the development of the CANDU nuclear power reactor system. As a result of this R & D investment, Canada now has a nuclear power industry with a capital value of about $30 billion. Ontario Hydro has already saved more than the federal government's $5 billion investment in R & D. By the early 1990s, Ontario Hydro will be saving about $1 billion *per year* in electricity generation costs by using nuclear power rather than the only practical alternative— coal. In addition, about $0.7 billion *per year* in foreign exchange will be saved by not buying coal from the U.S.A. to generate Ontario's coal-fired electricity.

Despite these facts, which show nuclear power to have been a highly successful economic endeavour, the anti-nuclear establishment regularly condemns nuclear power as an economic disaster.

"At present [Ontario] Hydro sucks up capital for projects that no sane investor would touch . . ." (David Poch, Energy Probe).[16]

This statement is inaccurate.

Ontario Hydro raises money from normal commercial lending institutions. It is hardly likely that these hard-headed investors are all insane. They know that Ontario Hydro, whose bonds are backed by the Government of Ontario, has been awarded a triple-A credit rating by the investment community.

"The annual fuel saving attributed to its nuclear program by Ontario Hydro would barely suffice to pay the annual operating budgets of Atomic Energy of Canada Limited (AECL) and the Atomic Energy Control Board (AECB), both of which come from the federal treasury" (Gordon Edwards, CCNR).[17]

This statement is inaccurate.

When Edwards made this statement (1982), AECL and AECB budgets were about $200 million and $20 million per year respectively. At that time, the annual saving to Ontario Hydro by using uranium instead of coal was about $600 million per year. In addition, by using Canadian uranium instead of U.S. coal, Canada was benefitting by about $400 million per year in avoiding foreign exchange outflow.

HIBERNIA—BRUCE

The public, and the anti-nuclear establishment, frequently do not realise the enormous contribution to our energy supplies made by nuclear electricity.

It has been pointed out by D. K. Evans of AECL that the potential production of oil from the Hibernia field off the east coast of Canada is 525–650 million barrels, which will produce thermal energy of 3–3.5 billion gigajoules.[18] The electrical energy from the CANDU reactors at Ontario Hydro's Bruce station, running at 80 per cent of capacity, will produce an equivalent amount of electrical energy in twenty to twenty-five years.

Since Hibernia is expected to be depleted in about eighteen years, the rates of energy production from Hibernia and Bruce are roughly the same. However, the total energy production from Bruce should be twice that of Hibernia since Bruce's reactors are expected to last forty years.

The Canadian government's share of the cost of Hibernia development will be up to $3.2 billion. The total cost to the federal government for the development of its nuclear power program since 1945 is about $5 billion, and that money covers the development of the Pickering and Darlington nuclear power stations too.

❖ ❖ ❖

". . . *nuclear power as it now exists cannot possibly replace oil, or even make a significant contribution in that direction*" (Gordon Edwards, CCNR).[19]

This statement is misleading.

The major advantage of oil as an energy source is its portability. When oil (and natural gas) supplies become depleted, portable energy could be provided by high-capacity electrical batteries. These batteries will be charged by electricity. An alternative energy medium, which will provide vehicles with a longer range than batteries, is hydrogen. This fuel is compact and clean burning. It is being increasingly regarded as the energy source of the future. The most convenient way to make hydrogen is to electrolyse water, using electricity from nuclear power. Once our supplies of oil and gas become depleted, electricity will be increasingly required not only as a primary energy source, but also to manufacture other fuels which will replace oil and gas.

"Moreover, alternative energy analyses indicate that non-nuclear approaches to the problem of satisfying our future energy needs are more economically sound than heavy reliance on nuclear power" (Gordon Edwards, CCNR).[20]

This statement is misleading.

As noted in chapter 7, alternative energy sources are not economically competitive with nuclear power in Canada and are not likely to be so for the foreseeable future. It is generally found that the "alternative energy analyses" which show the opposite have been carried out by ideological think-tanks whose primary motivation may be persuasion rather than research.

"It seems equally clear that the only rationale at this time for building the Darlington reactors in Ontario or a second Point Lepreau reactor in New Brunswick is to keep the nuclear industry alive. Neither province is short of electricity; in fact both provinces have substantial surpluses" (Gordon Edwards, CCNR, 1984).[21]

"Because the power produced by Darlington will not be needed by us . . ." (L. Solomon, Energy Probe, 1983).[22]

These statements are inaccurate.

During most of the 1980s, a common theme of the anti-nuclear "experts" was that the Darlington nuclear power station was surplus to requirements. Fortunately Ontario Hydro did not listen to these "experts," and by the end of the 1980s it has become apparent that Darlington's four units, which will come on stream between 1990 and 1992, will indeed be needed.[23] New Brunswick, too, will require additional electrical generating capacity in the 1990s,[24] but it is presently unclear whether it will be provided by nuclear or coal, or both.

Even with the additional supply from Darlington, if the Ontario economy continues to expand at the rate it has for the last few years, there could be brown-outs or even black-outs in the province by the mid- to late 1990s. It will be possible to delay the effect of these shortages for a few years by spending about $1.2 billion to upgrade some old, expensive, and environmentally dirty coal-fired power plants, but even with their assistance the time is fast approaching when new power plants will be required. It takes about ten years to plan and construct a nuclear power station, and some experts think it may already be too late to avoid serious energy shortages in Ontario in the 1990s and beyond. Meanwhile, it is believed that even the anti-nuclear establishment no longer makes any serious claim that Darlington is not required.

JAPAN

The actions of one country, Japan, clearly demonstrate the benefits of nuclear energy compared with alternative energy sources.

Japan possesses few conventional energy resources and must import almost all of its gas, oil, coal, and uranium. Thus it has a strong incentive to use alternative energy sources. Japan also has the innovative research sector, the industrial strength, and the economic resources to develop, manufacture, and employ alternative energy sources.

Despite these incentives and abilities, Japan has made nuclear energy its fastest growing energy source and rarely chooses alternative energy sources for electricity generation.

Japan obviously relies on reality rather than ideology to consolidate and expand its position in world markets.

"Since 1973 [Ontario] Hydro [electricity] rates have tripled . . ."
(L. Solomon, Energy Probe, 1983).[25]

This statement is misleading.

Energy Probe forgot to tell its audience that over the same period, 1973–1983, natural gas and oil prices also increased. Discounting inflation, hydro electricity rates went up by 40 per cent, natural gas by 198 per cent, and oil by 338 per cent.

". . . Ontarians pay more for electricity than the average Canadian . . ."
(L. Solomon, Energy Probe, 1983).[26]

This statement is inaccurate.

At the time this statement was made, the "average" urban Canadian who used 1,000 kilowatt-hours of electricity per month received a bill of about 5.2 cents per kilowatt-hour. In Ontario the corresponding bill was 4.2 cents in Toronto, 4.0 cents in Ottawa, and 4.4 cents in London. (These figures are for 1983.)

"After Darlington is built, only 300 full-time jobs will be needed to run and maintain it" (L. Solomon, Energy Probe).[27]

This statement is misleading.

Nuclear power stations are not built to provide jobs directly; they are built to provide electricity. However, employment is increased by the promise of cheap, reliable electricity. Low-cost electricity in Ontario has attracted many companies, such as automobile manufacturers, to locate in the province and thus provide jobs.

The anti-nuclear establishment is fond of pointing out that more jobs could be provided by using small-scale dispersed alternative energy sources rather than large-scale nuclear sources. This may be true, but it is also true that a major feature of alternative energy sources is the labour cost required to keep them operational. These labour costs help make alternative energy sources expensive compared with nuclear or even coal-powered facilities. The net result of changing to alternative energy sources would be increased energy costs resulting in reduced production and a reduction in available jobs.

"[Ontario] Hydro has already piled up a $16 billion debt—greater than that of most Third World countries" (L. Solomon, Energy Probe).[28]

This statement is misleading.

A company's debt must be compared to its assets, not with Third World countries, in order for any fiscal pronouncements to be meaningful. Ontario Hydro's assets, at $21.5 billion when the above statement was made, are always far in excess of its debts.

This statement is also a good example of providing misleading information by failure to make relevant comparisons—this time with other provinces. Ontario is Canada's most populous province. The *per capita* debt of its electrical utility, Ontario Hydro, is the third lowest of the electrical utilities in Canada's ten provinces.

"Even the market for medical radioisotopes has been declining" (Gordon Edwards, CCNR).[29]

This statement is inaccurate.

The market for medical radioisotopes has been expanding ever since they were first produced in quantity at Chalk River in 1947. There was a quantum jump in use after Canada first introduced the large-scale production of fission-derived molybdenum–99 (the source of technetium–99m) in 1974. Considering that many Third World countries will likely use medical radioisotopes when they acquire the technical facilities and capabilities, the scope for further expansion of the market is obvious.

". . . radioisotopes used in medicine, agriculture and industry do not require a nuclear reactor for their production. They can be produced in cyclotrons and in various other types of accelerators" (Gordon Edwards, CCNR).[30]

This statement is misleading.

Many types of radioisotopes can be produced in accelerators, but these devices are used mainly for producing short-lived radioisotopes, some of which are useful for medical diagnosis. It would be uneconomic to produce in an accelerator long-lived materials such as cobalt–60 (half-life about five years), which is used in medical therapy. The statement is misleading because although it may be technically feasible, it would be economically impracticable to replace reactor-produced radioisotopes with accelerator-produced radioisotopes.

> *"The Canadian nuclear industry and its government sponsors have never had a mandate from the Canadian people to pursue a nuclear option for Canada. Canada's involvement in the nuclear fuel cycle has been imposed on Canadians from above without public consultation"* (New Democratic Party [NDP]).[31]

These statements are unjustified by the facts.

All funds for the development of Canada's nuclear program have been provided by vote by the representatives of the people in Parliament. The votes, which usually provided funds to AECL, were normally approved by members of all parties. Approval was assisted by presentations made by AECL representatives to the House of Commons Special Committee on Research and later to the Natural Resources and Public Works Committee.

The members of today's NDP seem unaware that their predecessors in Parliament enthusiastically endorsed the setting up of Canada's nuclear power program in the 1950s.[32] Then party leader Tommy Douglas and energy critic Stanley Knowles always supported the nuclear program in the House. In the early 1960s, when the U.S.A. stopped buying uranium from Canada and it looked as if our uranium industry would collapse, it was the NDP members who took up cudgels on behalf of the uranium miners and urged the government to increase the pace of its nuclear power program in order to provide a market for Canada's uranium. In the mid-1960s, Tommy Douglas spoke in support of the construction of the Pickering reactors, noting that nuclear power was "a field of endeavour in which government planning and public enterprise can play a very important part."[33] In the mid-1970s, Tommy Douglas still supported nuclear energy, even though he claimed to speak as "a layman who is wallowing in a sea of abysmal ignorance in a field as complicated as nuclear energy."[34] The debates in Hansard would make interesting reading for some of today's NDP members who claim that the public has been excluded from nuclear decision-making.

CHAPTER 10

Who to Believe?

THE DECLARED PURPOSE OF THIS BOOK HAS BEEN TO PERSUADE the reader that the dangers of Canada's nuclear industry have been greatly exaggerated by the anti-nuclear establishment, to the extent that the public has been misled into believing that the nuclear industry is one of the more dangerous, rather than one of the safest, energy industries operating today.

However, no matter how persuasively this book has been written there probably remain some doubts in the minds of some people. How can the average reader judge between what he or she has read here and what he or she has been told by the anti-nuclear establishment? With limited expertise in these issues and a limited amount of time, how can the average reader assess the merits of the arguments on both sides?

A good way to decide this question of credibility would be to obtain a third opinion on the subject. This would be the opinion of someone who does not have an axe to grind, who has had access to all the relevant information and has studied all aspects of the issues impartially, and who has arrived at a considered and balanced judgement on the safety of nuclear power.

There are several ways in which a reliable and independent third-party opinion could be obtained. It would be possible, for example, to set up a commission presided over by a judge to receive evidence from all sides. A judge is familiar with the problem of distinguishing true evidence from false and with wading through massive quantities of complex arguments to arrive at an impartial judgement.

Or a commission could be set up presided over by a distinguished academic from one of our universities. Senior university professors are usually very intelligent people, well equipped to sort through all the facts presented to them in order to arrive at a conclusion.

A third possibility would be a commission of laymen representing us, the people. Such a group would consist of our elected representatives to Parliament drawn from each of the three major political parties, who would listen to the debate, question the proponents on each side, and then vote on the issues.

Any of these three types of commission would be a satisfactory way of deciding the pro- versus anti-nuclear arguments. In fact, all three types have been set up in Canada just for that purpose—and all three have decided in favour of Canada's nuclear power program. Although each has had reservations about some aspects of the nuclear power industry, all three commissions have given the nuclear industry what is basically a resounding vote of confidence. It is worthwhile studying these three commissions more closely.

THE CLUFF LAKE INQUIRY

In the mid-1970s a mining company proposed to exploit some of the rich uranium deposits at Cluff Lake in northern Saskatchewan. The anti-nuclear establishment in the province protested, claiming that the mining would contaminate the environment and that the uranium would be used in unsafe nuclear reactors or, worse, would be used to manufacture atomic bombs. There was sufficient public pressure that the Saskatchewan government set up a commission presided over by Mr. Justice Bayda of the Saskatchewan Supreme Court to advise it on this issue.[1]

Although the immediate issue was the opening of a uranium mine at Cluff Lake, the terms of the inquiry were extraordinarily wide. It was appointed "to conduct a public inquiry into the probable environmental, health, safety, social and economical effects of the proposed uranium mine and mill at Cluff Lake, as well as the social, economic and other implications of the expansion of the uranium mining industry in Saskatchewan."[2] These terms of reference allowed for evidence to be presented on all aspects of the nuclear controversy, and the anti-nuclear establishment brought its best efforts to bear in order to convince the commission of its views.

The inquiry sat in formal hearings for sixty-seven days and heard 138 witnesses. There were 39 intervenors from Saskatchewan, 30 from the rest of Canada, and 26 from overseas. These last included a number of the peripatetic anti-nuclear experts who have been mentioned in the Introduction of this book.

One of the imported experts was Amory Lovins, representing the Friends of the Earth. Lovins presented his case in favour of soft path energy strategies and against the use of nuclear power, but the commission was not impressed. In its report the commission stated that ". . . Lovins has made a moral judgement that nuclear energy is not only bad for society but is also unnecessary and, therefore, the motives or intentions of those who promote the use of nuclear power are also suspect. The standards which he uses are, in our view, too simple to answer the ethical questions of nuclear power in today's world."[3]

In addition to listening to the experts, the commission also criss-crossed the province listening to the concerns of the ordinary citizen. For consideration of the moral and ethical issues relating to nuclear energy, the commission hoped for guidance from the churches. However, the Inter-Church Energy Committee of Saskatchewan, whose members are appointed by the Anglican, Lutheran, Presbyterian, Roman Catholic, and United Church of Canada denominations, boycotted the inquiry. Although the commissioners wrote to each of the churches requesting assistance, they received none. Nonetheless one of the denominations published a pamphlet against the use of nuclear energy, and of the fourteen clergymen who voiced their personal views, the commission noted that ten presented the same anti-nuclear viewpoint as the pamphlet.

The commission was set up in February 1977 and did not report until fifteen months later, in May 1978. The transcripts of the hearings ran to 13,524 pages with an additional 337 exhibits. The final report of the commission contained over 400 pages and it provides one of the best expositions of the pro- and anti-nuclear arguments ever produced. As might be expected from a commission presided over by a judge, the arguments in the final report are detailed and clear. After examining all aspects of the nuclear scene from mining to wastes disposal, from health and safety to moral and ethical issues, the final conclusion of the commission is worth quoting:

> To address ourselves finally to the last question posed in our opening chapter—are the negative broader implications of mining uranium of sufficient force to warrant not proceeding with the mine and, if they are, do they continue to be so even after they are balanced against the broader positive implications?—we conclude that the broader negative implications when balanced against the positive ones are not of sufficient force to warrant not proceeding with the Cluff Lake mine/mill or other uranium mines/mills in Saskatchewan.[4]

THE PORTER INQUIRY

Another commission of inquiry into nuclear power was set up under a distinguished academic, Dr. Arthur Porter, professor emeritus of industrial engineering at the University of Toronto, and reported in 1980. The commission was the Royal Commission on Electric Power Planning, which was asked by the Ontario government to examine the long-range electric power planning concepts of Ontario Hydro. Since nuclear power figures prominently in Ontario Hydro's future plans, the opportunity was taken to explore the whole nuclear option.[5]

The Porter Commission took considerable pains to see that the public was informed of the issues being discussed and assured it of participation in the discussion. A consulting firm hired by the commission studied awareness, attitudes, and expectations of the public with respect to energy. A Public Interest Coalition was created to provide the public and those groups not already identified as "interest groups" with enough information to allow them to participate in the hearings.

The inquiry was conducted in three stages. In the first, exploratory stage a comprehensive view of the issues to be addressed was developed. In the second stage, information was gathered concerning these issues, and in the third stage the issues received detailed consideration in the form of a debate between those holding opposing viewpoints.

Greatest attention was given by the commission to the safety of Ontario's CANDU nuclear reactors. Despite the efforts of the anti-nuclear establishment, the commission found that these reactors are safe within reasonable limits and that continued operation should be allowed.[6]

The commission also found that the present methods of storage of spent fuel at reactor sites will be satisfactory for the next thirty years, but a long-term disposal plan was called for with the recommendation that a moratorium on the further development of nuclear power be imposed if satisfactory progress towards a permanent waste disposal solution is not achieved by 1990.[7] From the pro-nuclear viewpoint this is a fair recommendation, particularly since progress in this issue since the commission reported has been uniformly rapid and successful.

It is worth noting that some of the same overseas anti-nuclear activists who gave evidence to the Bayda Commission also did so at the Porter Commission. Amory Lovins was there again, and the commission recommended further research into soft energy sources. However, Lovins was unsuccessful in persuading the Porter Commission that nuclear power should be abolished.

THE ONTARIO SELECT COMMITTEE

The third investigation into nuclear power in Canada was carried out by members of the Ontario Legislature sitting as the Select Committee on Hydro Affairs. This committee was established in December 1977 with Mr. Donald C. MacDonald (NDP, York South) as chairman. The committee consisted of fourteen members, six from the then majority Progressive Conservative Party and four each from the two other parties, the Liberals and the New Democratic Party (NDP).[8]

Its mandate was to examine and report on several matters relating to the activities of Ontario Hydro. Among the topics first examined by the committee were Ontario Hydro's proposed uranium contracts with both Denison and Preston mines, and the construction of heavy-water plants at the Bruce nuclear site. The committee then turned its attention to the safety of Ontario's nuclear reactors. In sixteen weeks of exhaustive hearings which spread over a full calendar year, and which spanned the serious nuclear accident at Three Mile Island in the U.S.A., all aspects of Ontario's nuclear reactor safety, design, licensing, practice, and compliance were thoroughly examined.

Nearly 100 witnesses appeared before the committee, and 150 exhibits were tabled. Much information from the nuclear industry and the Atomic Energy Control Board, which had hitherto been treated as "commercially confidential," was disclosed to the committee. This information, amounting to 436 volumes, was placed for public reference in the Legislative Library and in the Ontario Hydro Public Reference Centre.

The most significant conclusion of the members of the committee was that Ontario's nuclear reactors (CANDU reactors) were "acceptably safe." They came to this conclusion after a detailed examination of all the evidence and after considering the arguments for and against the safety of the reactors presented by the pro- and anti-nuclear advocates.

They went into the technicalities of nuclear reactors in greater depth than the Porter Commission, mainly because they were offered so much more technical information on the operation of CANDU reactors by Ontario Hydro. The committee concluded that the chance of a serious accident occurring in a nuclear reactor is extremely small and that the benefits derived from nuclear power are worth the very small risks incurred. They explicitly noted that, in dealing with safety, absolutes are misleading, and they made themselves familiar with the scientific concept of risk.

They also noted that their judgement that nuclear reactors are acceptably safe must be a political/societal judgement of the ratio of benefits to risks. The risks were judged to be very small and were outweighed by the benefits of nuclear power, which they described as competitively priced, Ontario-based energy from generating stations that are relatively non-polluting in normal operation.

Three of the fourteen members put in a dissenting opinion to the statement that Ontario's reactors are "acceptably safe." They argued that since Ontario already has a nuclear power program, the risks associated with it must, by any reasonable person, be accepted. Therefore the conclusion by the other members that the reactors are acceptably safe had been conditioned by supply and financial considerations and not solely by safety considerations.

The three dissenting members belonged to the NDP. Before the committee hearings on nuclear reactors began, the Ontario NDP (but not the federal NDP at that time) had adopted a policy statement condemning the use of nuclear power in Ontario. The fourth NDP member on the committee did not sign the dissenting opinion.

THE SIZEWELL B INQUIRY

The most recent large-scale public inquiry into nuclear power was conducted not in Canada but in the U.K. from January 11, 1983 to March 7, 1985. It was known as the Sizewell B Inquiry and was presided over by Sir Frank Layfield, Q.C.

The inquiry had been asked to report on an application by the U.K. Central Electricity Generating Board (CEGB) for consent to construct a pressurised-water reactor at a site in Sizewell, Suffolk. The terms of the inquiry were very wide, covering the technical and economic as well as the social and ethical aspects of the complete nuclear fuel cycle from mining, through reactor safety and waste disposal, to nuclear proliferation.

The U.K. anti-nuclear establishment, assisted by some overseas colleagues, objected to all aspects of nuclear energy connected with the building of the reactor. The inquiry listened to evidence presented on both sides of all the issues, and counsel for the inquiry questioned the evidence in detail. As a result, the inquiry lasted 340 days, spread over more than two years, and collected 16 million words of evidence. The final report, published in 1986, is exceptionally thorough in its treatment of the issues and is decisive in its favourable view of the merits of nuclear power compared with alternative energy sources.[9]

Many of the arguments used against the Sizewell reactor are similar to those used against Canada's domestic nuclear industry, demonstrating the international homogeneity of the anti-nuclear game. Some of the relevant conclusions and recommendations of the report with respect to those arguments are listed below.[10]

NUCLEAR SAFETY

"The safety criteria for both normal operation and for accidents are likely to be generally satisfied by the design."

"An accident at Sizewell B, if built, would almost certainly have tolerable consequences, at worst requiring measures such as the banning of milk near the station."

"The probability of an uncontrolled release as the result of a degraded core is probably between once in ten million years and once in a million years."

"Theoretically possible accidents which could cause hundreds or thousands of deaths would almost certainly not occur."

RADIATION RELEASES FROM NORMAL OPERATION

"The maximum additional individual dose to a member of the public from Sizewell B would be no more than of the order of 1% of the dose from natural background radiation."

WASTE DISPOSAL

"The CEGB's conclusion that the safe disposal of all types of radioactive waste was technically feasible was not disputed."

"There are no reasons connected with the management of radioactive waste why consent for Sizewell B should be refused."

SPENT FUEL TRANSPORTATION

"In comparison with most other safety issues considered in the report, the safety of spent fuel transport gives extremely little justification for anxiety."

DECOMMISSIONING

"The CEGB demonstrated that the safe decommissioning of Sizewell B would be feasible."

THREE MILE ISLAND (TMI)

"The TMI accident showed that even an accident involving a large number of serious shortcomings and errors affecting design, human factors and the arrangements for regulating nuclear safety does not necessarily cause significant harm to people."

RENEWABLES

"I therefore conclude that renewable energy sources do not provide an alternative to Sizewell B, either as a cost-saving investment or to meet capacity need."

COSTS

"My conclusion is that Sizewell B is likely to be the least cost choice for new generating capacity. The probability of a coal station having lower costs is remote."

CIVIL LIBERTIES

"Grant of consent for Sizewell B would not, in my opinion, lead inevitably to a great expansion in the production of plutonium with an attendant need for increased security and potential restriction of civil liberties."

CONCLUSION

The average reader who feels confused by the nuclear issues should consider seriously the results of these inquiries. There is no doubt that nuclear power has its risks, and they need to be carefully controlled. But whenever the risks have been compared with the benefits carefully, conscientiously, and competently by independent inquiries, the result has always been the same. The use of nuclear power has been endorsed.

It is not likely that all these inquiries have been wrong. It is more likely that the anti-nuclear game, when examined by intelligent, informed people, will always stand revealed for what it really is, a game only.

There is a role, and an important one, in today's society for critics of nuclear power. The need for the nuclear option and the safety of the nuclear option must be questioned continually by critics outside the nuclear industry. The present anti-nuclear establishment has forfeited playing a legitimate role in this exercise by its reliance on dubious methods to convince the public of its cause. Until the anti-nuclear establishment abandons its current methods of persuasion, it will not, and should not, be taken seriously by the nuclear industry, the government, or the public.

Notes

CHAPTER 1: INTRODUCTION

1. Atomic Energy of Canada Limited, *Technical Summary: CANDU Nuclear Generating Station* (Mississauga, Ont.: n.d.).
2. Samuel McCracken, *The War against the Atom* (New York: Basic Books, 1982), particularly chapter 6.
3. Mark P. Mills, "Journalism and Nuclear Energy," *The Health Physics Society's News Letter*, 15, no. 2 (1987), p. 2.
4. U. Hans Behling and James E. Hildebrand, *Radiation and Health Effects: A Report on the TMI-2 Accident and Related Health Studies* (n.p.: GPU Nuclear Corporation, 1986).
5. Atomic Energy Control Board, *The Accident at Chernobyl and Its Implications for the Safety of CANDU Reactors*, INFO–0234(E) (1987).
6. Amory B. Lovins and L. Hunter Lovins, "Nuclear Bomb and Nuclear Power," *Foreign Affairs* 58 (1980), p. 1137
7. Frank A. Iddings, "Doubts about New Technologies Old Hat, History Shows," *Montreal Gazette*, 26 February 1984, Sec. I, p. 26.
8. Geoffrey Greenhalgh, *The Necessity for Nuclear Power* (London: Graham and Trotman, 1980), pp. 229 ff.
9. *Energy Probe Research Foundation* [brochure] (Toronto, 1987).
10. Private communication with Energy Probe.
11. House of Commons, Standing Committee on Environment and Forestry, *Proceedings*, no. 7, 3 February 1987, p. 19.
12. *International Institute of Concern for Public Health* [brochure] (Toronto, 1987).
13. John W. Gofman, *Radiation and Human Health* (San Francisco: Sierra Club Books, 1981), p. 698.
14. Rosalie Bertell, "X-Ray Exposure and Premature Aging," *Journal of Surgical Oncology*, 9 (1977), p. 379.
15. Elaine Carey, "Honors Piling Up for Rebel Nun," *Sunday Star*, 25 January 1987, Sec. D, p. 5.

16. Robert Bott, David Brooks, and John Robinson, *Life after Oil* (Edmonton: Hurtig, 1983).
17. Interfaith Program for Public Awareness of Nuclear Issues, *Final Report*, November 1985.
18. Walter Robbins, *Getting the Shaft* (Winnipeg: Queenston House, 1984).
19. House of Commons, Standing Committee, *Proceedings*, p. 43.
20. "Eurobarometre Survey, no. 17," sponsored by the Commission of the European Community, April 1982, as cited in Ronald Inglehart, "The Fear of Living Dangerously: Public Attitudes toward Nuclear Power," *Public Opinion*, February/March 1984, p. 41.
21. Quoted in "Former NRC Member, Ahearne, Speaks Out on Nuclear Energy," *Atomic Industrial Forum*, 2/INFO 179 (1986).
22. World Health Organization, *Mental Health Aspects of the Peaceful Uses of Atomic Energy*, WHO Technical Report Series, no. 151 (1958).
23. E. Sokolowski, "Can Fear of Nuclear Power Be Met with Rational Arguments?" *Nuclear Europe*, 8–9 (1988), p. 10.
24. S. Rothman and S. R. Lichter, "The Nuclear Energy Debate: Scientists, the Media, and the Public," *Public Opinion*, August/September 1982, p. 47.
25. B.A.J. Lister, "Transuranium Nuclides in the Environment," *Proceedings of IAEA Symposium, San Francisco*, 17–21 November 1975, p. 641 [comment made during a panel discussion].
26. Daniel Machalaba, "Nuclear Fallout: Press Becomes a Big Factor in the Continuing Fight over Three Mile Island; Editor: 'We're Being Used,' " *Wall Street Journal*, 24 August 1983, p. 11.
27. Quoted in Leonard J. Theberge, "The Role of the American Media in Covering Nuclear Power: Where Is the Balance?" Seventh Annual Symposium of the Uranium Institute, London, 1–3 September 1982.
28. David Suzuki, in "Problems and Risks of Producing Nuclear Energy," *The Nature of Things*, CBC Television, 25 November 1987.

CHAPTER 2: RADIATION AND HEALTH

1. G. Agricola, *De Re Metallica*, trans. H. D. Hoover and L. H. Hoover (New York: Dover, 1950).
2. Ontario, Ministry of the Attorney General, *Report of the Royal Commission on the Health and Safety of Workers in Mines* (Toronto, 1976), usually referred to as the Ham Commission Report.
3. United Nations, Scientific Committee on the Effects of Atomic Radiation (UNSCEAR), *Ionizing Radiation: Sources and Biological Effects 1982* (New York: United Nations, 1982).
4. National Academy of Sciences, National Research Council, Advisory Committee on the Biological Effects of Ionizing Radiation (BEIR), *The Effects*

on Populations of Exposure to Low Levels of Ionizing Radiation (Washington, D.C., 1980).

5. American Medical Association, Advisory Panel, *Risks of Nuclear Energy and Low Level Ionizing Radiation* (1981), p. 13.

6. U.S.S.R., State Committee on the Utilization of Atomic Energy, "The Accident at the Chernobyl Nuclear Power Plant and Its Consequences," International Atomic Energy Agency Post-Accident Review Meeting, Vienna, 25–29 August 1986.

7. Recent re-evaluations of the data on the Japanese survivors indicate that the risk of a fatal cancer should be increased to two to three per 10,000 person rems. So far this data has not been accepted by the ICRP, and it has not been adopted in framing Canadian radiation protection regulations.

8. Arthur C. Upton, "The Biological Effects of Low-Level Ionizing Radiation," *Scientific American*, 246, no. 2 (1982), p. 41.

9. D. K. Myers and H. B. Newcombe, *Nuclear Power and Low Level Radiation Hazards*, AECL–6482 (1979), p. 3.

10. Bernard L. Cohen, "Genetic Effects of Natural Radiation," *Ascent* (1982), p. 9.

11. Lauriston Taylor, *Radiation Protection Standards* (Cleveland: CRC Press, 1971).

12. C. C. Wang and L. L. Robbins, "Biological and Medical Effects of Radiation," in Gerald H. Hine and Gordon L. Brownell, *Radiation Dosimetry* (New York: Academic Press, 1956).

13. A. Mutscheller, "Physical Standards of Protection against Roentgen-Ray Dangers," *The American Journal of Roentgenology and Radium Therapy*, 13 (1925), p. 65.

14. Lauriston S. Taylor, "Reminiscences about the Early Days of Organised Radiation Protection," in L. Kathren and Paul L. Ziemer, *Health Physics: A Backward Glance* (New York: Pergamon Press, 1980).

15. "International Recommendations for X-Ray and Radium Protection 1934," *Radiology*, 23 (1934), p. 682.

16. "International Commission on Radiological Units, 1953," *British Journal of Radiology*, 27 (1954), p. 243.

17. H. C. Marsh, in *Radiology*, 43 (1944), p. 275.

18. H. J. Muller, in *Science*, 46 (1927), p. 84.

19. "International Recommendations on Radiological Protection, 1950," *Radiology*, 56 (1951), p. 431.

20. National Academy of Sciences, National Research Council, *The Biological Effects of Atomic Radiation* (1956).

21. *Recommendations of the International Commission on Radiological Protection*, ICRP Publication, no. 26 (Oxford: Pergamon Press, 1977).

22. J. S. Mitchell, *Memorandum on Some Aspects of the Biological Action of Radiation*, Report HI–17, Montreal Laboratory, 20 November 1945, p. 5.

23. *The Atomic Energy Control Act*, Geo VI, Ch. 37, 31 August 1946.
24. Department of National Health and Welfare, Occupational Health Division, Radiation Services, *Summary of the Recommendations of the International Commission on Radiological Protection (1954)* (Ottawa, 1955).
25. "Atomic Energy Regulations of Canada," SOR/47–327, *The Canada Gazette*, Part II, 1 April 1947.
26. T. F. Mancuso, A. Stewart, and G. Kneale, "Radiation Exposures of Hanford Workers Dying from Cancer and Other Causes," *Health Physics*, 33 (1977), p. 369.
27. T. Najarian and T. Colton, "Mortality from Leukemia and Cancer in Shipyard Nuclear Workers," *Lancet*, 1 (1978), p. 1018.
28. John W. Gofman, *Radiation and Human Health* (San Francisco: Sierra Club Books, 1981).
29. Rosalie Bertell, *Handbook for Estimating Health Effects from Exposure to Ionizing Radiation* (Toronto: International Institute of Concern for Public Health, 1984).
30. D. P. Geesaman, *UCRL–50387 and Addendum*, Lawrence Livermore Laboratory, 1968.
31. George L. Voelz, Louis H. Hempelman, J.N.P. Lawrence, and William D. Moss, "A 32-Year Medical Follow-Up of Manhattan Project Plutonium Workers," *Health Physics*, 37 (1979), p. 445.
32. J. H. Fremlin, "Radiation Hormesis," *Atom 390*, April 1989, p. 4.
33. Jack Harris, "Is Radiation Good for You?" *New Scientist*, 28 May 1987, p. 63.
34. J. K. Brown, "Does a Little Radiation Do You Good?" *Nuclear Spectrum*, 3, no. 1 (1987), p. 8.
35. Bernard L. Cohen, *Before It's Too Late: A Scientist's Case for Nuclear Energy* (New York: Plenum Press, 1983), p. 31.
36. *Report of the President's Commission on the Accident at Three Mile Island* (Washington, D.C.: U.S. Government Printing House, 1979), usually referred to as the Kemeny Report.
37. Mark Roth of the Pittsburgh *Post-Gazette*, quoted in Peter Beckman, *Access to Energy*, 12, no. 6 (February 1985).
38. "Testimony by Morgan, Gofman Thrown Out of Court by Judge," *Atomic Industrial Forum*, INFO 196 (February 1985), p. 2.
39. Sir Frank Layfield, Q.C., *Report of the Sizewell B Public Enquiry*, presented to the Secretary of State for Energy, 5 December 1986.
40. Ibid., 3, Section 6, chapter 30.
41. Rosalie Bertell, "Submission to the Ontario Nuclear Safety Review," International Institute of Concern for Public Health, 1987.
42. Ontario Hydro, "Detailed Response to the IICPH Submission to the Ontario Nuclear Safety Review," 1987, pp. A5–4/5.
43. Quoted in "Review of the Evidence of Rosalie Bertell," *Sizewell B Public Enquiry: Transcript of Proceedings*, 27 February 1985.

44. Bertell, "Submission to the Ontario Nuclear Safety Review," p. 13.
45. Rosalie Bertell, *No Immediate Danger? Prognosis for a Radioactive Earth* (Toronto: Women's Educational Press, 1985), p. 1.
46. Ibid., p. 2.
47. Ibid., p. 65.
48. Ibid., p. 73.
49. D. Reid, *A Textbook of Obstetrics* (Philadelphia: W. B. Saunders Co., 1962), p. 259.
50. Bertell, *No Immediate Danger*, p. 55.
51. Ibid., p. 87.
52. Ibid., p. 17.
53. Ibid., p. 170.
54. Ibid., p. 39.
55. Rosalie Bertell, "X-Ray Exposure and Premature Aging," *Journal of Surgical Oncology*, 9 (1977).
56. Rosalie Bertell, "Environmental Influence on Survival of Low Birth Weight Infants in Wisconsin, 1963–1975," *International Perspectives on Public Health*, 1, no. 2 (1984).
57. David Poch, *Radiation Alert* (Toronto: Doubleday Canada Ltd., 1985).
58. Ibid., p. 9.
59. Ibid., p. 27.
60. Ibid., p. 28.
61. Ibid., p. 30.
62. Ibid., p. 45.
63. Ibid., p. 66.
64. Ibid., p. 66.
65. Ibid., p. 66.
66. Ibid., p. 67.
67. Ibid., p. 91.
68. Ibid., p. 69.
69. Gordon Edwards, "Estimating Lung Cancers; or, It's Perfectly Safe, but Don't Breathe Too Deeply," CCNR, 3 (1978). Reprinted and updated August 1985.
70. Ibid., p. ii.
71. J. Svec, E. Kunz, and V. Placek, "Lung Cancer in Uranium Miners and Long-term Exposure to Radon Daughter Products," *Health Physics*, 30 (1976), p. 433.
72. F. E. Lundin, J. K. Wagoner, and V. E. Archer, *Radon Daughter Exposure and Respiratory Cancer: Quantitative and Temporal Aspects*, National Institute of Occupational Safety and Health/National Institute of Environmental Health Services, Joint Monograph, no. 1 (1971), p. 138.
73. V. E. Archer, J. K. Wagoner, and F. E. Lundin, "Lung Cancer among Uranium Miners in the United States," *Health Physics*, 25 (1973), p. 351.
74. Rosalie Bertell, Evidence given under cross-examination, Waste Not Wanted

Inc. versus HM the Queen, Court of Ontario, 18 April 1984.

75. Bertell, "Submission to the Ontario Nuclear Safety Review," p. 56.
76. *Radiological Significance and Management of Tritium, Carbon–14, Krypton–85, Iodine–129, Arising from the Nuclear Fuel Cycle* [report by an NEA group of experts] (Paris: OECD/NEA, 1980).
77. Bertell, "Submission to the Ontario Nuclear Safety Review," p. 63.
78. See *Radiological Significance*.
79. American Nuclear Society, *Nuclear Power and the Environment* (1976).
80. Bertell, "Submission to the Ontario Nuclear Safety Review," p. 33.
81. David Poch, *Brief to the IPPANI Hearings*, 1–29 (1984), p. 4.
82. Thomas J. Connolly, "Reflections on the Second Nuclear Coming," *Nuclear News*, April 1986, p. 45.
83. Bertell, Evidence given under cross-examination, 18 April 1984.

CHAPTER 3: NUCLEAR POWER REACTORS

1. W. Eggleston, *Canada's Nuclear Story* (Toronto: Clarke, Irwin, 1965); Margaret Gowing, *Britain and Atomic Energy 1939–45* (London: Macmillan, 1964); Margaret Gowing, *Independence and Deterrence* (London: Macmillan, 1974).
2. Von O. Hahn and F. Strassman, "Uber den Nacheweiss und das Verhalten der bei der Bestrahlung des Urans Mittels Neutronen Enstehenden Erdalkalimetalle," *Die Naturwissenschaften*, 27 (1939), p. 11.
3. Lise Meitner and Otto Frisch, "Disintegrations of Uranium by Neutrons: A New Type of Nuclear Reaction," *Nature*, 143 (1939), p. 239.
4. H. von Halban, F. Joliot, and L. Kowalski, "Number of Neutrons Liberated in the Nuclear Fission of Uranium," *Nature*, 143 (1939), p. 680.
5. Neils Bohr and John Archibald Wheeler, "The Mechanism of Nuclear Fission," *Physical Review*, 56 (1939), p. 426.
6. H. Halban, F. Joliot, L. Kowalski, and F. Perrin, "Mise en évidence d'une réaction nucléaire en chaîne au sein d'une masse uranifère," *Le Journal de Physique et le Radium*, 10 (1939), p. 429.
7. R. Peierls, "Critical Conditions in Neutron Multiplication," *Cambridge Philosophical Society*, 35 (1939), p. 610.
8. Samuel L. Glasstone, *Sourcebook of Atomic Energy* (Princeton: D. van Nostrand, 1958), p. 449.
9. Ibid., p. 469.
10. Peter de Leon, *A Cross-National Comparison of Nuclear Reactor Development Strategies* (Santa Monica: Rand Corporation, 1976), p. 5739.
11. Irvin C. Bupp and Jean-Claude Derian, *Light Water* (New York: Basic Books, 1978), particularly chapter 4.
12. de Leon, *A Cross-National Comparison*, p. 20.

13. R. M. Brown, E. Robertson, and W. M. Thurston, *Deuterium Content of Canadian Waters*, AECL–3900 (1971).
14. W. B. Lewis, *An Atomic Power Proposal*, AECL–189 (1951).
15. House of Commons, *Debates*, 17 February 1953, p. 2011.
16. Gordon H. E. Sims, "The Evolution of AECL" (M.A. Thesis, Carleton University, 1979), p. 97.
17. W. B. Lewis, *The Accident to the NRX Reactor, Part 1*, AECL–232 (1953); D. G. Hurst, *The Accident to the NRX Reactor, Part 2*, AECL–233 (1953).
18. G. C. Laurence, "Nuclear Power Station Safety in Canada," a paper presented to the Niagara-Finger Lakes Section of the American Nuclear Society, 26 January 1972 (also published as AECB–1058).
19. W. G. Morrison et al., "Containment Systems Capability," *Nuclear Journal of Canada*, 1, no. 1 (1987), p. 53.
20. D. G. Hurst and F. C. Boyd, *Reactor Licensing and Safety Requirements*, AECB–1059 (1972).
21. Gordon H. E. Sims, *A History of the Atomic Energy Control Board* (Ottawa: Supply and Services Canada, 1981), chapter 8.
22. United States Atomic Energy Commission, *Theoretical Possibilities and Consequences of Major Accidents in Large Nuclear Power Plants*, WASH–740 (1957). Despite its title, this report only dealt with consequences.
23. *Reactor Safety Study*, Nuclear Regulatory Commission Document, WASH–1400, NUREG 75/014 (1975).
24. George Tokuhata and Edward Digon, *Cancer Mortality and Mobility (Incidence) around TMI* (n.p.: Pennsylvania Department of Health, 1985).
25. L. Ray Silver, *Fall-Out from Chernobyl* (Toronto: Deneau Publishers, 1987).
26. "Chernobyl Babies," *New Scientist*, 19 February 1987, p. 22.
27. V. G. Snell and J. Q. Howieson, *Chernobyl: A Canadian Technical Perspective*, AECL–9334s (1987).
28. Atomic Energy Control Board, *The Accident at Chernobyl and Its Implications for the Safety of CANDU Reactors*, INFO–0234(E) (1987).
29. J.A.L. Robertson, *Nuclear Energy in Canada: The CANDU System*, AECL–6328 (rev. 1) (1984).
30. J. T. Rogers, "Candu Moderator Provides Ultimate Heat Sink in a LOCA," *Nuclear Engineering International*, 24 (1979), p. 280; R. A. Brown, "Consequences of Nuclear Accidents" [presentation to the Ontario Nuclear Safety Review Workshop on the Safety of Ontario's CANDU Reactors, Toronto, 1987]; Atomic Energy of Canada Limited, "The Safety of Ontario's Nuclear Power Reactors: A Scientific and Technical Review" [submission to the Ontario Nuclear Safety Review, Toronto, 1987].
31. F. Kenneth Hare, *The Safety of Ontario's Nuclear Power Reactors: A Scientific and Technical Review* (Toronto, 1988).
32. Norman Rubin, "Doubts About Candu Safety," *Toronto Star*, 18 July 1983, Sec. A, p. 12.

33. Norman Rubin, in "Problems and Risks of Producing Nuclear Energy," *The Nature of Things*, CBC Television, 25 November 1987.
34. David Poch, "Why Industry Faces Little Liability for Nuclear Mishaps," *Montreal Gazette*, 17 January 1987, Sec. B, p. 4.
35. National Academy of Sciences, *Air Quality and Stationary Source Emission Controls* (1975).
36. Margaret Laurence, Energy Probe fund-raising letter, Toronto, n.d.
37. J.A.L. Robertson, "An Open Letter to Margaret Laurence, C.C.," Atomic Energy of Canada Limited, 7 April 1983.
38. Kathleen Kenna, "Atomic Energy Report Is Too 'Soft' on Industry Lobby Charges," *Toronto Star*, 19 April 1988, Sec. A, p. 11.
39. Stephen Dale, "Probing Candu's Global Reactions," *Now Magazine*, 14–20 March 1985, p. 5.
40. Norman Rubin, *Background Information on Nuclear Power, Ontario and Darlington* (Toronto: Energy Probe, 1986).
41. Ibid.
42. Gordon Edwards, "A Chernobyl in Canada? It Could Happen," *Globe and Mail*, 22 August 1986, Sec. A, p. 7.
43. Gordon Edwards, "Cost Disadvantages of Expanding the Nuclear Power Industry," *Canadian Business Review*, 9, no. 1 (1982), p. 25.
44. Ibid., p. 1.
45. Ibid., p. 25.
46. Ibid., p. 21.
47. Royal Commission on Electric Power Planning, *A Race against Time: Interim Report on Nuclear Power* (Toronto, 1978), p. xiii.
48. Gordon Edwards, "An Open Letter to the Board of Directors of Hydro Quebec," 26 May 1986, p. 1.
49. Lawrence Solomon, "Reactor Sale to Ankara Is Really a 'Turkey,' " *Toronto Star*, 6 December 1985, Sec. A, p. 21.
50. David Poch, *Radiation Alert* (Toronto: Doubleday Canada Ltd., 1985), p. 77.
51. Edwards, "Cost Disadvantages," p. 23.
52. Poch, *Radiation Alert*, p. 77.
53. Rosalie Bertell, *No Immediate Danger? Prognosis for a Radioactive Earth* (Toronto: Women's Educational Press, 1985), p. 123.
54. Edwards, "An Open Letter," p. 2.
55. Poch, *Radiation Alert*, p. 78.
56. House of Commons, *Debates*, 15 May 1986, p. 13331.
57. Energy Probe, "Press Release Backgrounder," 3 March 1987.
58. Norman Rubin, Energy Probe fund-raising letter, n.d.
59. David Poch, "Parliament Shields Nuclear Industry from Damage Suits," *Ottawa Citizen*, 27 January 1987.
60. Ibid.

61. Energy Probe, "Press Release Backgrounder," 3 March 1987.
62. Poch, "Parliament Shields."
63. Edwards, "An Open Letter," p. 2.
64. Energy Probe, "Energy Probe's Challenge of Federal Law Could Shut Down Nuclear Industry" [press release], 3 March 1987, p. 6.
65. Poch, "Parliament Shields."
66. Rubin, Energy Probe fund-raising letter.

CHAPTER 4: NUCLEAR FUEL WASTE

1. L. R. Haywood et al., *Fuel for Canadian Power Reactors*, AECL–3979 (1971).
2. J.A.L. Robertson, "The Candu Reactor System: An Appropriate Technology," *Science*, 199 (1978), p. 657.
3. L. J. Clegg and J. R. Coady, *Radioactive Decay Properties of CANDU Fuel: Vol. 1, The Natural Uranium Fuel Cycle; Vol. 2, Irradiated Fuel*, AECL–4436/1 (1977).
4. Ontario Hydro, *The Management of Irradiated Fuels in Ontario*, 2 vols., Ontario Hydro Report, no. G.P.76014 (1977).
5. A. M. Aiken, J. M. Harrison, and F. K. Hare, *The Management of Canada's Nuclear Fuel Wastes*, Energy Mines and Resources Report EP 77–6 (1977).
6. T. E. Rummery and E.L.J. Rossinger, *The Canadian Nuclear Fuel Waste Management Program*, AECL–8374 (1984).
7. D. M. Wuschke et al., *Second Interim Assessment of the Canadian Concept for Nuclear Fuel Waste Disposal: Vol. 4, Post Closure Assessment*, AECL 8373–4 (1985).
8. W. T. Hancox, "Safe, Permanent Disposal of Nuclear Fuel Waste," *Nuclear Journal of Canada*, 1, no. 3 (1987), p. 256.
9. George A. Cowan, "A Natural Fission Reactor," *Scientific American*, August 1978, p. 36.
10. Wuschke et al., *Second Interim Assessment*.
11. Organisation for Economic Co-operation and Development (OECD), Nuclear Energy Agency, *Technical Appraisal of the Current Situation in the Field of Waste Management: A Collective Opinion by the Reactor Waste Management Committee* (1985).
12. House of Commons, Standing Committee on Environment and Forestry, *Proceedings*, no. 7, 3 February 1987, p. 28.
13. Dan Heap, *Brief to the IPPANI Hearings*, 1–33 (1984), p. 2.
14. Norman Rubin, "The Mismanagement of Canada's Nuclear Waste Management Program" [brief to the Standing Committee on Environment and Forestry], 3 February 1987, p. 3.
15. Gordon Edwards, "Cost Disadvantages of Expanding the Nuclear Power Industry," *Canadian Business Review*, 9, no. 1 (1982), p. 26.

16. David Hallman, *Brief to the* IPPANI *Hearings*, 1–8 (1984), p. 11.
17. David Poch, "Submission to the Standing Committee on Environment and Forestry" [enclosed letter to the Hon. Marcel Masse, 24 October 1986].
18. Gordon Edwards, "An Open Letter to the Board of Directors of Hydro Quebec," 26 May 1986, p. 1.
19. House of Commons, Standing Committee, *Proceedings*, pp. 30–31.
20. David Poch, *Radiation Alert* (Toronto: Doubleday Canada Ltd., 1985), p. 67.
21. Elinor D. U. Powell, "The Moratorium against Uranium Mining in British Columbia Should Be Continued" [brief to the Government of British Columbia, Physicians for Social Responsibility, February 1987].
22. House of Commons, Standing Committee, *Proceedings*, p. 23.
23. Rosalie Bertell, *No Immediate Danger? Prognosis for a Radioactive Earth* (Toronto: Women's Educational Press, 1985), p. 269.
24. Rosalie Bertell, *W-5*, CTV Television, 7 December 1986; Melta Spencer, "Low-Level Radiation and Species Death Syndrome" [interview with Rosalie Bertell] *Peace Magazine*, May 1985, p. 21.
25. House of Commons, Standing Committee, *Proceedings*, p. 36.
26. Ibid., p. 28.
27. Ibid., p. 13.
28. Ibid., p. 7.
29. Ibid., p. 53.
30. Gordon Edwards, quoted in Anne Weiser, ed., *Challenges to Nuclear Waste* (1987), p. 71.
31. House of Commons, Standing Committee, *Proceedings*, p. 28.
32. Ibid., p. 29.
33. Edwards, in *Challenges to Nuclear Waste*, p. 71.
34. Gordon Edwards, in Ronald Babin, *The Nuclear Power Game* (Montreal: Black Rose Press, 1985), p. 16.

CHAPTER 5: URANIUM MINING

1. D. M. Le Bourdais, *Canada and the Atomic Revolution* (Toronto: McClelland and Stewart, 1959).
2. O.J.C. Runnalls, "The Uranium Industry in Canada" [brief submitted to the Cluff Lake Board of Enquiry, Energy Mines and Resources, 1977].
3. C. G. Stewart and S. D. Simpson, "The Hazards of Inhaling Radon–222 and Its Short-Lived Daughters," in IAEA *Symposium on Radiological Health and Safety in Mining and Milling Nuclear Materials*, Vol. 1, STI/PUB/78 (Vienna, 1964).
4. *Royal Commission Report Respecting Radiation, Compensation and Safety at the Fluorspar Mines, St. Lawrence, Newfoundland* (Ottawa, 1969).
5. J. Muller and W. C. Wheeler, "Causes of Death in Ontario Uranium Mines," in *Proceedings of the International Symposium on Radiation Protection*

in Mining and Milling of Uranium and Thorium, Bordeaux, France, 9–11 September 1974.

6. Ontario, Ministry of the Attorney General, *Report of the Royal Commission on the Health and Safety of Workers in Mines* (Toronto, 1976), p. 81.

7. G. Bruce Doern, "Science and Technology in the Nuclear Regulatory Process: The Case of Canadian Uranium Miners," *Canadian Public Administration*, no. 21 (1978), p. 51.

8. Advisory Panel on Tailings, *The Management of Uranium Mill Tailings: An Appraisal of Current Practices*, AECB-1156 (1978).

9. David Hallman, *Brief to the IPPANI Hearings*, 1–8 (1984), p. 7.

10. House of Commons, Standing Committee on Environment and Forestry, *Proceedings*, no. 7, 3 February 1987, p. 21.

11. Sir Walter Marshall, "Address to the U.S. Atomic Industrial Forum Annual Conference," Washington, D.C., November 1984.

12. Norman Rubin, *Brief to the IPPANI Hearings*, 1–41 (1984), p. 3.

13. U.S. Nuclear Regulatory Commission, *Final Generic Environmental Impact Statement on Uranium Milling*, Vol. 1, NUREG-0706 (1980), p. 19.

14. Rubin, *Brief*, p. 3.

15. Anne Smart and Larry Mullen, "Greenpeace Action in Saskatchewan Opposed," *Saskatoon Star Phoenix*, 15 April 1981, Sec. A, p. 5.

16. Greenpeace, Nuclear Division, "Nuclear Exports and Government Secrecy" [leaflet], Toronto, n.d.

17. John Willis, "An Open Letter to the Members of the Legislative Assembly, Province of Saskatchewan," Greenpeace, January 1988.

18. Greenpeace, "Nuclear Exports and Government Secrecy."

19. House of Commons, *Debates*, 15 May 1986, p. 13297.

20. Hallman, *Brief*, p. 8.

21. New Democratic Party Inquiry, "Backgrounder," 14 July 1986.

22. Elinor D. U. Powell, "The Moratorium against Uranium Mining in British Columbia Should Be Continued" [brief to the Government of British Columbia, Physicians for Social Responsibility, February 1987].

CHAPTER 6: NUCLEAR PROLIFERATION

1. House of Commons, *Debates*, 15 December 1945, p. 2893.

2. R. W. Morrison, "Is Canada Peddling Nuclear Bombs Worldwide in the Guise of Nuclear Reactors?" *Science Forum*, 10 (1977).

3. See the statement to the House of Commons by Mackenzie King, House of Commons, *Debates*, 5 December 1945.

4. International Atomic Energy Agency, "International Atomic Energy Agency: What It Is, What It Does" [public information leaflet], Vienna, 1981.

5. *Statute of the International Atomic Energy Agency* (New York: United Nations, 1956).

6. Gordon H. E. Sims, *A History of the Atomic Energy Control Board* (Ottawa: Supply and Services Canada, 1981), p. 177.
7. House of Commons, *Debates*, 17 December 1945, p. 3635.
8. Gordon Edwards, *Brief to the IPPANI Hearings* (1984), p. 13.
9. Gordon Edwards, "Cost Disadvantages of Expanding the Nuclear Power Industry," *Canadian Business Review*, 9, no. 1 (1982), p. 29.
10. Ibid., p. 29.
11. Norman Rubin, *Brief to the IPPANI Hearings*, 1–41 (1984), p. 18.
12. Edwards, "Cost Disadvantages," p. 29.
13. Gordon Edwards, in Ronald Babin, *The Nuclear Power Game* (Montreal: Black Rose Press, 1985), p. 15.
14. Rubin, *Brief*, p. 19.
15. Ibid., p. 19.
16. Ibid., p. 10.
17. Dan Heap, *Brief to the IPPANI Hearings*, 1–33 (1984), p. 3.
18. House of Commons, *Debates*, 15 May 1986, p. 13306.
19. Ibid., pp. 13306–13307.
20. Heap, *Brief*, p. 3.
21. Ibid., p. 5.
22. Ibid., p. 3.

CHAPTER 7: ALTERNATIVE ENERGY SOURCES

1. National Research Council, *Alternative Energy Technology in Canada*, NRCC–26612 (1986), p. 16.
2. Ibid., p. 39.
3. P. Love and R. Overend, *Tree Power: An Assessment of the Energy Potential for Forest Biomass in Canada* (Ottawa: Supply and Services Canada, 1978).
4. R. Overend, "Biomass Conversion Technologies," in *Proceedings of the ISES Congress, Brighton, England, August 1981*.
5. Amory B. Lovins, "Energy Strategy: The Road Not Taken," *Journal of International Affairs* (1976), p. 56.
6. Ibid., p. 95.
7. Cluff Lake Board of Enquiry, *Final Report*, p. 275, note 55, and *Transcript of Hearings* (1978), p. 6610.
8. Lovins, "Energy Strategy," p. 77.
9. W. Kenneth Davis, "Conclusions of the Fourteenth World Energy Congress," Montreal, 22 September 1989.
10. Lovins, "Energy Strategy," p. 93.
11. Geoffrey Greenhalgh, *The Necessity for Nuclear Power* (London: Graham and Trotman, 1980), pp. 233 ff.
12. David Brooks, "Choices Range from Minimum Change Maximum Growth

to Maximum Change No Growth," 47th Couchiching Conference, Geneva Park, Ontario, 1978.

13. Robert Bott, David Brooks, and John Robinson, *Life after Oil* (Edmonton: Hurtig, 1983).

14. Amory B. Lovins and L. Hunter Lovins, *Brittle Power* (Andover, Mass.: Brick House, 1982).

15. David Brooks, John Robinson, and Ralph Torrie, *2025: Soft Energy Paths*, Report on the Friends of the Earth Energy Path Study (Ottawa: Department of Energy Mines and Resources, 1984).

16. David Fishlock, "Nuclear Could Learn From Warplanes," *The Energy Daily*, 2 May 1989, p. 5.

CHAPTER 8: RISKS OF NUCLEAR ENERGY

1. Herbert Inhaber, *Energy Risk Assessment* (New York: Gordon and Breach, 1982).

2. John P. Holdren et al., "Health and Safety Impacts of Renewable, Geothermal and Fission Energy," in Curtis C. Travis and Elizabeth L. Etnier, eds., *Health Risks of Energy Technologies* (Boulder, Colo.: Westview Press, 1983).

3. D. K. Myers and M. M. Werner, "A Review of the Health Effects of Energy Development," *Nuclear Journal of Canada* (1987), p. 14.

4. R. Wilson, "Analysing the Daily Risks of Life," *Technology Review*, February 1979, pp. 41–46.

5. Bernard L. Cohen, "A Catalogue of Risks," *Health Physics*, 36 (1979), p. 707.

6. Ernest Siddall, "Presentation to the NDP Inquiry into Nuclear Energy," 27 October 1986.

7. Ernest Siddall, *Safety Policy in the Production of Electricity*, AECL–7540 (1982).

8. Ernest Siddall, *Risk, Fear and Public Safety*, AECL–7404 (1981); Bernard L. Cohen, "How Much Should We Spend to Save A Life?" *Public Utilities Fortnightly*, 19 November 1981, p. 22.

9. Aaron Wildavsky, "No Risk Is the Highest Risk of All," *American Scientist*, 67 (1979), p. 32.

10. Gordon Edwards and H. Lajambe, "Reply to Hydro Quebec's Comments Re: Gentilly 2 Nuclear Reactor," CCNR, September 1986.

11. David Poch, *Brief to the IPPANI Hearings*, 1–29 (1984), p. 2.

12. David Poch, quoted in Thomas Claridge, "Health Risks Cited by Groups Opposing Hydro Tritium Plant," *Globe and Mail*, 17 December 1987, Sec. A, p. 20.

13. Patricia Adams, "Canada's Foreign Aid Flouts UN Environmental Plan," *Montreal Gazette*, 20 June 1988, Sec. B, p. 3.

14. Gordon Edwards, "Cost Disadvantages of Expanding the Nuclear Power

Industry," *Canadian Business Review*, 9, no. 1 (1982), p. 27.

15. H. E. Thexton, *The Cost and Financing of the Decommissioning of Nuclear Power Plants* (n.p.: Nuclear Energy Agency, OECD, 1986).

16. Rosalie Bertell, "Letter to the Delegates at the UN Conference on the Peaceful Uses of Nuclear Energy," IICPH, 4 February 1987.

17. Poch, *Brief*, p. 2.

CHAPTER 9: BENEFITS OF NUCLEAR ENERGY

1. *Estimates of Total and Nuclear Electricity Generation* (Paris: Nuclear Energy Agency, OECD, 1989).

2. O.J.C. Runnalls, "Canada's Nuclear Future," 29th Annual Conference, Canadian Nuclear Association, Ottawa, June 1989.

3. Canadian Nuclear Association, *Yearbook* (1989), p. 37.

4. Ibid., p. 37.

5. G. Subramanian et al., eds., *Radiopharmaceuticals* (New York: Society for Nuclear Medicine, 1975).

6. P. Richards, "A Survey of the Production at Brookhaven National Laboratory of Radioisotopes for Medical Research," *Transactions of the Fifth Nuclear Congress* (New York: IEEE, 1960), p. 225.

7. World Health Organization, *Report to the UN General Assembly Conference on PUNE*, A/Conf.108/PC/30/Rev 1 (1986), p. 6.

8. Ibid., p. 9.

9. M. G. Brown, "The Canadian Design Approach to Medical Product Sterilisation Plants," Conference on Radiation Sterilisation of Medical Supplies and Pharmaceuticals, Stockholm, April 1965.

10. K. J. Round, "Application and Opportunities for Radiation Sources," 1984 CNA Conference, Saskatoon, 3–6 June 1984.

11. "Reports on IAEA Activities and the Peaceful Uses of Atomic Energy," *IAEA Newsbrief*, 2, no. 15 (25 November 1987).

12. Frank M. Fraser, *Historical Overview and Potential of Food Irradiation* (Kanata, Ont.: AECL, Radiochemical Company, n.d.).

13. Gordon Edwards, in Ronald Babin, *The Nuclear Power Game* (Montreal: Black Rose Press, 1985), p. 14.

14. Ibid., p. 15.

15. David Suzuki, "Expect Side Effects from Irradiated Food," *Globe and Mail*, 7 September 1987.

16. David Poch, *Toronto Star*, 9 November 1987, Sec. A, p. 17.

17. Gordon Edwards, "Cost Disadvantages of Expanding the Nuclear Power Industry," *Canadian Business Review*, 9, no. 1 (1982), p. 20.

18. D. K. Evans, "Nuclear Energy Candu It Better," *Vancouver Sun*, 27 September 1988.

19. Edwards, in *The Nuclear Power Game*, p. 15.
20. Gordon Edwards, *Brief to the* IPPANI *Hearings*, 2–68 (1984), p. 12.
21. Ibid., p. 12.
22. Lawrence Solomon, Energy Probe newsletter, 1983.
23. *New Electricity Stations in Ontario: When Are Decisions Needed?*, UNEB Nuclear Notes (Ottawa: Energy Mines and Resources Canada, 1987).
24. *New Brunswick Electricity Supply and Demand*, UNEB Nuclear Notes (Ottawa: Energy Mines and Resources Canada, 1987).
25. Solomon, Energy Probe newsletter.
26. Ibid.
27. Ibid.
28. Ibid.
29. Edwards, in *The Nuclear Power Game*, p. 16.
30. Edwards, *Brief*, p. 12.
31. New Democratic Party Inquiry, "Backgrounder," 14 July 1986.
32. For example, see House of Commons, *Debates*, 1 February 1958, p. 4147.
33. House of Commons, *Debates*, 20 August 1964, p. 7053.
34. House of Commons, Natural Resources and Public Works Committee, *Proceedings*, no. 4, 2 December 1976, pp. 4–5.

CHAPTER 10: WHO TO BELIEVE?

1. Cluff Lake Board of Enquiry, *Final Report*.
2. Ibid., p. 6.
3. Ibid., p. 275.
4. Ibid., p. 288.
5. Ontario, Royal Commission on Electric Power Planning, *Report: Vol. 1, Concepts, Conclusions and Recommendations* (1980).
6. Ibid., p. 65.
7. Ibid., p. 72.
8. Ontario Legislature, Select Committee on Ontario Hydro Affairs, *The Safety of Ontario's Nuclear Reactors: Final Report* (Toronto, 1980).
9. Sir Frank Layfield, Q.C., *Report of the Sizewell B Public Enquiry*, presented to the Secretary of State for Energy, 5 December 1986.
10. Ibid., Vol. 7, Part VII, chapter 108, "General Conclusions."